Handbook of Commercial Underwriting

Edited by
Jess Lederman

Mortgage Lending Handbook Series

MORTGAGE BANKERS ASSOCIATION OF AMERICA
Washington, DC

Real Estate Finance Press
Mortgage Bankers Association of America
1125 15th Street, NW
Washington, DC 20005

Ron J. McCord, CMB, President

Warren Lasko, Executive Vice President
Joyce E. Kappeler, Vice President, Education

ISBN 1-57599-019-9

First Printing, November 1997

Disclaimer

This publication is designed to provide, as simply and as accurately as possible, a comprehensive resource regarding commercial underwriting. It should be noted that the information presented is not all inclusive. Forms, regulations, and overall processes may change because of changes within the industry. This publication should not be used as a substitute for referring to the applicable rules and regulations and is sold with the understanding that the publisher is not engaged in rendering legal or other personalized professional service. If legal or other expert assistance is required, the services of a competent professional should be sought.

Table of Contents

Section Two: Analyzing Property Sectors

About the Editor

JESS LEDERMAN

Mr. Lederman, a private investor and the editor and co-author of more than 30 books on the financial markets, is one of the pioneers of modern mortgage finance. He co-founded two of the largest private-sector counterparts to Fannie Mae and Freddie Mac, and was the architect of several innovative securities. Previously, Mr. Lederman was chairman of the Asset Backed Capital Group. He has also held positions as executive vice president with Bear Stearns Mortgage Capital Corporation, vice president of sales and marketing for Sears Mortgage Securities Corporation and director of pricing and research with the PMI Group.

Mr. Lederman received a B.A. from Columbia College, where he graduated Phi Beta Kappa and summa cum laude, and his M.B.A. from the Columbia University Graduate School of Business.

About the Authors

Steven J. Beauchamp

Mr. Beauchamp has been a managing director of Landauer Associates, Inc., for the past 11 years. Throughout his 20-year career, he has been involved in lending, brokerage, and consulting. Mr. Beauchamp has consulted and advised clients on many of the major office, resort, residential, industrial, hotel and retail facilities in Florida and the Caribbean. He has also coordinated the evaluation of major real estate portfolios throughout the United States. Mr. Beauchamp is a graduate of Albion College in Michigan, with a degree in economics. He is a licensed real estate professional in Arizona, Florida, Georgia, Michigan and Texas.

Peggy Berg

Ms. Berg is president and founder of The Highland Group, Hotel Investment Advisors. She founded the company to provide high-quality consulting services within the hotel industry in the areas of market, financial and feasibility analysis for hotel development, acquisition and disposition. Clients include major chains such as Hilton, Choice, Best Western and Holiday Inn, as well as individual investors and developers of hotels of all types. Ms. Berg currently chairs the International Society of Hospitality Consultants, and she is also a member of the American Hotel Motel Association and the Georgia Hospitality and Travel Association. Ms. Berg is a frequent speaker at industry conferences. She is a certified public accountant (CPA) and a graduate of Michigan State University's School of Hospitality Management. She also has a degree in business.

W. Thomas Gardner

Mr. Gardner is an investment officer and has worked for State Farm Insurance since 1969, spending his entire tenure in the mortgage loan division of the investment department. He has been responsible for company-owned real estate and loan production in the eastern half of the United States. As a member of the loan review committee, Mr. Gardner is responsible for investment approval.

Vernon George

Mr. George is president and CEO of Hammer, Siler, George Associates, a real estate and urban economic consulting firm with offices in Atlanta; Denver; Silver Spring, Maryland and Washington, D.C. Mr. George has taught at the University of Virginia and has authored numerous papers on market feasibility, development strategy and other related topics.

Jim Giegerich

Mr. Giegerich has been president of Giegerich & Associates in Bethesda, Maryland, for 17 years. The firm specializes in real estate economics, market feasibility and project planning for investment-grade commercial, office, industrial and residential real estate investments. His experience includes large-scale mixed-use communities, transit station air rights mixed-use projects, central business development (CBD) redevelopment and theme retail facilities. Mr. Giegerich has also been director of economic development, promoting and facilitating real estate development for a large Washington, D.C., suburban jurisdiction.

JAMES R. LAGASSÉ

Mr. Lagassé is vice president of the real estate division, acquisitions and dispositions at Cigna Investment Management, Inc. Mr. Lagassé holds a bachelor's degree from the University of Connecticut and an M.B.A. from Pennsylvania State University.

THOMAS Z. MINEHART III

Mr. Minehart is executive vice president of Legg Mason Real Estate Services, Inc., where he is in charge of the commercial loan production. Mr. Minehart has over 30 years of experience in the valuing, analyzing, structuring and financing of income property real estate investments. Mr. Minehart has a B.A. in political science from Ursinus College in Collegeville, Pennsylvania, and a master's degree in business administration from Temple University in Philadelphia. He is a licensed real estate broker in Delaware, New Jersey and Pennsylvania.

Richard E. Nichols

Mr. Nichols is president of Richard E. Nichols Associates, Inc., an appraisal and counseling firm based in Indianapolis, Indiana. The firm provides technical skills in the valuation of conventional subsidized multifamily properties, feasibility studies and a broad range of commercial and industrial special-purpose property valuations, as well as large agricultural holdings. Mr. Nichols is chairman of the Indiana Appraisers Certification Board and since 1990, has been a trustee to the Appraisal Foundation, where he served as chairman of the board of trustees in 1994.

Stephanie Polyzois

Ms. Polyzois is a senior mortgage analyst with Green Park Financial, a Fannie Mae Delegated Underwriting and Servicing (DUS) lender based in Bethesda, Maryland. Prior to joining Green Park, Ms. Polyzois was with First National Bank of Maryland in the commercial real estate lending division. Ms. Polyzois holds a bachelor of arts degree from Wake Forest University in North Carolina and an M.B.A. from the Sellinger School of Business, Loyola College, in Baltimore. She is a member of Beta Gamma Sigma, a national honor society in business and management, and Alpha Sigma Nu, the national Jesuit honor society.

Donald H. Schefmeyer

Mr. Schefmeyer is president of Action Mortgage Corporation, a commercial mortgage broker originating and placing loans nationwide since 1982, and Action Management, Inc., a commercial and multifamily property management firm. Both firms are headquartered in South Bend, Indiana. A graduate of Syracuse

University, Mr. Schefmeyer has been actively involved in commercial mortgage banking and real estate development since 1970. He is a Certified Mortgage Banker and holds the SRPA designation of the Appraisal Institute. Mr. Schefmeyer served on the Mortgage Bankers Association of America (MBA) Board of Governors, is past president of the Northern Indiana Chapter of the Appraisal Institute and has been designated a faculty fellow of MBA. He has lectured extensively for MBA.

Gary S. Smuckler

Mr. Smuckler is a partner in the Washington, D.C., office of Pepper, Hamilton & Scheetz. He has extensive experience representing lenders under the multifamily programs of Fannie Mae, Freddie Mac, and private mortgage conduits engaged in mortgage securitization. Mr. Smuckler had been deputy general counsel and managing attorney at Freddie Mac and, before that, in-house counsel and head of mortgage servicing at a large savings and loan association. He graduated from the University of Michigan and Wayne State University Law School in Detroit.

Mary E. Vander Linden

Ms. Vander Linden is president of Access Solutions, a real estate and urban consulting firm. She was formerly vice president and manager of research for Northland Financial Company, a real estate investment banker. Ms. Vander Linden provides macroeconomic, demographic and real estate market research for the company's seven regional offices and loan administration staff. Ms. Vander Linden's work has appeared in a number of national trade publications, including *Mortgage Banking* and *Development.* Ms. Vander Linden has an A.B. from Fontbonne College in St. Louis and an M.S. in urban studies from Washington University, also in St. Louis.

Stephen F. Wood

Mr. Wood is chairman of Vista Commercial Mortgage Group, LLC. In 1977, Mr. Wood founded Woodmark, Inc., a commercial mortgage banking firm, where he served as president. Mr. Wood also served as president and director of Nashville's largest savings and loan association. While he has been active in the financing of all types of commercial real estate, Mr Wood has been particularly active in the financing of nursing homes and other senior living facilities. Mr. Wood is a graduate of Vanderbilt University in Nashville. He has been active in trade association activities and has served as president of both the Nashville and Tennessee Mortgage Bankers Associations.

Introduction

Having been preceded by the MBA's 1995 release of the *Handbook of Commercial Real Estate Finance,* the *Handbook of Commercial Underwriting* is the MBA's third handbook concentrating on the commercial market. A companion reference to the MBA's newly released *Handbook of Commercial Mortgage Finance: Primary and Secondary Market,* this latest handbook examines functional areas in detail and explores the nuances of the different market sectors.

Section One provides an in-depth exploration of the tools of the trade, including income and expense and property analysis, market feasibility and forecasting, real estate appraisal, mortgage financing submission and critical legal issues. Section Two turns to specific property sectors, covering multifamily, shopping centers, office buildings, hotels, industrial properties and the senior care market.

Many thanks are due to the chapter authors, who took time from their hectic schedules to produce this contribution to literature on commercial real estate finance. Special thanks are owed to Donald Schefmeyer, who was invaluable in suggesting authors, and to MBA.

Jess Lederman

Section One: Tools of the Trade

1

Analyzing the Income and Expense Statement

James R. Lagassé, Vice President
Cigna Investment Management, Inc.

The Income/Expense Statement

The income/expense statement (income statement) is a representation of a property's sources of funds (derived from the building's tenants) and uses of funds (those expenditures of funds necessary to operate the property). While financing or purchasing a building includes evaluating the physical asset or "bricks and sticks," the underlying value is determined predominantly by analyzing the income stream produced by the leases in place and their associated expenses. The way to evaluate the income stream produced by the building and its leases is through understanding and analyzing the income statement.

In its most basic form, the income statement represents the following equation:

Revenues – Expenses = Net Operating Income

While historical or actual income statements are not perfect predictors of the future, as we have all learned over the past 10 years, they are helpful in the underwriting process. That is, in evaluating actual income statements, one can uncover trends and other telltale signs that will help to validate or support the underwriter's efforts in determining the property's ultimate value — upon which a financing or purchase offer can be based.

Income Statements

There are three basic forms an income statement can take: actual, pro forma and market effective. If the property being evaluated is an up-and-running property, there will be actual income statements available for the underwriter to review along with various other financial records, such as balance sheets, aged receivables reports, rent rolls, leases and invoices. These statements may be tabulated on a monthly, quarterly, semiannual or annual basis. Often, the actual results of a property are compared to the budget prepared for the property by the property or asset manager.

Exhibit 1 is an example of an income statement for a property for the full year as compared to the property's budget. While the comparison to budget might seem unnecessary, it is an interesting comparison to evaluate. If actual results are much better or worse than those predicted by the budget, the preparers of the budget may have been too optimistic or too pessimistic; may not have fully understood the property, market or their nuances; or may simply have been caught off guard by market forces over which they had no knowledge or control. In any case, the comparison of actual to budget results can be helpful in evaluating the overall quality of information supplied by the property or asset manager and also in evaluating how well the property or asset manager understands the property and the market. Remember, in underwriting a property for financing or purchasing, we are not blindly following the numbers but also making subjective judgments about many other aspects of the property. Evaluating actual and budget projections

EXHIBIT 1

Sample Income Statement — Actual vs. Budget

INCOME STATEMENT
ACTUAL vs. BUDGET

ABC OFFICE BUILDING
ANYTOWN, ANYSTATE

	ACTUAL 1995	BUDGET 1995	VARIANCE $	VARIANCE %
INCOME				
Base Rent	$3,140,674	$3,226,689	($86,015)	–2.7%
Parking Revenue	267,727	275,000	(7,273)	–2.7%
Expense Recoveries	131,040	90,000	41,040	31.3%
Other Income	1,794	0	1,794	100.0%
Total Income	$3,541,235	$3,591,689	($50,454)	–1.49%
OPERATING EXPENSES & TAXES				
Utilities	175,023	175,000	23	0.0%
Janitorial	223,449	220,000	3,449	1.5%
Maintenance & Repairs	244,101	210,000	34,101	14.0%
Security	101,275	80,000	21,275	21.0%
Management Fee	91,764	89,792	1,972	2.1%
Property Tax	276,145	288,096	(11,951)	–4.3%
Insurance	16,780	26,150	(9,370)	–55.8%
Advt. & Promotion	41,109	35,000	6,109	14.9%
General & Admin.	256,169	300,000	(43,831)	–17.1%
Other Expenses	36,442	15,000	21,442	58.8%
Total Op. Exp. & Taxes	$1,462,257	$1,439,038	$23,219	1.6%
NET OPERATING INCOME	$2,078,978	$2,152,651	($73,673)	–3.5%

is but one of the many pieces of information to analyze and about which objective and subjective conclusions may be drawn.

The second form of income statement, the pro forma income statement, relates to properties that are under development or in lease-up — properties for which there are no historical or actual results. A pro forma income statement is simply a projection of the income and expenses the property is expected to generate after construction is complete and the property achieves a stabilized occupancy level at market rents. Typically, a vacancy factor is applied to the income stream based on local market conditions including competing operating properties, properties under construction and future job growth projections which will translate into demand for additional office space.

Generally, vacancy assumptions range from 5% to 10% based on the factors described above. Prior to the real estate recession experienced in the late 1980s through mid-1990s, a 5% vacancy assumption was a standard assumption. However, there are other forces at work in the commercial real estate industry that have moved the "structural" vacancy from the 5% level to a higher level. These forces include changing work patterns (such as telecommuting, office hoteling and satellite offices), lower space requirements per employee and an oversupply of office space in many markets of the country. All of these factors and others have conspired to alter the landscape of pro forma analysis conducted in the commercial real estate industry.

The third form the income statement takes — a market-effective income statement — represents the property as if it were leased at current market-effective rents with a market vacancy level and market expenses. This form of income statement can be used for up-and-running properties or properties under development or in lease-up. With this type of income statement, if contract rents in the market are quoted at $20.00 per square foot per year with five months of free rent on a five-year lease, the market-effective rent is equal to $18.33 per square foot per year. (Here's how to calculate the market-effective rent: The tenant will pay rent for only 55 months of the 60-month term because of the 5 free months, effectively averaging the rent received over the entire lease term. Therefore, $20.00/square foot/year times the ratio of the number of months paying rent and the total number of months in the lease term equals the market-effective rent per square foot per year.) This rent stream is then offset by a vacancy factor equal to the vacancy found in the market at the time of analysis as well as a market level of operating expenses and taxes. A market-effective income statement is a what-if look at the property assuming it behaves exactly as the competitive buildings in the market in which it is located at a particular point in time.

It should also be noted that in underwriting an up-and-running or operating property, a seller or borrower often will provide not only the actual income statement but also a pro forma income statement for an analyst to review. In this case the pro forma income statement represents how the property will perform in the future based on the preparer's interpretation of historical, current and future market forces. If possible, the underwriter should then prepare a market effective income statement so that any combination of the three income statements can be analyzed. The underwriter must exercise extreme caution in evaluating the pro forma income statement because it really is just the preparer's best guess of the future. It is based on certain pieces of factual information but it is prospective and subject to different interpretations based on what the interpreter's ultimate goals are. As always, objective information undergoes subjective evaluation and cannot be analyzed in a vacuum. Comparing and contrasting any combination of the three income statements — actual, pro forma and market effective — brings up interesting issues the underwriter must resolve. For example, there may be significant differences between actual net operating income, pro forma net operating income and market-effective net operating income. When this is the case, the underwriter must uncover and understand the reasons for the discrepancies before drawing any conclusions and proceeding with the underwriting task.

In summary, no matter which type or combination of income statements is analyzed, the underwriter must consider many market and other assumptions during the process. While most of the information found in an income statement comes from verifiable financial data, the underwriter must use good judgment and factual information to develop, test and validate the information provided in the property's income statement.

Building Measures

Before starting a discussion of the components of an income statement, a review of building measurement methods seems advisable, since many income and expense items are determined by building area.

A building's size may be expressed in more than one way, depending on its use and on the conventions of the market in which it resides. There are two basic measures for any building:

- The overall building size — the square foot measurement of each of the floors to the outside surfaces of the building walls (see Exhibit 2).
- The size of the space leased or available to be leased — the square foot measurement of each of the floors to the inside surfaces of the building walls (see Exhibit 3).

The industry generally calls the first measure gross building area (GBA). The second measure, or the amount of space available to be leased to the tenants, can be defined a number of ways, depending on the type of property (retail, office, warehouse or residential), industry standards and local custom. Some of the most

EXHIBIT 2

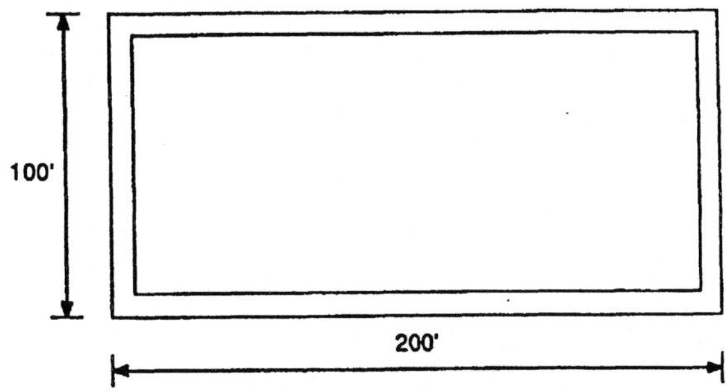

Area = 20,000 square feet per floor.

EXHIBIT 3

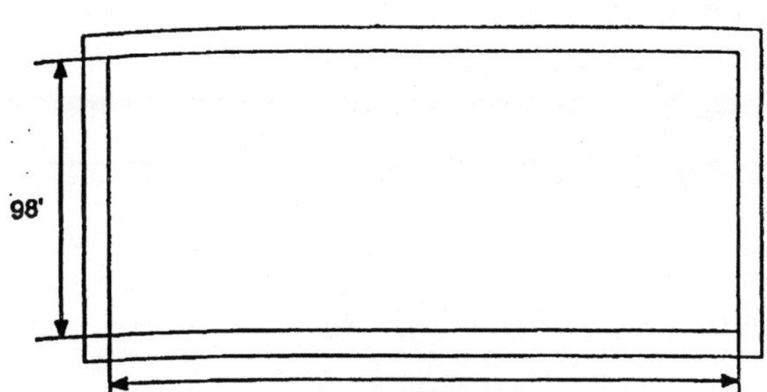

Area = 19,404 square feet per floor.

common definitions for the second measure include those shown below.

- *Gross Leasable Area (GLA).* This retail industry measure is the total floor area designed for tenant occupancy and exclusive use, including any basements, mezzanines or upper floors. In a retail mall, the GLA of the mall shops would be the product of the width of a tenant space measured to the centerline of the demising walls between tenant spaces multiplied by the depth of the tenant space measured from the exterior face of the mall wall to the exterior face of the rear wall. Exhibit 4 illustrates the GLA.
- *Usable Area (UA).* This office building industry measure is the area of a structure measured between the finished surface of the outside wall and the finished surface of the office side of the corridor times the width measured to the centerline of partitions that separate one office from another. No deductions are made for columns and projections necessary for the building. Exhibit 5, on page 10, illustrates the UA.
- *Rentable Area (RA).* Another office building industry measure, RA is the area of a structure measured to the major dominant element of the outside wall (which is not necessarily the finished surface) excluding any major vertical penetrations of the floor. Exhibit 6, on page 11, illustrates the RA.

A building's R/U ratio is the ratio of rentable area to usable area. The R/U ratio of the building illustrated in Exhibits 5 and 6 is approximately 116 percent. A building's efficiency factor is the ratio between the total lease measurement (GLA, NRA, UA, etc.) and the gross building area.

EXHIBIT 4

GROSS LEASABLE AREA

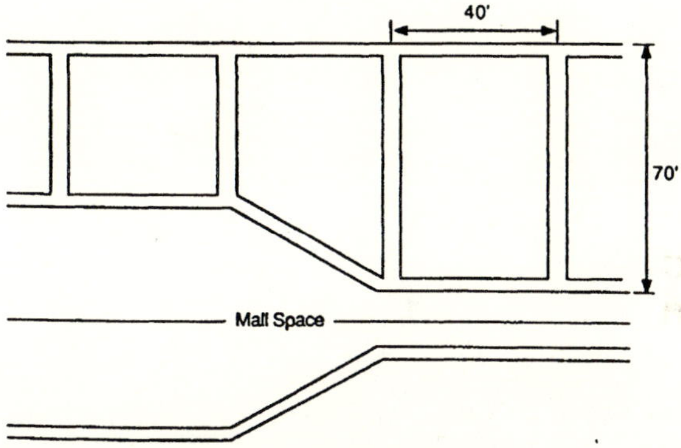

GLA (shop) = 2800 square feet

Underwriters should understand how buildings are measured and how markets allow buildings to be measured. A misunderstanding can lead to substantially different measures of space available to lease and estimates of potential income. In some markets, considerable concessions are granted (or premiums are gained) by manipulating measurement basis or add-on factors so that leases with comparable face rates have substantially different effective rates.

Revenues

The revenues in the income statement take various forms. The largest component of revenues comes from the property's underlying leases and any associated expense reimbursement income. Other sources of revenue include parking income, tenant service income, interest income and miscellaneous income.

EXHIBIT 5

USABLE AREA

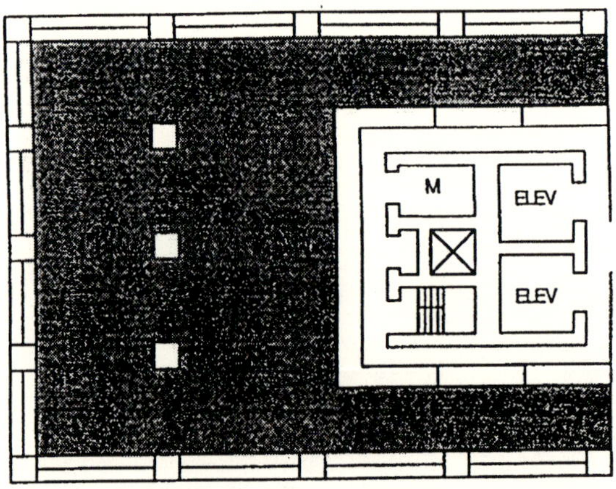

Usable area = 16,000 square feet per floor (approx.).

Lease and Expense Reimbursement

The income produced by the property's underlying leases found on the income statement can be verified by analyzing the rent roll, the actual leases and lease briefs prepared for each lease.

A rent roll is a chart that represents the basic business terms of a lease and is a convenient way to concisely view the terms of all leases to tenants in a building. A rent roll will typically contain the following information: tenant name, suite number, square feet occupied, lease start and end date, base rent, rent increases (if any), methods by which expense reimbursements are calculated (if applicable), the existence of options to extend the lease and any

EXHIBIT 6

RENTABLE AREA

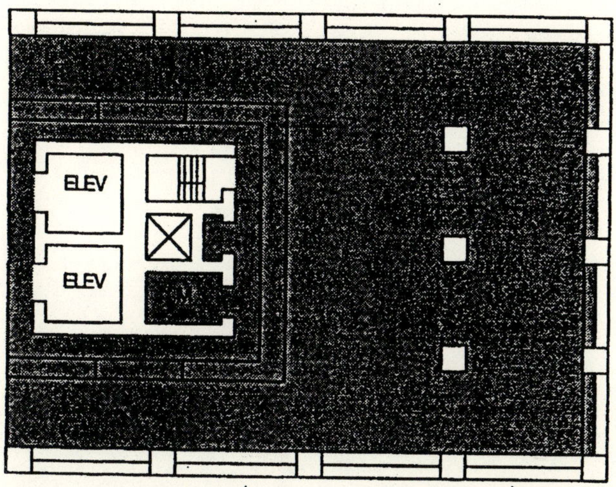

Rentable area = 18,500 square feet per floor (approx.).

other major business terms. Exhibit 7, shown on page 12, is a sample of what a typical rent roll might look like.

Most items are self-explanatory but the rent increase is a category not found in all leases. Sometimes, leases have provisions whereby the base rent is periodically increased. The increases can be stated as specific dollar amount increases (for example, $1 per square foot in lease years two and four) or as a percentage increase based on some popular index (for example, the lease rent will be increased in year three based on changes in the CPI). There may be caps or limits to the increase such as the rent will increase by the CPI amount but by no less than 2% and no more than 7 percent. The final form that a rent bump might take is entirely a function

EXHIBIT 7

SAMPLE RENT ROLL

Tenant Name	Suite No.	Square Feet	Lease Start	Lease End	Base Rent	Rent Inc.	Reimburse-ments	Options	Other
ABC	1	2,000	1/1/96	12/31/01	$20.00	Annual CPI increase	Base yr. 1996	1–5 yr. option at market rent	

of the market demand for the space, the desirability of the space and the landlord's and tenant's negotiating abilities.

The reimbursements category is a measure of how much of the property's operating expenses a tenant will be responsible for. These methods are completely negotiable and not subject to easy categorization, as each method can have numerous different assumptions and results. Some methods will include all expense categories, others will exclude some and still others will cap certain or all categories of expenses. There are myriad combinations of devising an expense reimbursement calculation with no one right way.

If the lease is a gross lease then the tenant pays a specified amount of lease rent to the landlord and nothing else. The presumption is that the rent charged is sufficient to pay all operating expenses attributable to the lease. These types of leases are becoming rare as markets evolve. At the other end of the spectrum is the net lease and the absolute triple net lease where a tenant pays base rent to the landlord and is responsible for the operating expenses associated with its space. These leases are typically found in industrial buildings. Most leases are a hybrid of gross and triple net leases that include an expense reimbursement income category.

For example, consider a net lease in which the escalation method is stated as base year 1996. This is interpreted as the tenant will pay its pro rata share of the increase in operating expenses over the base year of 1996. For instance, if operating expenses for the property in 1996 equaled $1,000,000 for a 100,000 square foot building (or $10/square foot) and the tenant in question leased 20,000 square feet, or 20% of the building, this tenant would be responsible for 20% of the increase in operating expenses in 1997. Should expenses for 1997 equal $1,100,000, then the tenant in question would be responsible for $20,000 [(1,100,000–1,000,000) x 20%] of the increase. However, if expenses were to be reduced (an interesting idea, but usually not the case) the tenant, in most cases, would not be entitled to a reduction in rent or rebate of rent.

Another common form of expense escalation is an expense stop amount. A stop is a stated amount of expenses over which the tenant is responsible for its pro rata share as they increase. For example, if there is a $10 expense stop for a particular tenant and expenses go up to $10.50/square foot in the next year, the tenant is responsible for $0.50/square foot of expense reimbursement. This method of expense reimbursement is becoming less prevalent due to the uncertainty and volatility of expense movements. However, the base year and expense stop methods are similar and, if carefully applied, produce similar results.

These are but two of the many expense reimbursement methods utilized today. These methods range from very simple to extremely complex. It is important to make sure the underwriters thoroughly understand the expense reimbursement method by fully investigating the mechanics of the reimbursement as found in the lease. Furthermore, when evaluating the expense reimbursement line item, underwriters must be sure to validate the existence of the income and its proper calculation. Remember, expense reimbursement methods are very important, completely negotiable and dependent on marketplace laws of supply and demand.

While the rent roll can be an extremely valuable tool in analyzing lease income, the corresponding leases will provide the details underwriters need to complete their analyses of this line item as found in an income statement. Another document that is more detailed than the rent roll but not as voluminous as the actual lease is the lease brief. It is, as its name implies, a brief description of the major lease terms. It is prepared by the property or asset manager, lawyers or the underwriters themselves after reading the lease. This document focuses on the business and/or unusual terms of a lease since much of a lease will be consistent from tenant to tenant. Exhibit 8 is a sample lease brief.

In any event, while it may seem tedious to analyze each and every lease, it is the most important document available to validate the largest revenue line items found on the income statement. After

EXHIBIT 8

LEASE BRIEF

PROPERTY NAME
PROPERTY STREET ADDRESS
PROPERTY CITY, STATE & ZIP CODE

Date of Lease Execution: ______________________________
Tenant Name: ______________________________
Suite #: __________ Use: __________
Tenant Rentable SF: __________ SF Bldg. Rentable SF: ____
Lease Term: __________ yrs __________ months
Commencement ______ Expiration ______
Base Rent: $ __________ (Mthly) ________ /SF Annual
Concessions (Free Rent): ______________________________
Rent Adjustment:

Date of Increase	New Base Rate (Mthly)	Annual
________	$________	$________ /SF
________	$________	$________ /SF
________	$________	$________ /SF

Renewal Terms: ______________________________
____
Ann. Op. Exp. Allowance: Exp. Stop $___ /SF Base Year ___ $___ /SF
Cap on OE & T? ______________________________
Exclusions? ______________________________
Prepaid Rent: $ __________ Security Deposit: $______
Parking Spaces: Reserved ________ Nonreserved ______

SPECIAL RIGHTS/OBLIGATIONS:

Holding Over: ______________________________
Assign/Sublet: ______________________________
Bldg. Plng. (Relocation): ______________________________
Termination Clause: ______________________________
Expansion/Reduction: ______________________________
Right of First Refusal: ______________________________
TI Allowance: ______________________________
Nonstandard TI Allowance: ______________________________
Moving/Buyout Allowance: ______________________________
Landlord Future $ Obligation: ______________________________
Tenant Future $ Obligation: ______________________________

all, the security for a loan or the asset purchased is only as valuable as the leases underlying the physical asset.

A lease-by-lease analysis is essential in real estate investment. Underwriters should be sensitive to what is "market" and how the property being analyzed measures up. Presumably, we deal in perfect markets and information is readily available to all tenants. Tenants usually act in their own best interests, seeking the most beneficial financial deal available. Underwriters must realize this and understand the implications to the actual leases. They must be able to trace information accurately from market information to tenant/landlord negotiation to lease document to income statement.

There are other reports available to underwriters that will help them understand and validate the existence and reliability of lease income. One example is the aged receivables report. This report will detail the accounts receivable for the property by various time periods (such as 0–30 days, 31–60 days, 61–90 days and 91+ days). If, for instance, the underwriter observes a particular tenant repeatedly showing up on the aged receivables report, then the long-term viability of that income should be questioned and investigated. There may be perfectly valid reasons for the tenant's tardiness but the underwriter must conduct the investigative work to satisfactorily understand the situation.

While this chapter is not intended to be an exhaustive analysis of all the various financial reports and their relationship to the income statement, the reader should be aware that there are myriad sources of related information available to corroborate, support and explain the income statement.

Other Income

Sources of income in an investment property other than lease and expense reimbursement income include:

- Parking income, derived from the operation of a parking facility.
- Tenant service income, generated from special tenant services provided to a tenant by the landlord. (This income is often in part or wholly offset by corresponding expenses.)
- Interest income, generated by the investing of excess cash flows from the property prior to distribution. (In most instances, interest income is not considered operating income; for the purposes of underwriting, it is not usually included as a source of income.)
- Miscellaneous income, derived from sources such as laundries, vending machines, furniture rental, late fees and deposit forfeitures.

Like base rent, other sources of income are often market and occupancy dependent. In the case of parking income, for example, parking charges are subject to supply and demand forces just as any other commodity; the proportion of short-term users to long-term monthly users relates to both market and occupancy conditions. Overall use is directly related to occupancy. If an office property is estimated to be at 95% occupancy, in most cases, the parking facility is not likely to be utilized at 100 percent.

Expenses

Expenses found on the income statement consist of a variety of categories. If the income statement covers an up-and-running or operating property, it will show the actual expenses incurred. These expenditures can be verified by auditing the property's backup documentation including accounting ledgers, bills and invoices as well as contracts and agreements that exist between the building owner and various service providers.

If the property is to be developed or is under construction, the pro forma income statement will show expense estimates based on market information gathered by the property owner. It is very important these expenses are estimated as accurately as possible and they reflect all the various expense items the property will incur.

Expenses can be classified as either fixed expenses or variable expenses. Examples of fixed expenses include insurance, property taxes and reserves. These expenses will be fixed (i.e., will not change) regardless of occupancy or usage. Variable expenses will vary with usage or occupancy or some other changeable element of the property's operation. Variable expense categories include management fees (usually calculated as a percent of revenues), administration, advertising and promotion, security, maintenance and repairs, utilities (water, sewer, gas and electric), cleaning and janitorial services, payroll and fringe benefits. Each of these expense categories is supported or backed up with written contracts or with bills/invoices provided by the particular service providers, or it is a function of property operations and is calculated on an as-used basis or according to the property owner's policies.

Again, the permutations of expenses and classifications are as varied as the number of property owners. However, accounting charts of accounts help to standardize the variation and do lead to some semblance of consistency in the industry.

One of the most important points to remember in analyzing the expense side of the income statement is to make sure it is a complete and accurate accounting of all of the expenses associated with operating a property. Furthermore, the backup documentation should be closely reviewed to validate the representations made on the income statement.

Large bodies of data concerning expenses have been accumulated by various groups concerning the operating costs of various types of real estate. These groups include trade associations, property-type associations, industry clearinghouses, institutional investors, owners and operators. These data sources provide a wealth of resource information and analytical tools for underwriters. Four such sources of comparative data are:

1. *Building Owners and Managers Association International (BOMA) Experience Exchange Report — Operating a Cost-Effective Office Building.* Published annually, the BOMA report provides published tables of operating income and expense data for over 4,500 office buildings located throughout North America. The 1995 report includes 3,600 U.S. private sector properties, 343 U.S. government office buildings, 194 privately held Canadian properties and 439 Canadian government buildings. This sample covers over 850 million square feet of office space in North America. The report contains information about a building's yearly operating costs and rental income as well as data on the building's use and operating characteristics.
2. *Dollars and Cents of Shopping Centers.* Published every two years by the Urban Land Institute (ULI), this report measures shopping center income and expenses to the point of net operating income. This figure is cross-referenced for four types of centers (superregional, regional, community and neighborhood), five age groups (1–3 years, 4–6 years, 7–9 years, 10–19 years and 20 years and over) and five geographic areas — four in the United States (East, South, Midwest and West) — along with Canada. Tenant sales and percentage rent figures are presented for each of the above subcategories.
3. *Institute of Real Estate Management (IREM) Expense Reports.* The IREM reports present median income and expense data by region and for the nation as a whole and in Canada. Each geographic area is further broken down by the property size, age group, rental range and building

type. The reports analyze various national income and expense trends and present special reports on current patterns in leasing fees, utilities consumption and tenant turnover rates. IREM publishes separate reports on apartments, office buildings and shopping centers and a combined report covering condominiums, cooperatives and planned unit developments (PUDs).

4. *National Apartment Association (NAA) Survey of Income and Expenses in Rental Apartment Communities.* Published annually, the NAA report is an income expense analysis for approximately 2,750 (as of 1995) properties containing in excess of 597,000 apartment units in the United States and Canada. The information is broken down by nation, region and metropolitan area. Furthermore, the information is presented for both garden and elevator properties and further separated into individually metered and master-metered properties.

There are various rules of thumb employed in analyzing operating expenses, including ratios, industry averages and other generally stated conventions for analyzing certain operating expenses. However, underwriters must recognize these rules are often based on averages and across property types and locations and therefore may become garbled in transmission and difficult to apply. Anecdotal information will not necessarily serve underwriters well. Diligently and relentlessly analyzing and validating income and expenses by combing over a combination of objective factual information (written agreements, invoices and so on) as well as subjective information will provide underwriters with a solid foundation for understanding the expenses related to property operations.

On the other hand, some expenses are quite easy to validate and predict. For instance, property taxes can be checked with either a visit or phone call to the local tax collector's office. Insurance costs are easily validated in discussions with insurance brokers or agents who sell policies to building owners. Underwriters will find most people consulted to confirm expenses are willing to help in any way they can.

This is not rocket science or nuclear physics. The operation of a property may appear confusing and disjointed but it is, in actuality, a rational, logical process that can be validated through a persistent, consistent and reasoned approach to analysis.

Net Operating Income

The easiest to understand of all the numbers on an income statement is the property's net operating income (NOI). Net operating income is a simple calculation — the result of subtracting expenses from revenues. The NOI is the amount of money available to the property owner to service debt obligations, make capital expenditures and improvements or distribute as the owner sees fit. It also represents a return on the property investors' original cash investment.

Applying a market capitalization rate (the cap rate) to the NOI is one way to produce an estimate of market value. There are other ways to estimate value, including discounted cash flow analysis, cost approach, replacement cost analysis and comparison of one property to other recent sales in the marketplace. This chapter does not discuss the various methods of property valuation. However, a full understanding of NOI — its accurate calculation and all its components — is one of the most critical elements of property valuation. The income statement is an invaluable tool in this pursuit.

Expanded Model

The income statement model can be expanded to include a number of income and expense categories. Because various leases and property types operate in different ways, their income statements are different. Typical operating statement categories for various types of real estate investment properties would include the categories shown in Exhibit 9 on the next two pages.

Reserves

As noted in the expanded model, reserves for replacements are included in the pro forma income statement. The rationale for including this noncash expenditure is that all properties are subject to a number of periodic expenditures for major replacements (roofs, parking lots and HVAC, for example). Rather than deducting 100% of expected costs in a pro forma income statement (which would severely diminish the amount of funds available to support debt obligations), an apportioned amount is usually included as an acknowledgment that prudent property owners and lenders should not use all available cash flow for the support of debt obligations.

Reserves are most often expressed as a per-square-foot cost and typically range from 10 cents to 20 cents per square foot for most investment types (other than hotels) in most markets. Assuming that nonrecurring expenses happen every 10 years, $1 to $2 per square foot is available over time for one-time expenses. Like all such rules of thumb, this cost varies according to building type, age and market.

Pitfalls

This chapter has dealt with the income statement for a property on a cash basis only — that is, the representation of the property's operation as reflected in terms of the actual cash dollars received by and expended by the property owners. This results in NOI that represents cash available to the property owner to service debt, make capital improvements or distribute as they see fit. There

EXHIBIT 9

TYPICAL OPERATING STATEMENT CATEGORIES FOR VARIOUS INVESTMENT PROPERTIES

Office	Retail	Apartment	Warehouse
		Revenues	
Base rent	Base rent	Base rent	Base rent
+ Escalation income	+ Percentage rent	+ Parking income	+ Escalation income
+ CPI increases	+ CAMM recovery	+ Late charges	+ CPI increases
+ Parking income	+ Escalation income	+ Deposit forfeit	– Parking income
+ Tenant services	+ CPI increases	+ Laundry	+ Tenant services
	+ Tenant services		
+ Other revenue	+ Other revenue	+ Other revenue	+ Other revenue
Gross income	Gross income	Gross income	Gross income
– Vacancy allowance*	– Vacancy allowance*	– Vacancy allowance*	– Vacancy allowance*
Effect. gross income	Effect. gross income	Effect. gross income	Effective gross income

*Not typically included in actual operating statements. Typically used in proforma statements.

(continued)

EXHIBIT 9 (cont'd)

TYPICAL OPERATING STATEMENT CATEGORIES FOR VARIOUS INVESTMENT PROPERTIES

Office	**Retail**	**Apartment**	**Warehouse**
Operating Expenses and Taxes			
Management fees	Management fees	Management fees	Management fees
+ Property insurance	+ Property insurance	+ Property insurance	+ Property insurance
+ Administration	+ Administration	+ Administration	+ Administration
+ Security	+ Security	+ Security	+ Security
+ Ads & promotions	+ Ads & promotions	+ Ads & promotions	+ Ads & promotions
+ Parking expense	+ Utilities	+ Utilities	+ Utilities
+ Utilities	+ Maint. & repair	+ Maint. & repair	+ Parking expense
+ Maint. & repair	+ CAM expense	+ Payroll & fringe benefits	+ Maint. & repair
+ Cleaning/janitor. work			+ Cleaning/janitor. work
+ Real estate tax	+ Real estate tax	+ Real estate tax	+ Real estate tax
+ Replacement reserves*	+ Replacement reserves*	+ Replacement reserves*	+ Replacement reserves*
+ Other expense	+ Other expense	+ Other expense	+ Other expense
Total OE&T	Total OE&T	Total OE&T	Total OE&T
Effect. gross income	Effect. gross income	Effect. gross income	Effect. gross income
– Total OE&T	– Total OE&T	– Total OE&T	– Total OE&T
Net operating income	Net operating income	Net operating income	Net operating income

*Not typically included in actual operating statements. Typically used in proforma statements.

are other variations of income statements that account for revenues and expenses slightly differently. The nature of these other types of statements require modification of techniques based on the cash basis statement.

For instance, GAAP requires rental income from leases which have free rent periods or step-up provisions be accounted for in a special manner. The free rent is spread out among all the years of the tenant's lease. Thus, a 60-month (five-year) lease that provides six months of free rent would provide the cash flow rent and GAAP accounting streams shown in Exhibit 10 on the next page. If an underwriter is looking at a GAAP statement in the first year, income is overstated. If it is the fourth year, income is understated. The effect is to smooth out the receipt of cash. This smoothing is also applied to expenses such as property taxes that might only be due twice a year but are accounted for on GAAP statements equally over 12 months.

Another example that would be different in a GAAP statement or tax statement is the treatment and recording of certain noncash expenses, such as the depreciation of capital expense items or the inclusion of interest expense (debt service interest) as an expense above net operating income. Adjustments should be made by the underwriter to account for them properly.

Lessons Learned

The late 1980s through the present have been particularly trying times as the commercial real industry has wrestled with a culmination of related factors: perhaps the worst real estate recession ever experienced; a tremendous oversupply of commercial real estate space; changing technological requirements and needs; environmental issues; changing work patterns, habits and space requirements; structural economic changes affecting the businesses that occupy

EXHIBIT 10

CASH FLOW RENT AND GAAP ACCOUNTING STREAMS

	Year 1	Year 2	Year 3	Year 4	Year 5
Actual Rent Cash Flow Stream					
Base Rents	$ 8.00	$ 16.00	$ 16.00	$ 16.00	$ 16.00
GAAP Accounting Stream					
Base Rents	$ 8.00	$ 16.00	$ 16.00	$ 16.00	$ 16.00
GAAP Adjustment	6.40	(1.60)	(1.60)	(1.60)	(1.60)
GAAP Income	$14.40	$ 14.40	$ 14.40	$ 14.40	$ 14.40

commercial space and many more governmental, economic and business-related issues.

Most of these issues have had an impact on property income statements in some way, shape or form. Some of the impact is obvious — such as the general acknowledgment that a 5% standard-vacancy assumption is, in most cases, no longer acceptable in pro forma analyses for most property types. History has shown that a 5% vacancy assumption is too aggressive. The particular vacancy assumption ultimately used will be based on a combination of market- and property-specific information.

Other impacts are much more subtle and require underwriters to truly understand the various elements of the income statement before using it in their analyses. For example, as markets have tightened and revenue streams from leases have, in some cases, dwindled, property owners have sought ways to augment their revenue streams. While this is not necessarily a bad thing to do, it is important to understand the root of the revenue enhancement. Let's say particular property owners have found a way to lease space on the side of a visible part of their property to a billboard company and the owners include the resulting revenue in the income statement. The underwriter examining this income statement must understand where this revenue comes from and assess the "quality" of this revenue. To carry this revenue through to the bottom-line NOI and then to apply the same cap rate to this income stream may not be the appropriate approach. Perhaps this revenue is more volatile, more short term in nature and therefore, more risky. If this is so, it should not be capitalized at the same rate as more "normal" property operations.

On the expense side of the equation, the analyst must consider whether all the expenses necessary to run the property have actually been included. Maintenance and the deferral of maintenance (i.e., neglecting the care and upkeep of a property) has been an issue since income statement analysis has been in existence, but it becomes more acute when times are tough.

Additionally, as local municipalities grapple with the realities of less funding from state and federal levels, there is more pressure on tax collections. There have been wild swings in property taxes. Underwriters analyzing a property's income statement must fully understand all the ramifications of local tax policy at the present time and how they may affect property taxes. Questions, such as "Will the property be reassessed immediately upon sale?" and "Will a financing event trigger a revaluation?" must be considered.

Underwriters should also fully understand the expense capitalization policy employed by the property owner. This is important in ascertaining whether expenses treated as capital expenditures truly are one-time nonrecurring expenses and whether the property owner is not understating operating expenses and thereby overstating NOI and possibly property values by misapplying capitalization policy.

Summary

Underwriters must carefully and completely review all objective and subjective information available to them, including market information comparison to industry standards and the like. While income statements are one of the most basic of documents reviewed in the underwriting process and seemingly one of the easiest to understand, underwriters must assess not only the accuracy of the information but also the quality and appropriateness of the revenues and expenses found in the reports.

There is no easy formula for understanding an income statement. It takes diligence, persistence, a keen eye for detail and completeness and qualitative judgments made by the underwriter to validate the property's NOI. Whether analyzing operating properties and their actual income statements or to-be-developed properties and their pro-forma or market-effective income statements, accurate income statement analysis is critical to the underwriting process.

2

Property Analysis

Thomas Z. Minehart III, Executive Vice President
Legg Mason Real Estate Services, Inc.

The purpose of this chapter is to discuss fundamental methods or means to critically examine income property. Keep in mind that each piece of income-producing real estate is a separate and distinct entity. Specific types of income-producing properties — including shopping centers, office buildings, apartments, hotels, industrial properties and medical facilities — should each be examined with specific criteria for these very different property types. This chapter will concentrate on four broad categories to describe various income property types and provide a general framework for examining any income-producing real estate project:

1. *Location of the Property.* This includes where the property is, the type of improvements at that location and the surrounding market characteristics that affect its marketability, such as supply and demand for that particular type of facility.
2. *Physical Attributes of the Project.* This includes such characteristics as the quality, size, composition, economic efficiency, architectural and structural design (such as external and internal building materials, heating,

air-conditioning and telecommunications) and parking capacities.

3. *Tenants and Use of the Facility.* This includes the mix of tenants, leasing structures and management's capacity to sustain financing.
4. *Basic Financial Data.* This includes operating statements of income and expenses and financial reports about the specific project and other similar properties.

These broad categories of information pertain to any type of property, from the smallest single-purpose sales outlet to a large, multipurpose office-retail-residential complex straddling several blocks of a downtown area.

While the principles may be similar, there are sufficient differences so that the characteristics of the borrower — and especially the manager — are important aspects of any financing. For example, a builder of an office building may not make a good developer of a shopping center; a typical real estate speculator or land developer should not be expected to be a good manager of a nursing home operation.

The mortgage banker's analysis of income-producing real estate is not an exact science. Subjective judgment, experience, and innovative ability all play their parts. However, each mortgage analysis involves certain fundamentals that create a framework in which the banker's assessments are presented.

The fundamental segments of an analysis are:

- Location
- Physical property description
- Sponsorship
- Appraisal
- Underwriting
- Loan structure

Location

Perhaps the oldest adage in real estate financing is that the three principles of success are location, location and location. Obviously, this is an exaggeration. A good location can be ruined by poor sponsorship, and some projects in marginal locations can succeed with special nurturing by strong knowledgeable sponsorship. The significant aspect of location is that it must be suitable for the project and property under discussion. The mortgage banker knows the aspects which make for a good apartment location in contrast to a good industrial or warehouse site.

Among the many location considerations are:

- Proximity to its market
- Compatibility with the surrounding environment
- Ingress and egress
- Visibility of the site, particularly in retail projects
- Transportation to the property
- Area demographics, such as work force availability, utilities, zoning and physical characteristics of the particular site

Physical Property Description

The information contained in a loan submission or property analysis should include the exact size of the facility, described by legal boundaries; gross and net rentable areas and other specifics, such as parking, amenities, physical and mechanical components, functional and economic utility and all aspects of physical and economic obsolescence.

Physical property characteristics shall be reviewed with respect to the particular property design and its ability to meet present and future tenant demands. A good mortgage banker should have either personal knowledge or available professional expertise for such matters as the adequacy of footings and foundations, heating and air-conditioning, load-bearing capacities, lighting, ceilings, floors, walls and windows. The analyst is responsible for making the judgment of whether or not the proposed project is adequate to function for the user successfully over time.

Sponsorship

Mortgage bankers need to know as much as possible about the sponsorship of the project: whether it is an individual developer, a partnership, a corporation or some other legal development entity. A prospective lender will be interested in the character, experience, ability, financial capability and dependability of the borrower or developer. Lenders must look beyond the collateral; they must also evaluate the borrower's capacity to succeed. Both the credit standing and track record of the project sponsor are important. Credit standing indicates whether the development entity will be responsible for its obligations. The track record helps determine if the developer can manage to complete the project and operate it profitably.

Evaluation of the development entity's financial stability requires a thorough financial investigation and analysis. Every effort should be made to obtain the best possible financial and credit information. Mortgage bankers should scrutinize the credit and financial statements of the corporation or partnership as an entity, as well as those of the individuals who comprise it, to determine the developer's capability to carry a project through to completion.

At the very least, assessment of the developer's track record should include the following questions:

- What other properties has this sponsor produced?
- What other properties of the same type as the subject property has this particular sponsor developed?

- How much real estate has been or is presently managed by the development entity?
- How well is the property maintained?
- What has been the payment record of the development entity?

Appraisal

Evaluation of a project's economic viability begins with the appraisal, which is an integral part of any income-producing financing submission. The mortgage banker must exercise good judgment in determining exactly how much importance to give the appraisal. Some lending institutions are appraisal oriented, while others place priority or equal emphasis on other factors, such as sponsorship and credit.

Appraisers use different methodology to appraise property depending upon the use of the appraisal — for example, appraisals for estates differ from those for condemnation and sale, insurance, local taxation and acquisition. Some lenders rely on the market approach; others rely on either the cost approach or the economic value approach. Some rely on the mortgage banker's appraisal; others require an independent, third-party appraisal. Mortgage bankers must know how particular lenders prefer to analyze certain aspects of the appraisal, such as rental rates, expenses, capitalization rates and discounted cash flow analyses.

No matter what method is used to determine value, most investors want to know the current market conditions for the particular property, including the current occupancy rate, absorption rates and effective rental rates for the property type in question. The mortgage banker's principal consideration should be that the appraisal provides a reasonable estimate of value upon which to base the loan amount. This estimate of value must be acceptable to the lender and the lender's many auditors and examiners. In addition, the information in the appraisal report should be consistent, with no unexplained differences in areas, sizes, room counts or any other facts.

Underwriting

The next step in evaluating income-producing real estate is underwriting. Underwriting is risk analysis. It is often the aspect of the evaluation process that lenders consider most important. Each lender tends to have its own underwriting pattern. Mortgage bankers should be familiar with the underwriting criteria of the particular lender or group of lenders with which they work. These criteria will vary from property to property and from one geographic location to another.

The mathematics of real estate finance is based on standard equations or ratios that apply to almost all types of income property — for example, loan-to-value ratio (LTV), loan-to-gross-income ratio, break-even occupancy, value per square foot and debt service coverage by the net operating income of the property. In underwriting a loan, each lender is likely to consider some ratios more important than others for each type of property. Almost all lenders consider debt service coverage a significant criterion. For each type of property, most have basic coverage requirements that they use to determine their preliminary interest in a loan.

Today, the mathematical analysis within the underwriting process is attracting more attention than in the past, due to the development of computer software programs — such as Argus, Pro-Ject, Lotus and Excel — that can be used for property analysis. These software packages can be used to create spreadsheets and databases that accept the basic cash flow assumptions (including rents, vacancies, expenses, capital improvements, costs and real estate or rental commissions) and can be easily adjusted for assumed inflation over any time period desired. Once the data is registered in the selected model, it only takes the click of a mouse button to try "what if" scenarios. Today, the computer and a good real estate software analytical package have become essential tools for performing property analyses.

Loan Structure

The final step in loan evaluation is structuring the loan. At this point, mortgage bankers must make significant judgments about the maximum amount of financing that a particular property can sustain. They must balance their figures against loan interest rates, terms and conditions. Based on a thorough analysis of the project's characteristics, this decision will influence the particular lender with which the mortgage banker is dealing.

For example, let's say the prospective lender never exceeds a 75% LTV for shopping center projects. The mortgage banker should know this when negotiating the application with the sponsor and when recommending a particular dollar amount to the lender. On the other hand, if the sponsor is willing to accept a lower LTV, but wants an interest rate lower than that generally offered by the lender for this particular type of project, the mortgage banker engages in negotiating the loan structure with both the borrower and the lender.

The changing environment in the money markets reflects changing expectations and leads to wide variations in negotiations. New products offered by lending institutions — such as short-term debt instruments based on the sponsor's credit, debt-equity instruments involving equity participations and convertible mortgages — will result in changing attitudes about the types of loans desired, as well as the terms on which loans will be granted.

To help the borrower structure the loan, the mortgage banker must be familiar with the changing world of real estate finance. Experienced mortgage bankers know that it is futile to try to sell a loan that does not fit a lender's pattern or to try to change a lender's investment policy. Nonetheless, mortgage bankers, borrowers and lenders can usually work together to develop new forms and ideas of creative mortgage financing to meet changing investment needs.

This chapter was based on information supplied by Angelo L. Dentamaro.

3

Market Feasibility

Vernon George, President and CEO
Hammer, Siler, George Associates

The first half of the 1990s has brought changes in the operations of the real estate business in the United States. Much greater importance is being placed on the determination of market feasibility as a part of the underwriting process for short- and long-term financing and equity investment. Significant losses on individual investments have encouraged lenders to move away from an asset allocation and risk averaging approach toward an overall assessment of the real estate portion of their total lending and investment portfolios.

Intermediate and longer-term good-project returns remain high for real estate investments relative to competing investment opportunities. As such, it is prudent for institutional investors to continue to build a real estate component into their total lending and investment portfolios. However, the experience of the first half of the 1990s makes it clear that to achieve high returns, lenders and investors must make a more rigorous effort to determine the probability that a project will achieve market success.

The immediate response has been for the lender to require substantial preleasing and/or sales before lending, as a technique for improving the probability of market success. And this practice will continue. However, even when the preleasing test is passed, the intermediate and longer-term ability of the project to remain leased — or to continue selling in the face of specific anticipated competition — is an essential part of the decision. Making these determinations requires effective market feasibility analysis.

Real estate product is described and measured in the kinds of units users typically perceive themselves buying or renting. These include housing units, office or industrial floor space, hotel rooms, retail floor space, entertainment floor space and other more specialized units, such as marina slips and parking spaces.

For many kinds of real estate products, the pace of leasing success is much greater once there is space in place, so that immediate/near-term occupancy is possible. This allows prospective tenants to see what the building space and project quality will be, so that they have a greater sense that there will be a critical mass of activity around them. Without the option of construction before substantial preleasing, this part of the market is threatened.

As of this writing, it is not clear when the Republican commitment to reduce taxes on capital gains will be fulfilled; however, when it is, a much broader range of potential investors will be attracted to real estate. Since these new investors will have less experience and fewer risk-analysis resources available to them, there will be much greater demand and fiduciary need for rigorous market feasibility analysis by those with a documented, strong track record of successful prediction.

The need for new investment in central cities and other older areas becomes ever greater as the role of government is reduced through revenue restrictions. The sharp reductions in federal programs to help produce economic development in cities will have a particularly strong negative impact. Banks and other lenders and investors are under pressure — and will be under greater pressure — to move in and play a much greater role in solving urban problems. Determining market feasibility is more difficult in these low-investment areas. Accurate market analysis is essential to achieving the results that will sustain and expand private investment, as well as to ensuring much greater leverage on scarce public capital.

Market Feasibility

There are many feasibility hurdles that must be overcome before a project moves to construction and operation. Market feasibility analysis determines which characteristics will make the project most marketable and then systematically predicts when various components will be absorbed in the market and at what price/rent levels.

This chapter addresses the market feasibility question in terms of:

- The importance of market feasibility analysis
- The steps in the market feasibility process
- How users should interpret the market feasibility report

The Importance of Market Feasibility Analysis

Market feasibility analysis enables the participants in the development process to estimate the absorption and capture rates. Absorption, as used here, is the calendar pace at which the units in a project could be marketed and sold or rented. Capture refers to the market share a particular project can attract, given the total amount of similar product type marketable in the market area. Knowing the capture rate gives the development participants some insight into how the project can be changed to be more successful in capturing a share of the market.

Market area refers to the geographic area within which other projects offering similar real estate product will compete with the subject project.

The most valuable answers generated by market feasibility analysis include the following:

- Market feasibility analysis identifies the characteristics a project should have in order to be successful in the market. Besides location, creativity and content are critical characteristics. Whether the users are employees, employers, hotel patrons, retailers, retail customers or residents, they expect something more than just physical facilities. High ceilings and atria, abundant glass, quality materials, abundant plantings, fountains and, in many cases, programmed entertainment activity have become very important, as the creativity and content in the project have become ever more essential to project success.

  The point is that the market is very competitive and will continue to be in the future. Those projects that are good lending risks in the short term and the long term are the projects that incorporate the features which have the strongest and growing attraction to potential users.
- Market feasibility analysis provides reliable estimates of present and future absorption levels of the relevant real estate product types in the metropolitan area and the market area during the proposed marketing period. The pace of office construction in most suburban and downtown office markets across the country and the resulting high vacancy rates are now finally reaching acceptable levels; this is an excellent example of how the total balance of space leased and space constructed can dominate the feasibility analysis, regardless of the quality of the individual project location and characteristics.
- Market feasibility analysis estimates the probable annual capture of each real estate product type over the proposed development and marketing period. How much real estate product in the subject project can be marketed, closed and

occupied and at what price/rents are key ingredients to total project feasibility.

- Market feasibility analysis is an initiative as well as an evaluative service. The feasibility analysis suggests the marketing and development strategy that will optimize market absorption. This means that, from a development and lending standpoint, the market analysts make their most valuable input to the successful project when they determine the project characteristics that will lead to the greatest marketing success. Objective evaluation and documentation is only one part of this service.

Market feasibility analysis is important to project success. In short, it provides estimates of the project revenues that will be generated and suggests key project, development and marketing characteristics that will optimize the project's revenue stream.

The Steps in the Market Feasibility Process

Market feasibility analysis is carried out as a series of systematic steps. It involves identifying, collecting and analyzing data in order to make market feasibility judgments. These steps include:

- Defining the market area
- Evaluating existing projects
- Identifying state-of-the-art design
- Analyzing the local economy
- Analyzing trends
- Defining the project concept
- Determining market share

Defining the Market Area

Various analysts have different labels for what we choose to call here the market area. Other labels used include the trading area (particularly for retail), the service area, the catchment area, the subarea and the competitive area. The label is not important, but the concept is. The market area is that geographic area within which other projects offering real estate product similar to the subject project will be competitive with the subject project.

The criteria and method for defining the market area relates to the characteristics of the project being proposed.

Retail Projects. For retail projects, the primary market area is often defined as that geographic area of residences within which the subject project is the most convenient location for the particular kind of retail store. The stores that have the greatest appeal, and therefore are most important in determining the market area, are the department stores in the regional malls, the supermarkets in community centers, major single-category outlets in power centers and free-standing clusters and, in some specialty centers, major theme restaurants and entertainment centers. These stores are called the anchors.

In the retail parlance, the "primary market area" is the contiguous geographic area that contains the consumers who are responsible for 75% to 90% (as specified in the particular analysis) of total sales. A secondary market area is often also defined. In this area, the proposed center typically has greater competition, and the residents do not find the proposed center to be in the most convenient location; however, substantial sales are still achieved. Sales to residents from outside the primary and secondary market areas is the third component of typical shopping center retail sales estimates and is often referred to as inflow.

The importance of the anchor stores in defining retail market areas is illustrated by a recent experience in a middle-sized, Mid-Atlantic community. With the completion of a planned expressway link, the proposed regional shopping center site will have the best highway access of any developed or proposed location to the entire urban region. There is also a large and growing expenditure potential in the part of the total region within a 15- to 20-minute drive time to the subject property. The center seems to be in a great location.

However, three of the four department stores now active in the region are already covering most of the residential area around the subject site from other centers. And, although these other sites are inferior to the subject site, these department stores are tied into their present locations with long leases. As a result, the trading area for this center, if based on the assumption of existing department store participation, would be quite small — too small for a feasible operation. The same situation could exist in a community center. Much of its logical trading area (typically much smaller than a regional center) might already be covered by the active supermarkets in other parts of the area.

In such situations, our HSG/Gould retail staff identifies anchor tenants that are not now in the market but could successfully compete. For such tenants, the subject site is superb, and because they currently do not have stores in the urbanized area, the logical market area is larger than for an anchor with other stores in other parts of the region.

Entertainment Projects. For entertainment projects, it is particularly important to identify the lifestyle characteristics of the probable market for the particular entertainment content and technology being proposed. If the location is well selected, these lifestyle characteristics will likely be prominent not only in nearby neighborhoods, but also in neighborhoods and employment centers in a number of the parts of the metropolitan market. Identifying these neighborhoods and employment centers and assessing their accessibility to the proposed location are essential to the process of defining the market area.

In our Charlotte Center entertainment project, the logical market area has a concentrated component and a dispersed component. The concentrated component is the employees, conventioneers and other visitors to downtown. The dispersed component is made up of the neighborhoods within the city and the surrounding region that have the age, income and household characteristics that would most likely be drawn to the virtual-reality-anchored entertainment content and technology.

Office Projects. For office projects, there are a variety of definition approaches based upon the market the office tenants intend to serve. For community-serving tenants — such as doctors, lawyers and real estate agents — the retail community center approach works best. In fact, such buildings are often located near or in community centers. For office tenants serving the entire city or major sectors of the city, the market area logically includes all those locations that could conveniently serve the residents and employees in the particular area. Major intersections are often preferred locations.

As our economy has shifted toward the services sector as the primary source of jobs, an ever larger share of office space has been occupied by firms that serve regional and national markets. As such, they can be located anywhere in a particular urban area. They chose their locations not from an orientation-to-customers standpoint, but rather based on factors such as proximity to quality residential areas (for their executives and other employees); proximity to expressways, airports and other intercity transportation facilities; image; and, of course, the quality of the space and the project.

There are often practical applied research considerations in determining the market area. Some of these are illustrated by a recent office park project carried out by our Atlanta staff. The project is located in a major Southeastern city and is aimed at the headquarters/research and development tenants. A reconnaissance of the area revealed that there are directly competitive facilities (that is, office buildings enjoying considerable success in the headquarters/research and development space market) in one downtown fringe location, in office parks near the airport and in two of the four geographic sectors of the suburban area.

A contiguous market area, including all these successful, and therefore competitive, nodes would include almost the entire urbanized area. To inventory all of the office buildings within it would be exhausting and misleading in implication. Thus, the market area was defined to include only those parts of the region which had either existing or probable future effective competitors for the headquarters/research and development market, in terms of their proximity to research institutions, quality housing and other R&D operations. Therefore, the market area was determined to actually include five discrete areas that demonstrated the market success and location quality to make them truly competitive.

Industrial Tenants. As with regional offices, some industrial tenants serve a local area, some serve the metropolitan area as a whole, and some serve both national and regional markets. The market area is best defined as the contiguous area offering the same general location characteristics in terms of expressway and other major transportation access, existing industrial zoning and use patterns and employee residential areas. Analyzing the potential for changing existing local community land use policies and zoning regulations can be particularly challenging for market feasibility analysts and is often important in industrial market analysis.

In a recent assignment that our Silver Spring, Maryland, staff carried out in a close-in suburb of Cleveland, most of the land in the logical path of industrial expansion was zoned agricultural but shown as industrial on the plan. Public facilities were not in place. The total industrial development pace in this suburb was modest.

Clearly, we had to assume that the subject land could be rezoned, or there would be no point in conducting the analysis. However, if we assumed from informally stated local policy that zoning would not be granted until major public infrastructure was in place, the competitive market area would be small. If we assumed, rather, that the courts would demand that land planned for a use must be zoned for that use, as the courts of this jurisdiction have in the past, then the market area would be very large and would result in a supply that far outstripped demand.

The optimum approach must define market areas based on each of the two sets of assumptions, and then use them as one tool in defining the reasonable range of market absorption for the subject project.

Hotel Patrons. Hotels cluster around traveler generators, including businesses, airports, expressway interchanges and tourist attractions. The market area for a particular hotel project includes all those locations that would be convenient to the same traveler generators as the subject site. Clearly, this is not a contiguous area but a series of individual high-accessibility nodes.

Residential Projects. For residential projects, image is an extremely important factor. Image is generalized by neighborhood and community names. To those living in the Washington, D.C., metropolitan area, McLean, Virginia, means something in desirability, price and school quality. To the well-informed or active house-seeking household, the selectivity of image is even more refined, with the Langley neighborhood within McLean having a special quality image. Definition of the market area here is created by the consumer. The analyst's job is to monitor, record and utilize the result.

The importance of neighborhood image requires a two-tier approach to residential market area analysis. In the primary tier, there is a McLean housing market. It is active, and the subject project in McLean can best have its success measured as a share of McLean activity. However, a large share of households considering a housing purchase in McLean are also looking in other prestigious residential areas in the remainder of Fairfax County, Virginia, and in adjacent Montgomery County, Maryland. Zoning, infrastructure and other policies and factors greatly change the relative desirability of these areas and the relative amount of housing product available. As a result, second-tier market analysis, which also requires careful market area definition, includes all those neighborhoods within the community that have substantial appeal to households seeking the good schools, quality amenities, shopping and other characteristics of prestigious communities. A careful examination of competitive projects and total sales pace in these other communities is important as well.

Evaluating Existing Projects

The systematic evaluation of the most comparable projects in the market area is often described as "surveying the competition," but it is really much more. From this evaluation, we learn:

- The project characteristics that have been most important to project success or lack of success in the market in terms of rent/price, amenity, location, marketing approach and so on
- The absorption rates projects have achieved and/or are achieving
- The amount of product projects still have to market and when it will be exhausted
- The total amount of product marketed by new, quality projects in the market area

Careful analysis of this data for individual projects and total market activity provides a good foundation for subsequent steps in the feasibility analysis.

The sources and methods of carrying out this existing project evaluation include:

- In-depth personal interviews with developers and marketing personnel at the projects
- Field surveys to examine and record project and location characteristics (photos are useful)

- In-depth interviews with development regulatory agencies and utilization of their GIS and total project data
- Interviews with Realtors, mortgage bankers and other informed industry personnel
- Door-to-door interviews with users to determine what they like and dislike about their projects
- Project data from data services and available databases

The results of this existing project evaluation will provide a good understanding of the project and user characteristics of the market area activity in each relevant real estate product type.

The existing project evaluation task is particularly important to users of market feasibility analysis. The market forecasts themselves must be judgments for which it is impossible to establish total certainty. The actual experience of the best projects — those that have been competing in the market and those that are most directly comparable to the subject property — provides an important base for user comparison and evaluation.

The importance of this test was illustrated in a recent assignment carried out by our staff in Florida for a major international equity investor. Although called in at the last minute, we were able to quickly determine that although the concept and location of the subject project were good, the projected project absorption would have to exceed the recent absorption in the total market by over 42% annually if it were to reach the financial projections on which the purchase price was based — clearly a red flag, at least until more detailed analysis could be carried out.

Identifying State-of-the-Art Design

At any point in time, developer efforts to meet the specific needs of various user groups are much more creative in some urban areas than in others. User needs are also constantly changing and some areas are "ahead" of others in this evolution. Identifying and utilizing the "state of the art" in this regard will often give a project an important edge in its market. Characteristics that have had leading-edge marketing leverage in recent years include:

- Flexible industrial/office space that often features a quality exterior finish but a wide variety of interior finishes to meet the specific needs of a wide range of potential tenants
- An atrium, providing an "entertainment" environment, in all types of non-industrial real estate product, providing an edge in creativity and content
- The university affiliation and campus design which are often used to establish instant image and momentum in the market
- Neotraditional design concepts, as a response to the planning concepts we have known in recent decades
- Smaller, high-quality, single-family detached product, created to reach a broader part of the market in areas with high land costs
- Restaurant- and entertainment-facility-anchored specialty retail centers

A comprehensive field trip would be a successful, but expensive, way to build this state-of-the-art database. More practical approaches include:

- Reviewing periodicals, newsletters and project files produced in the industry
- Attending conferences
- Involving consultants with national practices
- Conversing with regional affiliates
- Reviewing project promotional materials on the Internet

The point here is that maximum absorption will not necessarily come from following the most successful projects now in the market. There may be better techniques being used elsewhere.

The role of the market feasibility consultant bringing in successful new marketing and development concepts is well illustrated by a recent experience in Las Vegas. Diversification toward industrial development is proceeding at a healthy pace, but, until recently, product type offerings have been limited to high ceiling distribution facilities to serve the multistate region and low ceiling "incubator" space to accommodate the wide range of local serving businesses. The hoped-for spillover of research and development activity from high-cost California is occurring, but it is slowed by the limited available inventory of suitable space, largely because the development community was (understandably) unwilling to produce product for what was an undemonstrated local market. The solution was to draw on the experience of Atlanta, Washington and other cities. Market success was achieved when our clients began to build buildings that had the exterior quality and site control, which experience in other markets showed were required by many research and development firms, but that also had the high ceilings that were adaptable to distribution operations or, in the ground floor and mezzanine mode, to the combined office/light assembly needs of research and development firms.

Analyzing the Local Economy

Many market feasibility reports begin with a brief review of recent past and projected future population and employment growth from local planning agency reports and then never "visit" the data again. The more useful approach is to:

- Examine the trends and evaluate the forecasts for consistency with these trends. Where the forecasts deviate from the trends, determine if change factors that would logically account for these trend deviations are identified.

- Determine the dimensions of the economy and population most important to the real estate product type being analyzed (industrial employment to industrial land used, households and total personal income to retail potential and so on) and calculate the relationship between the absorption of the real estate product type and recent changes in the causal economic or population variables.
- Apply the relationships calculated for the recent past to the future projections of the appropriate population and economic variables. This enables you to develop one set of projections of future absorption.

There may be a considerable difference between availability and quality in local forecasts. By performing a common sense appraisal of the forecasts and building causal relationships, the economic and population projections can be an important part of the feasibility analysis process.

Determining the relationships between the appropriate characteristics of the economy and the future demand for a particular kind of real estate product is a useful way to detect overbuilding. In Denver, an analysis of in-depth energy-industry-outlook studies over recent years made it clear that, even without sharp energy price drops, the probable pace of projected employment growth is considerably slower than that of projected office space construction. Dramatic overbuilding was an almost certain result. These energy industry forecasts and the relationship between energy employment and office absorption provided the basis for our recommendation to clients that projects be deferred. The use of such symptomatic data to predict market balance is a technique that could be well used by the user too.

Analyzing Trends

There is often a user perception that the use of trends data is a substitute for better thinking. In reality, the expertise in any field is most heavily based on experience. No one looks forward to working with a brain surgeon or lawyer who has no real experience, regardless of the length of that person's training with secondary data.

Trends must certainly be analyzed and explained in terms of causal factors, and then adjusted — based on perceived changes in these or other causal factors — before they can be used as a forecasting technique. Trends in actual real estate product absorption and trends in economic and other causal or symptomatic data are useful as a foundation for market area absorption estimates.

The use of trends as a forecasting technique requires that the user understand the factors causing the trends. In a recent assignment in Pittsburgh, the office absorption trends had been heavily influenced by the expansion and space upgrading of major corporate headquarters. A series of in-depth interviews with senior officers of these corporations revealed that several were anticipating major corporate downsizing which would reduce their presence in the region and the downtown. By testing this and other underlying assumptions in the recent past, we were able to advise the client that renovation of older space was likely to be a competitive market since these corporations were poised to cut back. The used space absorption trend was an overly optimistic view of the future.

Defining the Project Concept

There is an adage that the answer to any question can never be any more precise than the question itself. This is certainly true of project capture estimates in feasibility analysis. A detailed description of the characteristics of the project being tested is an essential input to the project testing.

In order to understand this point, it is necessary to consider an example. In evaluating a potential shopping center acquisition in a small community in the Shenandoah Valley of Virginia for a major asset management firm, we were told that the completion of an interchange link to an existing expressway would make the center strong and lead to the filling of remaining vacant store spaces. The future construction of a major express street through the developing area to this interchange would expand the market area and support significant expansion of the center. Our conclusion was that if this street were built, the leasing predictions for the center would be achieved.

However, closer discussions with the highway department revealed that the interchange would not be complete by the opening of the center. Rather, the construction process would make even existing access to the center difficult during the first 18 months after its opening. Further, while the express street link is a high priority among local planners, the dean of the local legislative delegation held out little hope that it would be funded.

Clearly, in order for users to best interpret the results of a market report, they must know the assumptions made about the various important causal factors and the probability that those assumptions are correct.

Determining Market Share

Determination of the market share is a synthesis task and the culmination of a very important part of the feasibility analysis. Market feasibility work must build a strong bridge between analyses of the relevant factors and estimates of specific project capture. The high-confidence-level approach involves the following steps.

Determine Total Market Area Absorption. The first step in determining the market share (amount of a particular kind of real estate product that can be marketed at the subject property) is to determine the total amount of this type of product from all projects in the market area that will be marketed.

To do this, two approaches are used in tandem. First, the trends in total market area absorption of the particular real estate product type are analyzed. The total amount of product absorbed over the last five to seven years is analyzed, using both a total average and a three-year moving average. Factors that cause changes in absorption are determined, and the extent to which they will be operating in the future is judged. (Often called causal factors, these include the number of jobs and households created, changes in highway accessibility and other regional location factors.) Based upon this analysis, these past absorption trends are adjusted into projections for the future in terms of physical units that will be absorbed in each year or cluster of years.

In the second approach, the relationship between each of the real estate product types and the causal variables that operate at the metropolitan or market area level is established. For retail, this relationship is households and income in the market area. For most other uses, reliable projections are typically available only at the metropolitan level, in terms of employment by industry type. Here, the relationships between the recent past absorption in each real estate product type and change in the causal variable (office land and building absorption with office employment, for example) are calculated. Forecasts of those variables, made by responsible agencies, are then evaluated and adjusted for reasonableness, and the ratios are applied to estimate total metropolitan absorption.

These two approaches do not always result in similar absorption estimates for the total market area. This, in and of itself, is an important finding from the user's perspective. In a downtown project in a moderate-sized New England community a few years ago, trends in actual office and retail leasing were quite modest. However, an analysis of the broader New England economy revealed the beginnings of the broader technology-based upturn of which we are all now well aware. As a result, neither the trends nor forecasts developed by the local staff were judged reliable. However, properties assembled based upon these advance indications provided a quality development site at what was later to prove to be a bargain price.

The market area share of the metropolitan total is then determined using the trends approach previously described.

Determine Key Absorption Factors. Interviews with developers, industry experts and tenants/users all include questions on what factors were most important in their selection of a particular project. The answers to these questions are analyzed by the analysts, based on their previous project experience, and a set of location determinants are established and weighted for relative importance.

Each of the projects is then rated for each of the location determinants, and then, a composite score is calculated by applying the weightings to the ratings and summing the total. A rating range of 10 and a weighting range of 5 are often used. The multiplication of the rating by the weightings generates total location quality points for each project.

This judgmental model is tested and calibrated using the following steps:

- The total location quality points are calculated for each project using the rating and weighting approach.
- The total number of quality points for all projects competing in the market area during the last test period is tabulated. The percent share of the total market area quality points is calculated for each project.
- The actual absorption achieved by each project and the total absorption for all projects during recent periods are determined in the project evaluation step. At this point, the share of the market captured by each project is calculated.

- The share of the total market-area absorption captured by each project is compared to the share that project has of total location quality points. Where there are inconsistencies, the weightings of the factors are adjusted until the location model fits the actual absorption data.

For instance, a project that had 10% of the quality points for projects in the market during 1984–1985 should have captured 10% of the physical product absorbed during this period. The weightings of the factors are adjusted until the system results are consistent with the actual market performance of the recent past.

Determine Comparable Project Performance. This step involves a direct comparison of the subject project with the other projects that will be competing in the market during the period. Using the matrix of absorption factors, both rated and weighted, the subject project — as conceptualized — is rated for each factor and a cumulative score calculated. Each of the competing projects is likewise rated.

The point score of the subject project is compared to the point score for each of the successful projects currently competing in the market. The ratio of their point scores is then used to estimate market share for the subject project. For example, let's say that a residential project competing in the market area has been marketing 100 units per year and has a location point score of 80. Another more poorly located and developed project has a point score of 40 and has been marketing 50 units a year. Based on these numbers, if our own project — as conceived — has a point score of 60, we could expect an absorption of roughly 75 units a year. In other words, capture is a rational process related to location quality.

Determine Available Market Share. The direct comparable project absorption or head-to-head approach is valuable, and perhaps the most commonly used systematic market share approach. It is particularly useful in a balanced market. However, in a market where product production levels are increasing, or overall area and subarea absorption levels are decreasing, there may well be too many good projects in the market; that is, the market may be overbuilt. To test for this possibility in the future market, a share-of-the-market approach must also be used. The steps in this process are as follows:

- All existing projects are rated for each important location factor.
- All proposed projects that are judged likely to be in the market during the proposed marketing period for the subject project are also rated.
- Relative importance weights are assigned to the various factors and the location evaluation point scores totaled. These scores might be called location quality points.
- The share of the total location quality points for all projects are calculated. These shares change over time as projects enter and leave the active marketing phase.
- The shares are applied to the previously projected total subarea potential absorption, and the capture is estimated for the subject project in terms of the appropriate units of that particular kind of real estate product.

Combining the project-comparable and share-of-market approaches, each systematically applied, increases the probability that the absorption estimate accuracy will be good.

Optimize the Project's Market Appeal. There are two primary purposes for market feasibility analyses. The first is certainly to determine the capture or absorption that can be achieved by the project, if built. Equally important is the role of feasibility analysis in optimizing the market appeal of the project.

Basis for Project Optimization. The careful examination of existing projects in the market, the state-of-the-art review and the experience of the senior analyst are all important inputs to the conceptualization of the optimum project offering for the subject property. The design, traffic engineering, planning, financing and other members of the project team likewise bring this experience.

Interdisciplinary Sessions. Each of the disciplines — market feasibility, planning and design, engineering, traffic, finance and others — makes the greatest contribution to project success not in independent reports, but in "over the board" work sessions with the client developer and team as a whole.

Optimum Project Strategy. Through a series of these sessions with the developer, the optimum project/marketing strategy evolves. This process combines marketing strategy, probable market response, relative development costs, environmental constraints and other factors, using the expertise of planners, transportation experts, legal experts and market analysts.

Testing Strategy. Having devised what appears to be the optimum strategy, each expert must objectively test it and be prepared to justify the results.

Sensitivity Analysis. This analysis tests the impact of different levels of achievement for each of the critical variables, such as a slower or faster absorption pace, lower price/rents, a less-preferred zoning category, a more costly sewer solution, a delay in expressway construction and so on. Sensitivity analysis is often called downside or upside analysis. It is important to analyzing the risk characteristics of the project.

Market feasibility analysts are often chided: "If you're so objective, why do we never see negative reports?" The first answer is obvious: When the answer reported to private clients is negative, they seldom wish to incur the additional cost of writing and printing the report. Less obvious, but more important, is the answer that comes from the market-iteration process: Seasoned market analysts do not limit their thinking to the specific market question asked; and, particularly when the market for the client's preferred use is weak, the analysts do their best to define, at least in general terms, what uses make better sense for the property.

This market analysis role is illustrated by a recent assignment carried out by our firm's Denver office. A primary client objective was to generate additional income from the fourth and fifth floors of a department store building it owned and leased to a national chain operator. The objective was exhibition or trade mart space in support of an adjacent hotel. The vertical goods and people movement problems caused us to recommend against this use. However, in the process, our staff identified the potential to develop the space for a food court and other retail support activity, particularly if this department store building could be tied into a major, publicly funded, two- or three-level retail specialty mall being planned for downtown.

The rigorous application of these steps in the market feasibility analysis will result in an accurate set of market feasibility estimates that are easily understood.

Interpreting Market Feasibility Analysis

Users of market feasibility analyses must know the market feasibility characteristics of the project, understand how they were derived and be able to convincingly present these findings to lenders. As such, they need to address the following issues:

- Key assumptions
- Probable absorption level
- Project comparables
- Assumptions about competition

Understanding the Key Assumptions

The description of the detailed assumptions about the project being made in the capture determination is a very important part of the communication between the market analyst and the user. These assumptions include:

- *Timing.* What will the calendar marketing period be, and how does this relate to the competing projects?
- *Project and Facility Amenities.* What amenities are recommended and assumed? What is the impact on absorption if key amenities will not fit into the project budget?
- *Marketing and Promotional Strategy.* Will the project marketing be handled by the most successful marketing firm in town? Will there be an adequate promotional budget? Or, will the developer handle it in-house on a shoestring budget?
- *Timing of Public Improvements.* Which roads, sewers and other public improvements, not now in place, are key to the project? What completion timing is the analyst assuming?
- *Financing.* Are development, permanent- and end-user interest rates assumed to remain about where they are at the time of the analysis? Or, will they rise or fall?
- *Economic Trends.* How will economic growth in the region during the marketing period compare with that of the recent past? Why?
- *Supply/Demand Balance.* What will the total absorption of the particular real estate product type(s) in the market area be during the proposed marketing period? How will this compare to projected competitive supply?

The point here is that the user is not testing for clairvoyance. Rather, it is essential that he know what the analyst has assumed so that he or she may evaluate these assumptions for reasonableness as a part of determining the reliability of the forecasts. Other important assumptions include the project's probable absorption level and the market absorption levels of comparable projects.

Probable Absorption Level

Users must understand not only the probable absorption level, but the reasonable range. The downside and what could cause the downside are particularly important.

Market Absorption Levels of Comparable Projects

It is useful for users to compare the actual market absorption of the most successful comparable projects with the projections for the subject property. Users should examine and test assumptions about the number of competing projects that will be in the market and what will happen to their absorptions for reasonableness.

Importance to the Appraisal

The needs of users of appraisal estimates of project market value, primarily lenders, have become much better focused in the last decade or so as the troubled project has become a more common term in the industry. In the past, comparable sales and replacement cost were common phrases. Today, lenders must know not what the project would be worth when fully leased and/or what the land would be worth at that time when someone chooses to buy it for its most profitable permitted use. Rather, the lender must know, if the issue is land, the total absorption pace in the competitive subarea; how other tracts on the market and/or potentially on the market in the future compare in location quality with the subject site; and, therefore, what the probable sales pace of the subject property would be if sold to short-term users at short-term user prices. Finally, the lender must know the price that the total tract would bring in a single sale today; acknowledging that the purchaser would have to take into account the carrying or opportunity cost of each portion of the land prior to development.

In short, lenders on land have learned that to have an estimate of price without specific absorption and terms is no more useful from a real or present-value standpoint than an estimate of absorption without price. Likewise, the estimation of completed project value based upon what comparable projects up and fully leased are selling for "cash on cash" is almost academic in a competitive market. Lenders can make little use of value estimates that "jump over" the risk and timing hurdles of successful project marketing. Clearly, any estimate of the value of a project once it is fully marketed must be discounted by the probability of the successful marketing, and the probable time required for marketing. The market feasibility analysis tells the developers, lenders and appraisers what project absorption, price and terms should be used in their analysis and decisions.

4

Market Forecasting

James F. Giegerich, President
Giegerich & Associates

Understanding the market economy in general and the real estate market in particular is an essential fiduciary responsibility of mortgage lenders. Since there are so few advanced academic programs in real estate, many real estate lending professionals are not highly trained in market analysis or skilled in forecasting the changes in real estate markets. Much of this analysis is contracted to third-party independent consultants who specialize in this small but important slice of property valuation and project financing evaluation.

In the mid-1970s, undiscriminating bank lending and expanding real estate investments led to one of the worst financial reversals in real estate markets. As the markets recovered, many new factors entered the marketplace, including the 1981 tax legislation, severe inflationary concerns, comparatively disappointing corporate securities performance, new pension legislation suggesting that diversified portfolios include real estate, substantially increased offshore investor interest and economic expansion. Together, these factors contributed to real estate becoming a favored investment for both institutions and individuals through the use of real estate securities.

The favored status of real estate led to growing investor acceptance, which translated into booming capital inflows to real estate investments. Although the investor frenzy signaled over supply problems in the middle and late 1980s, financial institutions continued to pour money into speculative, investor-driven real estate deals. The market was sustained, not by the demand of tenants to occupy space in buildings, but by investors seeking to commit capital to finance and own buildings.

As lenders reviewed their real estate lending problems in the late 1980s and early 1990s, it became clear that many lending decisions had been based on unrealistic market assumptions and faulty risk analyses. The drive to increase bottom-line profits led lenders to generate large volumes of real estate investments that ignored the economics of the market place and the cyclical nature of real estate. When the inevitable downward market cycle arrived, some banks and savings and loans and a few life insurance companies found that their investments in real estate and real estate mortgages had resulted in government intervention or that the poor performance of these investments had pushed them into failure. In reviewing the resulting problems in financial institutions' commercial real estate portfolios, some lenders were unable to provide even the most basic data about the current condition of their portfolios or what was going to happen in the future.

This has led to a changing role for mortgage bankers. Today, mortgage bankers and asset managers are expected to better understand their real estate investment portfolios. Better knowledge of portfolio quality requires much more emphasis on fact finding, knowledge of market data, market forecasts and asset information concerning realistic rents, vacancy factors and operating costs.

Changing Market Trends

In the fast changing and dynamic era of the 1990s, market forecasting is complex and requires close attention to dramatic new trends in business, human behavior at home and work and overarching societal trends. Market studies and appraisals that utilize past trends to forecast the future are problematic because historic trends, especially from the roaring investor-driven real estate markets of the 1980s, are not generally good indicators of the current market forces or those anticipated during the 10-year pro forma period covering the end of the 1990s and beyond.

Fundamentally, the mid-1990s economy reflects uncertainty. The pace is fast and dynamic, and communications are instantaneous. The market structure is fragmented and fluid. The financial and investor base is global with a major institutional investor presence and increasing interest in real estate securitization.

One example of the changing real estate scene is in the dramatically changing retail markets. Retailing is now subject to factors that fundamentally change the long-held assumptions about the demand for, the characteristics of and the location of retail space. These factors include:

- Travel time
- Entertainment
- Sanitized replications of the urban experience
- Value-based retailing
- Individualized marketing
- Future retailing strategies

Travel Time

Studies of time allocation show that acquiring goods and services requires as much time as leisure activities. As individuals increasingly value personal priorities and lifestyle considerations over work and consumption, reduced shopping time is becoming a quality of life goal. Compelling priorities for enhanced effectiveness and efficiency in the allocation of personal time are changing traditional living patterns and, therefore, the retail real estate which is dependent upon them.

Traditional retailers are feeling pressure from Internet-shopping, television-shopping-channel and mail-order-catalog sales. The information highway, interactive video technology and changing social patterns are moving information about retail merchandise to the consumer. This is a dramatic departure from the traditional requirement that the consumer travel to where the merchandise is displayed. Transportation to a retail store to personally touch and feel the product, while still important to some, will no longer be the primary focus of the merchandising process.

Entertainment

Beyond pure convenience, people favor shopping facilities that enhance the social and entertainment experience of shopping. The success of the Mall of America in Minnesota has initiated interest in creating entertainment value associated with the shopping experience to add a destination magnet value to the location.

Sanitized Replications of Urban Experience

Consumers are interested in getting the convenience and variety of urban shopping, without the hassles and fears associated with going into the city. Replicas of urban shopping provide a protected shopping experience that responds to heightened concerns about crime and security issues.

Value-Based Retailing

In a more competitive, less forgiving, retailing environment, consumer choices and options will proliferate while undifferentiated offerings and mediocre quality will be eliminated. Successful retailers will increasingly emphasize the extra value they offer.

Individualized Marketing

The marketing priority has moved from mass marketing to individualized marketing. Mass marketing emphasized the product and sought to sell it to as many customers as possible. In contrast, individualized marketing — made possible by technological advances — focuses on one customer at a time and tries to sell as many products and services as possible to that customer.

Future Retailing Strategies

In the future, retailing strategies will have to embrace such themes as value, quality, service, convenience, style, entertainment and price. A property that is not strategically positioned to adapt to these priorities will have trouble sustaining a tenant's successful business and will therefore have a limited role as a retail facility.

Changing Workplace Trends

Trends in the workplace have also changed. The real estate market now reflects dramatically different types of space preferences, requiring new design configurations and location criteria. Accordingly, space-use patterns and real estate economics are inherently different today than during prior cycles of economic activity in the following ways:

- More production does not necessarily require more jobs. The information age, with its increase in computers and communication networks, has raised productivity to higher levels.
- More job titles do not necessarily lead to increased space requirements due to the changing dynamics of the workplace. Downsizing and corporate reengineering have resulted in greater outsourcing, increases in home businesses and the introduction of space-saving concepts such as office hotels and telecommuting.

- Even if more space is occupied, this does not necessarily translate into higher rents. Consider big box discounters and factory direct retailers, for example.
- Higher rents and increasing cash flows do not necessarily translate into higher property values in the face of escalating costs of capital.

Accordingly, new market forecasting models — models that are more descriptive of the present economy and real estate markets — are needed to provide better market forecasting results. The often used market-performance models that were based on previously relevant theoretical constructs and traditional explanations are no longer applicable.

Incorporating Market Cycles in Market Forecasts

Recent research studies document the effects of cyclical macroeconomic factors on real estate performance. Researchers have found that significant real estate and cash flow value differences occur when analyses incorporate cyclical economic factors rather than the simple trend patterns typically used in the constant-growth discounted cash-flow (DCF) analysis models of the 1980s. Analysis models that assume constant rates of change and rely on only past experience are clearly inappropriate in forecasting market values and supply and demand.

Incorporating economic cycle analysis results in market forecasting requires consideration of the following exogenous factors:

- Inflation
- Supply and demand relationships
- Changes in rental rates and vacancies
- Effect of interest rate changes

- New construction, vacancy rate and rental rate linkages
- Asset prices and rents
- Capitalization rates
- Unique regional geographic characteristics

In the Summer 1994 issue of the *Journal of Real Estate Research*, Waldo L. Born and Stephen A. Pyhrr illustrated the use of a cycle valuation model to evaluate linkages between real estate supply and demand cycles, equilibrium price cycles, inflation cycles, rent rate catch-up cycles and property life cycles. Their study demonstrated the differences of standard trend DCF valuation studies with a cyclic model and the significant impact of economic cycles on asset value.

Born and Pyhrr found that traditional real estate valuation models assume efficient markets, stabilized cash flow variables in single-year and multiyear pro formas and impute property return/risk expectations into current overall market capitalization rates to determine value. This traditional valuation framework is biased toward trend analysis and often assumes constant annual changes in rents and expenses and constant terminal value capitalization rates over 7- to 10-year projection periods. Economic cycles are not explicitly addressed by the valuation framework or models of the 1980s.

Based on this, Born and Pyhrr concluded that economic cycle impacts are significant and can dramatically alter valuation conclusions, especially at the bottom (trough) or top (peak) of the market supply/demand cycle. Traditional appraisal analyses that use linear models in DCF projections produce results that substantially undervalue property in the early recovery phase of the real estate cycle. On the other hand, when the real estate cycle is near or at its peak, linear "trend" projections lead to overvalued properties.

Phases of the Real Estate Supply/Demand Cycle

The analysis of a typical cycle of supply and demand, shown in Exhibit 11, indicates three important points:

- In a growing economy, the long-term trend line for both change in demand and supply is upward sloping. At the peak of each new cycle, the additions to supply and demand reach new peaks as compared to the previous cycle. The opposite occurs in a declining economy.
- Change in supply is somewhat more volatile than change in demand. Developer/lender enthusiasm causes supply to rise above demand during the peak phase, and developer/lender pessimism causes supply to fall below demand during the trough phase of the cycle.
- The demand cycle leads the supply cycle by a period of time. The lengthy process of planning and financing a new project makes it difficult for development to begin as soon as the market demonstrates a need or to stop as quickly as demand begins to decline.

Summary

Today, mortgage lenders are expected to understand their real estate investment portfolios better. Requirements for improved knowledge of the portfolio quality of real estate investments will mean more emphasis on market forecasts than in the past.

The impacts of economic cycles are significant and can dramatically alter the results of traditional real estate operating incomes and valuation conclusions. The market research and forecasting process is being redefined to produce information and data for use in economic cycle models so that real estate investment valuations can account for cycles in the economy.

EXHIBIT 11

PHASES OF THE REAL ESTATE SUPPLY/DEMAND CYCLE

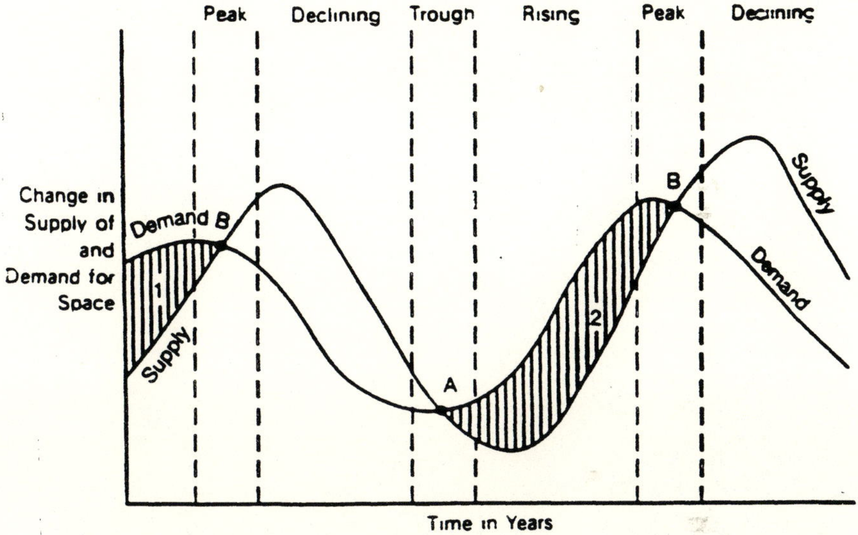

Economic Characteristics of the Real Estate Cycle (Pritchett, 1984. Wheaton, 1987. Written, 1987)

There are significant changes taking place in society in general, and in the home and workplace, thanks to the ready availability and use of communications, interactive video and computer technologies. These changes are resulting in fundamental changes in real estate requirements. Accordingly, it is becoming necessary to modify many of our past assumptions about the way real estate investments will perform in the future. Traditional market forecasting, based substantially on historical trends, is no longer appropriate.

5

Information: What You Know Is As Valuable As Who You Know

Mary E. Vander Linden, President
Access Solutions

For years, commercial mortgage bankers provided information by presenting facts about a property and region and then responding to investor questions. Confidence in the relationship between investor and mortgage banker made the information sufficient.

Today, the real estate industry is described as "information driven" — a term that has become almost a cliché. Every business and trade magazine carries articles on the significance of information as the personal computer and Internet push everyone — including mortgage bankers — into the information age. Nowadays, mortgage bankers are measured not only by who they know but also by what they know — the information they can provide. Mortgage bankers analyze the facts thoroughly and then offer the information to the investors.

The commercial real estate industry has always relied on facts and data about properties, markets and economies. The industry was not necessarily driven by information, however. The industry was principally entrepreneurial. Information supplemented what was primarily a relational (who you knew) and transactional business among owners, mortgage bankers and investors.

Although relationships remain fundamental, the industry has changed.

What Has Changed and Why Is There a Greater Need for Information?

The commercial real estate industry has undergone a fundamental change since the late 1980s. Faced with empty buildings and collapsed sales prices, the industry had no choice but to change. Relying only on facts and relationships became inadequate. Information gathering and analysis are now necessary parts of interactions between mortgage bankers and investors.

Information enhances the success of both mortgage bankers and investors in a number of ways. For instance, having information about all parts of an economy or a transaction helps reduce risk and provides competitive advantages. Like relationships, information brings confidence to a transaction. Information, combined with understanding and prudence, can keep markets in balance.

As an example, consider how retail markets in some regions are being overbuilt. It is not the real estate industry that has forgotten the lessons about the value of information. Retailers themselves continue to build big-box stores and power centers despite recent bankruptcies and consolidations. Supply and competition — not information about reduced disposable incomes, declining retail sales and changing customer habits — are driving the retailers. Knowing this can help the real estate industry in its decision making.

Why Should Mortgage Bankers Provide More Information?

Mortgage bankers need to provide more information because investors need more information. Experience has taught investors that they need to know all they can about the region, the market and the property. In the past, available real estate data was subjective and hard to compare. Today, as more data goes through the system, information quality, timeliness and accuracy are improving.

Competition is driving the need for information. Abundant competition exists for limited product. Investors and lenders must use accurate information quickly to capture the best transactions. Owners and borrowers also seek information — about financing, market conditions and when new product will become available. With appropriately analyzed information, all parties can make better decisions that improve business outcomes.

Competition from outside the traditional lending areas has also added to the need for better information. Real estate has lagged behind other asset forms in both research and information availability. Securitizations by Wall Street and increasing institutional ownership of real estate are causing that to change. Voluntary information standards have been assembled by the National Council of Real Estate Investment Fiduciaries (NCREIF), the Pension Real Estate Association (PREA) and the National Association of Real Estate Investment Managers (NAREIM). The Mortgage Bankers Association of America (MBA) has also worked on information standards, and members must begin working within these guidelines if they are to meet investor needs.

Real estate is local. Mortgage bankers are local and therefore can provide what national firms cannot. Mortgage bankers know the market and the principals. Mortgage bankers want long-term relationships with customers; with accurate information, they can provide well-founded market conclusions for investment decisions. The difference between closing a deal and losing a deal may be how good the information is and how quickly it can be obtained.

Canned or packaged information supplied by chambers of commerce or other organizations was once used as the primary source for regional and general real estate market data. However, this is no longer sufficient. Data is becoming a commodity.

Mortgage bankers must add value to it. Each piece of data must be multisourced, interpreted and analyzed; essentially, it must be condensed into a usable, well-organized format. Sources must be scrutinized for reliability and timeliness.

To compare how a region is performing to how the nation as a whole is performing requires familiarity with the gross domestic and state products, the consumer price index, job growth and analyses of these elements' effects on the economy and real estate markets. Supply-and-demand influences within a region and within a neighborhood, whether it be existing or proposed, should be known and understood.

Local information must include negative as well as positive aspects of the economy. The focus has been on jobs and how job growth affects real estate usage. As new construction occurs, however, micro (local) information will become more valuable. Information on supply-constrained markets or areas where a product can have functional or value advantages will become more important.

The industry will not go back to the 1980s. Although relationships are still fundamental, the ability to provide quality information will determine a mortgage banker's value and long-term customer loyalty.

What Kind of Information Must Be Provided and Analyzed?

Micro Information

Local, professional mortgage bankers are the main sources of investment information. They must provide large quantities of materials to meet underwriting standards, including details on borrowers. Everything that affects supply and demand for a particular property is included. Reports contain trends and competition within market areas and explain how the property and submarket work within the regional economy.

Macro Information

Mortgage bankers must fit a specific property into the context of the macro (regional) economy and the specific real estate market. A shopping center has to be analyzed in terms of population, employment and retail sales growth in its region; it also has to be analyzed as part of a neighborhood, considering household types, income levels and existing and potential competition.

A macro view of the entire economy is necessary. Where is the region's economy heading? What changes (for example, base closings, new companies or tax changes) could affect the economy, the real estate markets and the project in question?

Market or Property Types

Commercial real estate markets vary not only by region and location but also by property type. Knowing what is happening within a property type — on both a national and a local scale — is important. For instance, the office market is divisible into locations and classes. Rent differentials between classes of office space affect how rapidly space is absorbed. Class C space, while much less expensive, may be functionally obsolete or in a less desirable location. New space may have to be constructed even though Class C space is available.

As a further example, the St. Louis office market has received poor ratings in some articles because of its downtown vacancy rate. However, Class C and D buildings are included in that vacancy rate even though the properties are not considered investment-grade real estate and have little impact on market conditions. In addition, most national readers do not know about the continuing political struggles over demolition of possible historic landmarks included in the inventory. Such information can be supplied by local mortgage bankers, giving potential investors a better understanding of true market conditions.

Accurate, reliable, trustworthy sources are vital. A one-stop, readily accessible source would be perfect, but at this point, such a source is not available. Several national companies and magazines, such as the *National Real Estate Index* and *National Real Estate Investor,* provide helpful overviews, but these publications cannot offer the specific information required for analysis.

Government Agencies

Government agencies are making data acquisition easier through bulletin boards and Internet locations. California's Labor Market Information Department has one of the best bulletin boards (now on the Internet) — the California Economic Database System (916-262-2BBS) — for employment and population data. It has 16 phone lines and is available 24 hours a day, seven days a week. Data is placed on the bulletin board as soon as available, eliminating phone tag with analysts and long waits for printed information. Current and historical materials are easy to download.

FedWorld, a U.S. bulletin board and Internet site, is not as simple to use, yet it too can be helpful when searched. FedWorld (bulletin board 1-703-321-8020 or www.fedworld.gov on the Internet) provides access to a wide variety of government data sources, including the Department of Labor, the Census Bureau of Economic Analysis, the Federal Register and even the Federal Real Estate Sales bulletin board. Labor market information from several states can also be accessed through FedWorld. The Census Bureau also furnishes demographic information at its own Web site (http://www.census.gov).

Federal Reserve bulletin boards (FRED, St. Louis, 314-621-1824) and Internet sites (http://woodrow.mpls.frb.fed.us) provide interest rates, consumer price indices and other economic information. If a state or agency is not on-line, analysts within an organization can be found to provide the data required.

Economic factors are paramount in analyzing real estate markets. For example, employment changes are known to have significant impact on real estate supply and demand. Growth in labor force and jobs in distinct industry sectors have been the main measures used to determine regional demand. Slower FIRE (finance, insurance and real estate) and services sector growth are considered indicators of lessening demand for office space.

Demographic forecasts also need to be analyzed carefully. All numbers are not equal. Some forecasts are marketing tools rather than objective estimates. Understanding the marketing aspects of forecasts is important, as slower population growth in many locations will limit labor force increases over the next few years. This, in turn, could also slow office-space absorption and ultimately reduce rental increases.

It is important to look beyond population estimates and growth into areas such as migration sources and types and age distribution characteristics. In Denver, for example, many recent newcomers sought lifestyle changes rather than jobs; they had higher incomes and a greater impact on retail sales, home purchases and luxury apartment rents than traditional job seekers. In Phoenix, strong job creation has brought many educated, young people to the city; however, the national media often focuses on the region as a retirement center.

Councils of governments, regional planning agencies and economic development and planning departments of cities and counties are good sources of activities and plans relating to real estate in a specific region and neighborhood.

Academic Sources/Trade Magazines and Associations

Academic sources in the real estate field are still primarily print. Local libraries have Info-Trac, ABI/APO, the index for *The Wall Street Journal,* local newspapers and other databases that can be easily searched for recent studies and articles. In addition, many universities have data centers, business and economic research organizations and public policy departments that can be of assistance.

You also can find some materials on the Internet. Services such as Argus RE-View Online (1-800-947-9257), available with modem and communication package, are forerunners of the future. This toll-free service offers access to demographic and retail database services, Argus real estate publications (*National Real Estate Investor, Retail Store Image, American City & County,* and so on), trade associations and property listings. It also offers E-mail and search capabilities. RE-View is also on the World Wide Web at http://www.argusinc.com.

Real Estate Markets

Obtaining reliable real estate market information can be a problem, depending upon the region. Market information is still primarily from commercial brokerage firms. Some brokerages provide a great deal of information; others are secretive.

Brokerages that publish accurate and timely information provide a valuable service to the industry. While private data providers are available in a few markets, information from local commercial brokerage firms is still essential in understanding a market. Commercial real estate brokers, like mortgage bankers, need to know what is occurring in a marketplace and why.

Varying definitions and building survey criteria can make it difficult, if not impossible, to compare data between commercial brokerage firms. For example, some firms include sublease space in office vacancy rates, and others exclude it; office surveys may contain both single-use and multitenant buildings or only multitenant buildings. For another example, California brokerages report rent on a monthly basis while brokers in most of the country report rent on an annual basis.

Some terms have different meanings in different areas. For example, in some markets, the word "speculative" means available space in a multitenant building. In others, "speculative" means only space under construction that has not been preleased; after a space is leased, it is no longer considered speculative and is included with vacant space.

Some terms are used in particular regions but not elsewhere. For example, the term "shadow space" is used in the Minneapolis-St. Paul region to denote office space that is currently leased but not occupied. Rent is paid but the space may or may not be available for sublease. In industrial markets, some brokerage firms report availability rather than vacancy. Availability means that the space is currently occupied but can be leased. Vacancy refers to the space that is unused.

Definitions can change over time even within the same firm. Company buyouts and consolidations can cause familiar sources and terms to disappear or change, making years of prior data useless for comparison. Definitions and terms can differ between regions even among national commercial brokerage firms. Because of the type of industrial usage in Orange County, California, for instance, multitenant industrial space is specifically defined as highly finished research-and-development (R&D) and incubator space and is not included in inventory or vacancy rate. However, more traditional multitenant space is included with data from other Southern California counties.

Some of the definition and survey problems will be resolved as data sources join organizations like the Real Estate Information Network, an international association of commercial real estate publishers and information providers, or REI-NET, a network of commercial real estate providers. Definitions will become standardized, and all buildings in a market will be surveyed, rather than just a few selected buildings. Survey data will be verified through tenant follow-up.

How to Provide Information

The simplest and most common form of investor information comes from phone contacts, trade magazines and business or real estate journals. More formal information sources used by mortgage bankers include investment reports (preliminary briefs and final submissions on individual properties), appraisals and publications.

Investment reports must deal with the strengths and weaknesses of the property and trends in the marketplace. They also must describe how quantitative facts support qualitative statements about the transaction and the recommendations made. Computers and modems have facilitated the delivery of information, allowing for quicker, easier review. Discounted cash flow analysis software, such as Argus and Pro-Ject, enable local mortgage banking offices to produce spreadsheets for investors, showing the data under various assumptions. Econometric financing and forecasting models for specific properties are now being added into analysis software programs.

Conclusion

Mortgage bankers can obtain vast quantities of helpful information from multiple sources, in many forms. The first step into the information age is discovering what is available and how to access the data. The second step is determining how best to add value to the information collected. In whatever form information is furnished, it is important to remember two things: *Why* is more important than *what,* and data sources must be accurate and current.

Armed with traditional relationships and well-analyzed information, commercial mortgage bankers can compete effectively in today's information-driven industry. Mortgage bankers will know — and will provide — what it takes to make their customers and themselves successful.

6

Real Estate Appraisal

Steven J. Beauchamp, Senior Managing Director
Landauer Associates, Inc.

**All quoted information in this chapter was obtained from two sources: The Appraisal of Real Estate, Tenth Edition, and The Dictionary of Real Estate Appraisal, Third Edition, both published by the Appraisal Institute, Chicago, Illinois.*

The appraisal of real property is an evolving process that involves collecting, researching, analyzing and correlating information into an opinion of value. The Appraisal Institute defines an appraisal as "(1) An analysis, opinion, or conclusion relating to the nature, quality, value or utility of specified interests in, or aspects of, identified real estate. In this usage, appraisal covers a variety of assignments, including valuation, consulting and review. (2) The act or process of estimating value; an estimate of value."

Prior to 1950, the cost approach was extensively utilized as one of the primary methodologies. As the appraisal profession progressed in the 1960s and 1970s, the sales comparison and income approaches became the dominant methodologies. This trend was spurred by the rapid expansion of the real estate industry and the spread of data pertaining to markets and property transactions. In the 1980s, the entry of large numbers of institutional investors into the real estate industry pushed the appraisal profession into a computer analysis age. The 1990s have introduced electronically transmitted appraisal reports and on-line computer services and data banks. Despite these advances in technology, an appraisal is still an art form that expresses an opinion of value. New computer applications will aid appraisers in conveying information to clients in a more comprehensive and timely manner. In many instances, the rapid advances in technology will reduce the need for appraisals of homogenous forms of real estate (such as residential). However, appraisals will continue to be needed for complex real estate and when external issues (such as bankruptcies) require specific appraisal expertise.

Today's appraisal is a written or oral communication of an opinion of value. The opinion of value is supported by appraisal standards that set guidelines designed to create uniformity in the methodology and reporting process. The objective of these standards is to provide reliable and supportive opinions of value.

Picking an Appraiser

The selection of an appraiser is no different than the evaluation process performed to pick an architect, attorney or physician. The selection process is expedited by soliciting recommendations from other users of appraisal services. To determine which of the short list of recommended appraisers is the best qualified, you can ask the following questions:

- What is the total number of years of real estate appraisal experience of the appraisal professional?
- How many years has the professional been appraising similar properties?
- What is the professional's appraisal experience within the property's neighborhood, city and county?
- Does the professional have a recent appraisal example that can be submitted for review and that would

demonstrate the ability to perform the appraisal assignment?

- If not, can the professional explain orally the appropriate procedure for appraising the property?
- Will the professional be performing all of the appraisal services or will there be others performing or assisting in the appraisal? If others are involved, the following questions are appropriate:
  - What portions of the appraisal will the other professionals perform?
  - How many years of appraisal experience do the other professionals have?
  - Who will be involved in forming the final opinion of value?
- Is the appraiser licensed or certified?
- Does the appraiser hold a designation from a nationally recognized appraisal organization?

Although many clients select appraisers based on fees, expenses and timing, the best possible results will be achieved by a careful review of the appraiser's reputation, references and responses to the above questions. It is important to remember that the lowest fee and quickest turnaround time for an appraisal may not be provided by a qualified appraiser. Typically, qualified appraisers base their professional charges on time and expenses required to perform the requested services.

Appraisal Structure

Regardless of the form of the communication, there are several items that must be addressed within an appraisal. These appraisal requirements include:

- A definition of the appraisal problem
- A collection and analysis of the most relevant information
- A study of the highest and best use of the property
- Utilization of the most appropriate valuation methodology
- The reconciliation of the value conclusions from the three classical approaches (if appropriate) into a value estimate
- The communication of the opinion of value

Defining the Appraisal Problem

The definition of the appraisal problem should include "identification of the real estate, a discussion of the property rights to be valued, purpose of the appraisal, definition of value, date of the value estimate, the scope of the appraisal and limiting conditions." Form and narrative appraisal reports should include these topics in written form, while oral reports must also cover these topics and must be backed up by a written set of documents that support all of the findings and conclusions in an organized work file.

Identification of the real estate should include one or more sources. The most common sources are property name, street address and legal description (metes and bounds, rectangular survey system and lot and block). The vast majority of appraisals include all three of these sources and generally less-common forms of identification such as the tax folio number, property survey or photographs (aerial or street level). In more elaborate narrative reports, a brief description of the physical improvements and tenancy may be presented.

The property rights to be appraised may involve a wide variety of physical and legal property ownership types. The most common form of physical ownership is fee simple real estate. Other property ownership types include the subdivision of the property rights through legal conveyances such as mortgages, leases, and easements.

The purpose of an appraisal is "the stated reason for an appraisal assignment, i.e., to estimate the defined value of any real property interest or to conduct an evaluation study (consulting assignment) pertaining to real property decisions." This purpose is established by the clients or users of the appraisal. Mortgage lenders generally require appraisals for underwriting or asset monitoring purposes. The purpose established by other clients may be for a tax appeal, liquidation, bankruptcy, sale, acquisition, or to determine insurable value. The motivation of the clients is an important starting point in understanding the appraisal problem. Therefore, it is critical to establish the purpose of an appraisal before commencing an assignment. Determining the clients' requirements at the beginning of the assignment should aid in preventing any misunderstandings among the clients, users and appraisers.

The definition of value is "(1) the monetary worth of a property, good or service to buyers and sellers at a given time; (2) the present worth of the future benefits that accrue to real property ownership." Market value is the predominant property value requested by clients and users of appraisals. Market value is defined as "the most probable price, as of a specific date, in cash, or in terms equivalent to cash, or in other precisely revealed terms for which the specified property rights should sell after reasonable exposure in a competitive market under all conditions requisite to a fair sale, with the buyer and seller each acting prudently, knowledgeably and for self-interest, and assuming that neither is under undue duress."

Other forms of value requested by clients include value in use, investment value, going-concern value, insurable value and assessed value. Investment value is a specific value of a property investment to a particular investor or groups of investors. This value may result in a conclusion that is significantly different from market value. Going-concern value involves the combination of real-estate and business values. Hotel properties are excellent examples of properties that should be valued as a going concern.

Insurable value provides a value of the property improvements that could be destroyed by fire, wind, flood or other forms of destruction. This value estimate is commonly based on the replacement or reproduction cost, less nonperishable items. Assessed value is the value placed on a property by an assessor or property appraiser for the taxing entity. This form of value is generally set by government statute and may be lower than the market value.

The date of the value estimate is most often the date of inspection, but it can also be based on the requirements of the user of the appraisal. For active markets where property values are rapidly increasing or decreasing, a date of value that is more than 60 days prior to the issuance of the appraisal report may make the opinion of value unreliable. In more stable markets, where transactions occur infrequently and property values remain flat for extended periods of time, a date of value that is several years old may still be reliable. Retrospective dates of value may be appropriate for assignments involving past property claims. A bankruptcy case is one of a variety of sources for a back-dated appraisal. A future-value date may be useful to a lender's understanding of the potentials of a proposed property at completion or stabilization. Future dates of value are highly speculative and require detailed explanation. The client and appraiser should decide at the beginning of an assignment as to the appropriate date of value.

Scope of the appraisal is a very important part of the definition of the appraisal problem. It should clearly present the level of data collection, verification and analysis to be performed by the appraiser. This discussion should provide the readers of the appraisal report with sufficient information on the limitations to the opinion of value that are created by the appraiser's level of research, level of analysis and communication format.

Basic assumptions and limiting conditions are the key qualifiers of an appraisal. They are designed to inform and protect the client and other users of the appraisal. Some examples of standard assumptions and limiting conditions are as follows:

- This appraisal is prepared by, or under the supervision of, members of the Appraisal Institute in accordance with the Institute's Standards of Professional Practice and Code of Professional Ethics.
- Title to the property is assumed to be good and marketable unless otherwise stated. No responsibility is assumed for the legal description or any legal matter. The property is assumed to be under responsible ownership and competent management and free of all liens and encumbrances, except as specifically discussed herein.
- The definitions and assumptions upon which our analyses, opinions and conclusions are based are set forth in appropriate sections of this report and are to be part of these general assumptions as if included here in their entirety.
- The sketches, plot plans and drawings included in this report are included only to assist the reader in visualizing the property and are not meant to be used as reference in matters of survey. The legal description furnished should be verified with the aid of competent legal counsel.
- The appraisal was prepared for the function stated and should not be used for or relied upon for any other function.
- The distribution, if any, of the total valuation in this report between land and improvements applies only under the stated program of utilization. The separate allocations for land and buildings must not be used in conjunction with any other appraisal and are invalid if so used.
- Possession of this report, or a copy thereof, does not carry with it the right of publication. It may not be used for any purpose by any person other than the party to whom it is

> addressed without the written consent of the appraisers and, in any event, only with proper written qualifications and only in its entirety.

Specific limiting conditions may also be presented in this section of the report. The purpose of these conditions is to highlight their potential impact on the opinion of value. A statement, such as "the value estimate is based on the property being renovated at a cost of $600,000 within the next six months to comply with current building codes," is an example of a specific limiting condition that aids clients in understanding the reliability of the opinion of value.

A certification is required in all appraisals. The certification should follow the strict guidelines of the Appraisal Foundation. The Appraisal Foundation is an oversight organization that has a uniform standard for the appraisal process and certification. These guidelines require certification stating whether or not the appraiser has an independent third-party role in an appraisal. Without such a signed document within an appraisal, the users of the appraisal cannot be confident that the appraisal is free from bias.

The presentation of limiting conditions and certification is usually located within the front section of the appraisal report following the transmittal letter. However, it may be located directly after the reconciliation of value at the end of the appraisal report.

Collecting and Analyzing Information

County and City Analysis

The county/neighborhood data sections of an appraisal establish the rationale for external influences on a property's value. In many instances, this section of the appraisal report is subdivided into multiple subsections. Exhibit 12, shown on the next two pages, provides an example of a regional economic and demographic fact sheet.

EXHIBIT 12

BROWARD COUNTY, FLORIDA — REGIONAL ECONOMIC & DEMOGRAPHIC FACT SHEET (1990–2000)

	1990	1995 (est)	2000 (proj.)	Compound Annual % Growth 1990–1995	Compound Annual % Growth 1995–2000
Population					
Broward County, FL	1,255,488	1,411,661	1,553,823	2.4%	1.9%
Fort Lauderdale, FL, PMSA	1,255,488	1,411,661	1,553,823	2.4%	1.9%
State of Florida	12,937,926	14,174,341	15,274,681	1.8%	1.5%
United States	248,708,990	262,775,323	275,551,045	1.1%	1.0%
Households					
Broward County, FL	528,442	595,772	656,028	2.4%	1.9%
Fort Lauderdale, FL, PMSA	528,442	595,772	656,028	2.4%	1.9%
State of Florida	5,134,869	5,645,031	6,089,600	1.9%	1.5%
United States	91,947,195	97,413,803	102,233,962	1.2%	1.0%
Avg. Household Income					
Broward County, FL	$39,813	$45,961	$53,256	2.9%	3.0%
Fort Lauderdale, FL, PMSA	$39,813	$45,961	$53,256	2.9%	3.0%
State of Florida	$36,508	$42,377	$49,305	3.0%	3.1%
United States	$38,464	$44,436	$51,520	2.9%	3.0%
Per Capita Income					
Broward County, FL	$16,757	$19,498	$22,599	3.1%	3.0%
Fort Lauderdale, FL, PMSA	$16,757	$19,498	$22,599	3.1%	3.0%
State of Florida	$14,490	$17,057	$19,858	3.3%	3.1%
United States	$14,220	$16,654	$19,320	3.2%	3.0%
Aggregate Income (000)					
Broward County, FL	$21,038,212	$27,524,566	$35,114,846	5.5%	5.0%
Fort Luaderdale, FL, PMSA	$21,038,212	$27,524,566	$35,114,846	5.5%	5.0%
State of Florida	$187,470,548	$241,771,734	$303,324,615	5.2%	4.6%
United States	$3,536,641,838	$4,376,260,229	$5,323,646,189	4.4%	4.0%

(continued)

EXHIBIT 12 (cont'd)

BROWARD COUNTY, FLORIDA — REGIONAL ECONOMIC & DEMOGRAPHIC FACT SHEET (1990–2000)

	1990	1995 (est)	2000 (proj.)	Compound Annual % Growth 1990–1995	Compound Annual % Growth 1995–2000
Retail Sales (000)					
Broward County, FL		$17,368,935	$20,931,607		3.8%
Fort Lauderdale, FL, PMSA		$17,368,935	$20,931,607		3.8%
State of Florida		$137,811,945	$160,020,279		3.0%
United States		$2,241,319,080	$2,733,157,094		4.0%

Source: Urban Decision Systems; Market Statistics *Retail Sales data is for 1994 and 1999*

Socioeconomic trends (employment and population demographics), government and social factors, local and regional economic conditions, construction activity, taxes and availability of mortgages should be studied, analyzed and discussed. Much of the information for this section of an appraisal is abstracted from secondary sources such as government (federal, state and local), quasi-government agencies, trade associations and organizations that survey property markets. This information should be presented only if it is relevant to the property being appraised.

County data should present information that allows the reader of the appraisal to understand the level of diversity, work force size, unemployment rate and prospects for future expansion or contraction of companies and industries within the employment base. A comprehensive evaluation of the population size and composition — possibly including trends in population growth and distribution of population by age, income levels and household size — should also be presented. Government regulations (such as zoning and building codes) are important to investigate to determine their impact on the property. Social issues may involve presenting information pertinent to the property's ability to be successful in the market area. Buying power, general price levels and cost-of-living issues should be presented to aid in evaluating the capacity of the county to economically support the property. Development activity is a valuable indicator of the growth of an area and the prospects for an oversupply or supply shortage of public and private sector real estate. The tax base is important in evaluating whether a county/city has sufficient revenues to provide the essential public services and the prospects for future tax increases. The availability of financing in a particular region has a major impact on a property and its comparison to properties outside the region.

Neighborhood Analysis

Neighborhood data should provide the reader of the appraisal with a clear understanding of the subject property's relationship to its surroundings. A neighborhood is defined as "A group of complementary land uses; a congruous grouping of inhabitants, buildings, or business enterprises." The boundaries of a neighborhood are determined by a transition such as a natural or man-made boundary. A transportation arterial, a business district or property market (such as office, retail or apartment), bodies of water and physical topography (valleys and mountains) are good examples of boundaries between neighborhoods.

Neighborhoods are generally described as being in one of four stages of development: growing, stable, declining or revitalizing. The stage of development of a neighborhood may influence the future performance of the property being appraised. Neighborhood data should include a discussion of the forces influencing value including supply and demand factors.

The extent of the collection and analysis of relevant information is based on the impact of outside forces on the appraised property. It is important to focus or concentrate the analysis on the information that has the greatest impact on the property. For example, an apartment-building appraisal should focus on collecting employment, population and buying-power data. The number of apartments in a neighborhood and whether the basic needs of renters are provided for in a neighborhood should also be researched and analyzed.

Property Market Analysis

Property market analysis became an integral part of most appraisals after the collapse of the real estate industry in the late 1980s. It is the section of the appraisal that provides the reader with a historical perspective, as well as a forecast. The property market analysis may be presented as an independent section or as part of the county/neighborhood data, highest and best use or valuation sections.

This analysis provides the basis for determining the likelihood that the property may be stable or in transition. It may also be utilized to support the highest and best use and to support estimates of functional or external obsolescence. It is a critical element for forecasting revenues and expenses within the income approach.

A property market analysis section can be addressed by answering the following six questions:

1. What are the physical boundaries of the property market in which the property is located?
2. What is the size (number of buildings, square footage, number of dwelling units or hotel rooms and so on), quality level (Class A, B or C) and age of the inventory?
3. What is the occupancy level of the inventory?
4. What are the prospects for demolition or expansion of the inventory?
   (a) What is the impact of changing employment and population patterns on these prospects?
   (b) What is the availability of land in the market?
5. What are the historical, present and potential rental rates, lease terms and operating expenses?
6. What is the current and forecasted health of the property market?

After these questions are answered and the analysis is completed, a microevaluation of the competitive properties should be presented. In many cases, this microanalysis is presented at the beginning of the income approach to establish market rent, occupancy and operating expenses.

Property Data Analysis

Property data is generally presented in two parts: land and building descriptions. A discussion of property data must include descriptions of the land, site and building improvements and the direct impacts of legal and environment issues. This is commonly followed by a presentation of the site and building improvements. Property descriptions are based on physical inspections and third-party information, such as local building department plans and records.

Site Description

The site description should present the appraiser's physical observations, along with information provided by property surveys, zoning, soil tests, topography maps, environmental studies, legal documents and public records. A physical inspection is essential to understanding studies, surveys, maps and county records. Physical characteristics are based primarily on observation and available surveys and studies which should include size and shape, location, environment, frontage, access, view and topography. Surveys may provide the dimensions and elevation of a site and indicate easements and encroachments that can be helpful in understanding the value. A title policy may present information on deed restrictions, easements and encroachments. Zoning and land-use data may establish the starting point for the highest-and-best-use analysis for the property. Property taxes and assessment are generally presented in this section of an appraisal report and are routinely utilized in the income approach.

Site Improvements Description

Site improvements consist of landscaping, paving, sidewalks and utility infrastructure. These improvements may also include retention ponds, berms, bridges and other permanent improvements to the land. The interrelationships of the subject property to off-site improvements such as public roads, city sidewalks and utility hookups should also be presented.

Building Description

A building description should present the size, design and construction type in a detailed narrative or outline format. Details on the various building components including roof, exterior walls, interior space, mechanical, plumbing and electrical systems and special features should be discussed. Furniture, fixtures and equipment must be catalogued. A survey should be conducted to evaluate the quality and condition of the building improvements. These physical evaluations of the building and site improvements will result in an estimate of deferred maintenance and estimates of physical depreciation of short-lived and long-lived building improvements. Functional utility must be assessed based on the property inspection and an analysis of the market acceptance of their improvements. External obsolescence is measured in the approaches to value, and its impact is evaluated in the highest-and-best-use section.

Studying the Highest and Best Use

Highest and best use is the linchpin of an appraisal. It is defined as "the reasonably probable and legal use of a vacant or an improved property, which is physically possible, appropriately supported, financially feasible and that results in the highest value." An appraisal must possess a highest-and-best-use analysis. Without this analysis, the opinion of value may not represent market value.

The highest-and-best-use analysis is a two-phase analysis. It provides for a determination of the highest and best use as if vacant and as if improved. A four-step test is employed in each phase to evaluate which of myriad potential land uses is the optimum use. It is possible that the highest and best use of the land as vacant may be different from the highest and best use as improved. This occurs when the improvements are an underutilization or an overimprovement of the land.

Answering four questions is essential to determining a real property's highest and best use. These questions are:

1. What are the legally permissible land uses?
2. What are the physically possible land uses?
3. What are the financially feasible land uses?
4. What is the maximally productive land use?

The first question is based on research of the subject property and its development rights, taking into consideration current zoning and approvals. The second question is based on a rigorous evaluation of the physically possible land uses. Question three requires an analysis of the property markets associated with the land uses that appear viable. Question four is an evaluation of these potential land uses and a determination of which potential use is the optimum, or maximally productive, land use. This is estimated by performing an economic analysis of each of the financially feasible land uses. The land use that generates the highest potential land value is considered the highest and best use.

Determining the Valuation Method

There are three traditional approaches utilized in the valuation of a property: cost, sales comparison and income. In many cases, all three approaches are applicable and provide independent avenues to arrive at a value estimate for a property. In some cases, however, the use of all three approaches to value may be inappropriate or misleading. The defined scope of services and reporting requirements may also dictate the use of one or more of these three approaches. The appraiser is required to explain why an approach is omitted. It is also helpful to discuss any unusual procedures performed in preparing these approaches.

Cost Approach

The cost approach is defined as "a set of procedures through which a value indication is derived for the fee simple interest in a property by estimating the current cost to construct a reproduction of, or replacement for, the existing structure; deducting accrued depreciation from the reproduction or replacement cost; and adding the estimated land value plus an entrepreneurial profit. Adjustments may then be made to the indicated fee simple value of the subject property to reflect the value of the property interest being appraised."

This approach involves two separate analyses: estimating the value of the land and estimating the value of physical improvements. The value estimate of the land is based on one or more techniques: sales comparison, allocation, extraction, subdivision development, land residual or ground-rent capitalization. Estimating the value of the improvements is accomplished through physical observations and analysis of building-cost information.

Land valuation is second only to the highest-and-best-use analysis in degree of difficulty and propensity for error within the appraisal process. Comparable land sales may appear uniform and similar to the untrained eye, but as a rule, each parcel of land is unique. Therefore, subjectivity may play a role in the analysis. The broad array of market perceptions may, in fact, create a different land price for each and every potential seller or buyer. As a result, it is imperative that the appraiser establish the highest and best use of the land before proceeding with the cost approach.

Land Valuation via Sales Comparison Approach. Of the valuation techniques, the sales comparison approach is by far the most commonly used. It requires the appraiser to compare and adjust the most similar land sales to the subject site. The appraiser is charged with gathering market information on land sales, offerings and contracts. This information is verified and then analyzed. During the analytical process, physical, legal and economic factors are reviewed. These include property rights, legal issues, financial considerations, conditions of sale, market conditions at the date of sale, location, physical characteristics, utilities, zoning and highest and best use. These factors are distilled into adjustments that are utilized to aid in comparing each land sale with the subject site. Adjustments are abstracted from the market using the actual land sales and interviews with market participants (buyers, sellers and brokers of land). The adjusted land sales result in a range of potential value estimates for the subject land. If the range is narrow, the appraiser is apt to select a value estimate that is representative of the central tendency of the sales. However, when the resulting value range is wide, the appraiser is advised to place greatest weight on the one or two most comparable land sales. The most comparable land sales are those that require the fewest and smallest adjustments and appear to be most similar to the subject.

Land Valuation via Other Techniques. Other, less common land-valuation techniques are allocation, extraction, subdivision development, land residual and ground-rent capitalization. These five techniques are utilized in special situations and, in some cases, more than one may be relevant.

- The allocation method is based on the concept that there is a common relationship between land and an improvement value. It is generally utilized when there is an inactive land-sales market and an active property-sales market. The technique requires the appraiser to establish the ratio of land value to total property value based on the ratios of similar properties that have been recently developed and sold.

- Extraction is a variation of the allocation method; it requires the appraiser to estimate the replacement costs of the improvements and then deduct this estimate from the comparable property sale, thus abstracting the land value.
- The subdivision development technique involves determining the number of lots that can be created from a tract of land, calculating the development costs to create the lots, estimating the market value of each lot based on the sales comparison approach, projecting the absorption period for selling the lots, providing an estimate of the cost associated with selling the lots and operating a land-sales program (such as real estate taxes, supervision fees and operating costs) and creating a cash flow model that discounts the future cash flows based on a risk and profit rate.
- The land residual approach is a technique for determining land value that involves abstracting the improvement value. In order to perform this technique, the appraiser must treat the existing or proposed improvements as the highest and best use to the site and then estimate the total property net income and the income attributable to the improvements. The resulting income is the income attributable to the land, and it must be capitalized at a market-derived land rate in order to estimate the land value.
- Ground-rent capitalization is a technique that involves capitalizing the rent of a piece of land by a market-derived capitalization rate.

Reproduction and Replacement Costs Estimates. The next step of the cost approach is to determine the value of the improvements. The improvements include site and building improvements. The procedure requires a value estimate based on either reproduction or replacement cost. "Reproduction cost is the estimate of cost to construct at current prices as of the effective appraisal date, an exact duplicate or replica of the building being appraised, using the same materials, construction standards, design, layout and quality of workmanship and embodying all the deficiencies, super adequacies and obsolescence of the subject building." Replacement cost is defined by this source as "the estimated cost to construct, at current prices as of the effective appraisal date, a building with utility equivalent to the building being appraised, using modern materials and current standards, design and layout." In most instances, the replacement cost method is the preferred technique because it incorporates modern building materials and building skills, while reproduction cost may involve antiquated construction procedures and obsolete building material. Replacement cost may also be utilized to factor out functional obsolescence that results from outdated building methods and materials which would otherwise be difficult to measure and calculate later in this analysis.

To estimate replacement or reproduction costs, the appraiser must depend upon publications of building-cost data (which include materials and labor, but generally do not include profit). These sources include the Marshall and Swift Publication Company, Boeckh Publishing and F.W. Dodge/McGraw-Hill. Several of these sources provide costs on a comparative-unit, unit-in-place and quantity survey basis. The comparative-unit method is the simplest technique, while the quantity survey is the most comprehensive technique. The comparative-unit method involves an aggregated costs estimate of an entire building based on the actual construction costs of similar buildings, with adjustments for dissimilarities that would influence costs, such as building size, shape and special features. The unit-in-place method, which is also referred to as the segregated-costs method, is based on the actual cost of an installed component such as a window, wall or patio. The quantity survey method provides for a detailed cost estimate based on labor and materials, and it is the typical form in which a contractor provides a cost estimate.

Upon establishing the value of the site and the cost of the building improvements, the appraiser must estimate the depreciation resulting from physical deterioration and functional and external obsolescence. Curable physical deterioration should be estimated by observation and input from cost estimators. Long-term physical depreciation may be estimated using the economic age-life method, modified economic age-life method or breakdown method. Functional obsolescence can be curable or incurable. Both types can be estimated based on the cost to correct the deficiency in the existing improvements versus the cost to install the missing component in a proposed building or based on the capitalization of the rent loss associated with the deficiency. External obsolescence should be estimated based on a comparison of the subject property to properties that are similar but do not have external obsolescence; it can also be estimated by capitalization of rent loss.

The next step is to estimate entrepreneurial profit. Profit should be estimated based on interviewing developers, abstracting profit information from recent transactions and reviewing profits from alternative investments. The profit estimate should be applied to the depreciated estimate in order to avoid calculating the depreciation associated with profit. Applying a profit to the land value should be avoided in most instances, as the land value is based on its current value. The cost approach is complete when all of the sources of depreciation are deducted from the estimate of building and site improvements and when the land value and entrepreneurial profit are added.

Sales Comparison Approach

The sales comparison approach is defined as "a set of procedures in which a value indication is derived by comparing the property being appraised to similar properties that have been sold recently, applying appropriate units of comparison, and making adjustments to the sales prices of the comparables based on the elements of comparison. The sales comparison approach may be used to value improved properties, vacant land, or land being considered as though vacant; it is the most common and preferred method of land valuation when comparable sales data are available." This approach is based on the relationship of several real estate principles: supply and demand, substitution, balance and externalities. It requires researching the competitive market for sales, contracts, and listings pertaining to similar properties; verifying this information; utilizing units of comparison abstracted from these sales, listings, and contracts; adjusting the information based on elements of comparison (similar to land valuation analysis) and reconciling the comparable sales into a single value indication or a range of value indications.

Exhibit 13 shows a market data grid used in the sales comparison approach. The elements of comparison are based on factors relied on by buyers and sellers. These factors may include property rights (such as existing leases and liens), financing, conditions of sale, market conditions, location, physical characteristics and economic characteristics. An analysis of the appropriate factors should result in a set of meaningful adjustments. The adjustment may be based on a percentage or a dollar figure.

There are several techniques utilized within the sales comparison approach: unit of comparison, gross income multiplier and net income multiplier. In most instances, the appraiser will attempt to utilize all of these techniques. The greatest weight, however, should be placed on the technique or techniques utilized by buyers and sellers in the market.

The unit-of-comparison method involves abstracting a factor or rule-of-thumb measurement from sales. It may be the sales price per square foot, sales price per room (hotel), sales price per unit (residential) or, in the case of land, the sales price per front foot, square foot or acre. These abstracted units of comparison are then adjusted based on a comparison to the subject property. The

EXHIBIT 13

MARKET DATA GRID FOR RELATIVE COMPARISON ANALYSIS
MULTITENANTED OFFICE BUILDING

Element of Comparison	Subject	Comparable A	Comparable B	Comparable C	Comparable D	Comparable E
Sale Price	–	$2,930,000	$2,120,000	$2,450,000	$2,160,000	$2,470,000
Property Interest	Leased Fee	Leased Fee	Leased Fee	Leased Fee	Leased Fee	Leased Fee
Age	5 Years	6 Years	4 Years	5 Years	6 Years	4 Years
Sq. Ft. of GBA	36,000	40,000	32,000	35,000	30,000	38,000
Sq. Ft. of Rentable Area	31,800	37,600	29,700	32,200	26,700	33,800
Rentable Area Ratio	88%	94%	93%	92%	89%	89%
Price/Sq. Ft. of Rentable Area	–	$77.93	$71.38	$76.09	$80.90	$73.08
Occupancy Rate	90%	87%	85%	90%	95%	90%
Construction Quality & Condition	Average	Average	Average	Average	Average	Average
Ratio of Parking Space to Rental Area	Good	Same	Same	Same	Inferior	Same
Average Rent per Sq. Ft. of Rentable Area	$12.60	$12.80	$11.80	$12.60	$13.00	$12.30
Location	Average	Superior	Inferior	Average	Superior	Inferior
Expense Ratio	Market Norm	Similar	Similar	Higher	Similar	Similar
Net Adjustment	–	Negative	Positive	Negative	Negative	Positive

appraiser should place the greatest weight on the most comparable sale or group of sales.

The gross income multiplier is a widely used method for estimating value of income-producing properties. It is most accurate when it is one of the principal methods used by buyers and sellers. It is most commonly used in valuing small rental properties, such as apartments, stores and warehouses. The quality of the value estimate derived from this method is based on the uniformity of the operating expenses and occupancy levels between the subject property and the comparable sales.

Income Approach

The income approach is defined as "a set of procedures through which an appraiser derives a value indication for an income-producing property by converting its anticipated benefits (cash flows and reversion) into property value. This conversion can be accomplished in two ways. One year's income expectancy can be capitalized at a market-derived rate or at a capitalization rate that reflects a specified income pattern, return on investment and change in the value of the investment. Alternatively, the annual cash flows for the holding period and the reversion can be discounted at a specified yield rate."

This approach attempts to estimate the value of property based on four basic principles:

1. Anticipation and change
2. Supply and demand
3. Substitution
4. Balance and externalities

It is typically the most direct approach to estimating the value of a portion of the bundle of rights.

When utilizing this approach, it is appropriate to evaluate the leases in place and their relationship to market-oriented rents. A complete analysis of the historical and budgeted revenues, generated from scheduled rents and other sources of income, must be performed. Projections of contract and market rent must also be made for each rentable space within the property. An estimate of vacancy and collection loss is created based on historical performance, current market conditions (reflecting supply and demand balance or imbalance) and anticipated future market conditions and lease potentials within the subject property.

Deducting the vacancy and collection loss from gross potential income produces an effective gross income. Operating expenses must be examined to determine their current and probable future levels. These expenses are generally composed of fixed and variable operating costs. A review of historical costs, current costs, budgeted costs and comparable property costs are essential in estimating the stabilized or projected operating expenses of a property.

Deducting operating expenses from the effective gross income results in an estimate of net operating income which can be the basis for direct capitalization into value or a projection of future streams of net operating income found in a multiyear model. The utilization of an NOI figure that is comparable in methodology to that which was abstracted from comparable sales is imperative to the creation of a valid value estimate.

The most common problem results when reconstructed revenue and expense statements of the subject property are not consistent with those of the comparable sales. A potential difference may occur when capital reserves are treated as expenses in one or more of the comparable sales and as capital expenditures in other comparable sales. As a result, it is imperative that the appraiser analyze the subject and comparable sales in a similar manner.

The conversion of a stabilized income stream or a variable income stream may be accomplished using either the direct capitalization method or the discounted cash flow method.

Direct Capitalization Method

The direct capitalization method is simplistic in application and therefore easy to understand. This approach is based on abstracting overall capitalization rates from comparable property sales. Overall capitalization rates can be derived directly from comparable sales, or indirectly through the bands of investment or gross income multipliers.

Rate Abstraction from Comparable Sales. The overall capitalization rate may be abstracted from overall sales. This approach requires the appraiser to divide the net operating income (numerator) by the sales price (denominator) to produce a factor called the overall rate. The procedure is represented by the algebraic equation of $R = I/V$, where R is the overall rate, I is the NOI and V is the sales price.

This approach is useful when the income stream is relatively stable or when it has a modest growth rate. When the income stream is fluctuating or the growth rate is rapid, this procedure is still valid. For instance, if the overall capitalization rate of a sale is lower than the norm for the market, this may suggest that the buyer thought there was significant potential to improve the income stream (through higher occupancy, lower expenses or higher rents) of the purchased property. The reverse logic would be anticipated for an overall capitalization rate that is above the norm of the market.

Band of Investment. This is a process of building an overall capitalization rate from two methods: land-and-building components or mortgage-and-equity components. The mortgage-and-equity-component method weights the components based on contribution to the overall investment. The appraiser must determine the loan to value in order to establish the percentage of debt and equity. This relationship may be provided by the lender and borrower, or it may be based on the typical market relationship. The appraiser must determine the appropriate equity and debt rates of return. The debt rate is generally the mortgage constant (defined as the ratio of annual debt service to the principal amount of the mortgage loan) derived from the terms of the proposed mortgage or from a market-oriented mortgage, while the equity rate must be abstracted from the yield rates of actual sales or from yields required by buyers and sellers of property investments possessing similar risk. The land-and-building-component method applies the same techniques, but replaces debt and equity with land and building. In this analysis, the appraiser must estimate land and building rates of return based on the market and other appropriate sources: the appraiser must then apply these rates to the established land-to-building ratio.

Discounted Cash Flow Analysis

A discounted cash flow analysis is more appropriate when the annual flow of revenues, expenses, and net incomes fluctuate during the course of a projected holding period. Typically, a discounted cash flow analysis is the preferred income approach technique when the property being valued contains numerous leases of varying durations that are above or below market rates. This technique is also very useful when the property has not achieved a stabilized operating level. The main drawbacks to this approach are:

- It is dependent upon projecting future events.
- The longer the projection period, the lower the degree of accuracy.
- The complexity of the analysis is not easily communicated to those who are not familiar with this methodology.

To perform this technique, an appraiser must evaluate the appropriate investment (holding) period that a buyer would require. The appraiser must then estimate the prospects for the existing income stream to change over time and the risk associated with achieving these projections. The evaluation starts with a determination of market rent and terms. Next, the appraiser evaluates whether the existing contract rents will continue as prescribed by lease and determines the probability that leases will roll to market. The appraiser is required to estimate the potential vacancy and collection losses that may occur over the holding period, based on historical trends in the property and projections for the competitive market. The appraiser must then project expenses based on varying occupancy levels anticipated to occur in the property. The growth rate of operating expense must also be determined by historical trends and forecasting of economic conditions that may affect these cost items. The level of reserves must be estimated on a year-by-year basis or through the use of a straight average of the anticipated cost over the holding period. Finally, the appraiser must estimate the required reversionary capitalization rate and discount rate to be applied to the sales price and the cash flows using rates abstracted from actual sales or rates provided through surveys of market participants.

There are numerous software packages, such as ProJect, Argus, Office II and Dynalease, that facilitate lease-by-lease analysis. These and other software packages are designed for inputting individual contract rents, other income streams (such as escalation rent, parking fees and miscellaneous income) and operating expenses over a prescribed holding period.

Exhibit 14, on pages 113 and 114, demonstrates some of the things you can do using a good computer software package. Computer applications speed up the evaluation process and eliminate the operator errors inherent in preparing individual discounted cash flow models using programs such as Lotus 1-2-3 and Excel. The specialized software programs can also aid in determining the revenue, expense and rate (reversionary capitalization or discount rate) items that have the greatest impact on value. It is very important — an ethical requirement — for appraisers to fully understand how the software processes the data, as they will be

EXHIBIT 14

22-Nov-96

Property Name:	
Owned NRA:	**311,718 sf**
Direct Capitalization Rate:	**9.50%**
DCF Capitalization Rate:	**10.00%**
DCF Discount Rate:	**12.50%**
DCF Sales Commission:	**2.50%**
Direct Cap. Value:	**$27,027,768**
DCF Value:	**$27,256,294**
DCF Value PSF:	**$87**
% of Value in Reversion:	**49.55%**
Avg. Annual NOI Growth:	**5.77%**
Avg. Annual CF Growth:	**7.08%**
Comments:	**12/31/95**

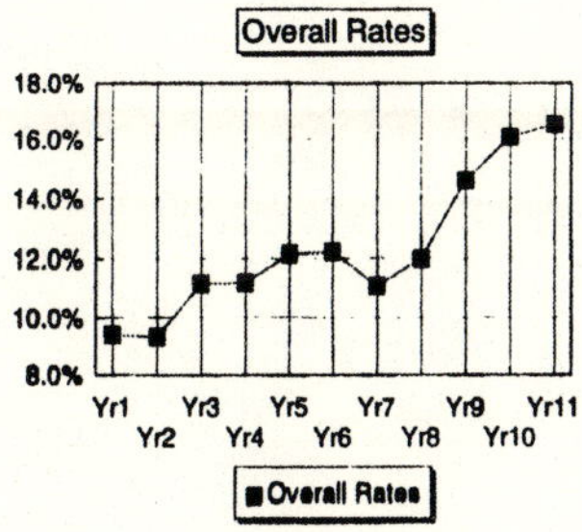

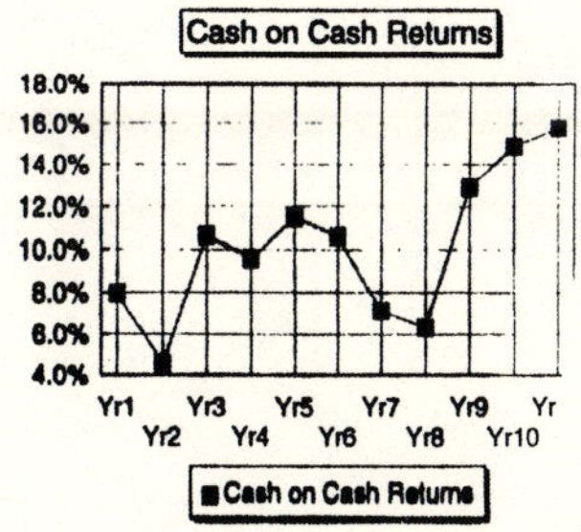

EXHIBIT 14 (cont'd)

DCF Capitalization Rates

DCF Discount Rates	9.25%	9.50%	9.75%	10.00%	10.25%	10.50%	10.75%
11.00%	$31,412,314	$30,972,931	$30,556,081	$30,160,073	$29,783,382	$29,424,629	$29,082,563
11.25%	$30,873,272	$30,443,663	$30,036,086	$29,648,888	$29,280,577	$28,929,805	$28,595,348
11.50%	$30,346,169	$29,926,096	$29,527,566	$29,148,962	$28,788,827	$28,445,841	$28,118,807
11.75%	$29,830,704	$29,419,935	$29,030,231	$28,660,012	$28,307,853	$27,972,463	$27,652,673
12.00%	$29,326,583	$28,924,891	$28,543,799	$28,181,762	$27,837,385	$27,509,407	$27,196,683
12.25%	$28,833,521	$28,440,686	$28,067,997	$27,713,943	$27,377,159	$27,056,413	$26,750,585
12.50%	$28,351,240	$27,967,048	$27,602,559	$27,256,294	$26,926,920	$26,613,231	$26,314,132
12.75%	$27,879,470	$27,503,713	$27,147,225	$26,808,562	$26,486,419	$26,179,616	$25,887,083
13.00%	$27,417,950	$27,050,424	$26,701,745	$26,370,500	$26,055,413	$25,755,331	$25,469,206
13.25%	$26,966,424	$26,606,930	$26,265,873	$25,941,868	$25,633,668	$25,340,144	$25,060,273
13.50%	$26,524,643	$26,172,990	$25,839,371	$25,522,432	$25,220,954	$24,933,832	$24,660,064
13.75%	$26,092,367	$25,748,367	$25,422,008	$25,111,966	$24,817,049	$24,536,175	$24,268,365
14.00%	$25,669,361	$25,332,831	$25,013,558	$24,710,249	$24,421,736	$24,146,961	$23,884,967

Direct Capitalization

	9.00%	9.25%	9.50%
Value	$28,529,311	$27,758,249	$27,027,7[illegible]
Yr 1 OAR	9.00%	9.25%	9.50%
Yr 2 OAR	8.92%	9.17%	9.42%
Yr 5 OAR	11.59%	11.91%	12.24%
Yr 10 OAR	15.34%	15.76%	16.19%

	9.75%	10.00%	10.25%
Value	$26,334,749	$25,676,380	$25,050,127
Yr 1 OAR	9.75%	10.00%	10.25%
Yr 2 OAR	9.66%	9.91%	10.16%
Yr 5 OAR	12.56%	12.88%	13.20%
Yr 10 OAR	16.61%	17.04%	17.47%

	Yr1	Yr2	Yr3	Yr4	Yr5	Yr6	Yr7	Yr8	Yr9	Yr10	Yr11
NOI	$2,567,638	$2,544,723	$3,045,307	$3,052,469	$3,307,040	$3,326,974	$3,021,800	$3,265,186	$3,973,063	$4,375,116	$4,497,733
Cash Flow	$2,170,558	$1,245,283	$2,914,711	$2,605,865	$3,136,700	$2,898,488	$1,943,047	$1,724,882	$3,527,149	$4,053,258	$4,301,535
OAR	9.42%	9.34%	11.17%	11.20%	12.13%	12.21%	11.09%	11.98%	14.58%	16.05%	16.50%
C on C	7.96%	4.57%	10.69%	9.56%	11.51%	10.63%	7.13%	6.33%	12.94%	14.87%	15.78%

5 Yr. Avg. OAR:	10.65%	10 Yr. Avg. OAR:	11.92%
5 Yr. Avg. ConC:	8.86%	10 Yr. Avg. ConC:	9.62%

Source: Landauer Real Estate Counselors

responsible for the errors that result from faulty computer programs or input errors.

Reconciling Value Conclusions

The reconciliation should present the strengths and weaknesses of the approaches employed within the appraisal. The approach that provides the greatest degree of reliability should be given the greatest consideration in the final opinion of value. Although more than one approach may be considered to have similar degrees of support, it is not appropriate to average the findings of multiple approaches into a final opinion of value. In the final analysis, the appraiser should select the approach that best represents the method by which buyers and sellers evaluate a property.

Communicating the Opinion of Value

There are three main report formats: oral, form and narrative. The most comprehensive is a narrative appraisal report. The other formats tend to be less complete, but the opinion of value should be equally reliable, regardless of the content of the reports, unless specific limitations are cited.

- Oral reports should contain a discussion of the property, data utilized, analysis performed, conclusions, and limitations on the opinion of value. They should be backed up by a file that contains written support for all of the information provided orally.
- Form reports are designed for standard property types. They contain all the requirements of an appraisal if they are properly filled out by the appraiser. However, the form is often too limited in presentation and may require

numerous narrative attachments if utilized for complex residential properties and the majority of income properties.

- Narrative reports are comprehensive presentations. They may be prepared in an abbreviated or lengthy format. Regardless of the length, they must contain all the basic appraisal requirements and sufficient discussion to allow the reader to draw the same value conclusion as the appraiser.

Some of the appraisal organizations have approved specific format guidelines to meet the evolving needs of clients. The Appraisal Institute has three appraisal formats: self-contained appraisal report (which is a full narrative report), summary appraisal report (which is an abbreviated narrative report) and restricted appraisal report (which is a report limited in scope of work and presentation). The summary appraisal report and restricted appraisal report are useful for providing knowledgeable real estate clients with an opinion of value in a cost-effective, timely manner. Unfortunately, these formats may not provide sufficient detail to allow the client or other users of the report to understand the rationale for the final opinion of value.

Reviewing an Appraisal

Clients should take an active role in reviewing appraisals performed for them. Although a review of the appraisal by another third-party appraiser may be the most practical procedure to undertake, the more informed the client is of the process, the better the final conclusions. The Appraisal Institute has a set of standards and ethical rules that must be complied with to perform an appraisal review. In addition to these rules, the following questions should be answered when reviewing an appraisal:

- Does the appraiser's description of the property match the actual description?
- Is the appraiser estimating the value for the correct property interest?
- Did the appraiser correctly utilize the information provided?
- Does the scope of services cited in the engagement letter match the services performed in the report?
- Does the data and analysis presented in the appraisal support the conclusions for each section of the report and the final opinion of value?
- Do the limiting conditions weaken the opinion of value to such a degree that its usefulness is in doubt?
- Does the appraiser's certification indicate that the appraisal was conducted by a disinterested third-party appraiser?

After these questions are answered and the appraisal has been proofread for material errors and inconsistencies, the reviewers will know the quality level of the opinion of value. If the reviewers believe that there are sufficient reasons why the appraisal does not appear to be supportable or reasonable, they should begin a dialog with the appraiser in order to resolve the issues. In the majority of cases, appraisers are able to present additional information to support their conclusions. The remaining situations may require an independent third-party appraisal review.

Conclusion

In summary, the real estate appraisal profession and real estate professionals are evolving. This evolution has mirrored the practices of buyers and sellers of real property over the years and will continue to do so. Computer technology will create new opportunities for the profession to serve clients, but in ways and forms that are still being developed. In the future, massive data banks and computer analysis of valuation matrices may replace the good, old-fashioned appraisal practices that are used for the relatively homogenous inventory of single family housing. However, the complex interaction of income-producing properties and their markets will always be difficult to evaluate without an expert from the real estate industry.

Selecting an appraiser is a due diligence process similar to that of hiring other professionals. Finding the best qualified professional requires soliciting recommendations and asking the right questions about appraisal experience.

The appraisal process is one of the best training grounds for systematically evaluating a problem. The process has structure and form based on professional standards and ethical guidelines. Although there is an element of subjectivity in an appraisal, these guidelines minimize the differences in the scope of work and that clients should expect.

The critical elements of an appraisal are determining the purpose of the assignment and establishing the appraisal procedure. The single most important element of the appraisal process is the highest-and-best-use analysis. Without such an analysis, an appraiser may not be able to determine the true value of a property. It is also very important to evaluate the competitive market and the property's interrelationship with this market. County, city or neighborhood analysis should be germane to the property being appraised. The property description should be of sufficient detail to allow readers to understand it without physically inspecting the property. Although there are three traditional approaches to value, the appraiser and client should evaluate whether all are appropriate to the development of an appraisal of the property. In some cases only one or two approaches may be warranted. This selection process should mirror the process that buyers and sellers utilize. Reconciling the various value estimates into a final value conclusion should be based on the strengths and weaknesses of the approaches used.

The report format utilized should be tailored to the needs of the clients. Narrative reports should be used to aid clients who have little understanding of the appraisal process or when there will be multiple uses of the report or multiple clients and or users of the report. Oral reports serve a niche role in the real estate industry, but should be carefully communicated and documented. Form reports are an acceptable manner in which to convey an opinion of value for simple residential and income properties. Other report formats, such as summary and restricted appraisal, may be utilized for specific client objectives; however, the client must be very familiar with both the property and the appraisal process in order for these formats to be useful and not misleading.

All appraisals should be reviewed to some extent. Although differences of opinion may arise from a review of the appraisal, dialog generated from the review process leads to enhanced understanding of the opinion of value. The more involved appraisers and clients are in this process, the better the final results.

7

Best Use of Appraiser, Appraisal and Appraisal Report

Richard E. Nichols, President
Richard E. Nichols Associates, Inc.

During the late 1970s and early 1980s, there was rampant lending and appraisal/appraiser activity. Many mistakes were made, and serious consequences followed. Large numbers of loans went into default, causing huge financial losses. Many changes have been implemented since in an attempt to prevent a similar situation from occurring in the future. One of these was the establishment of The Appraisal Foundation.

The Appraisal Foundation was founded in November 1987 by eight appraisal organizations. As a not-for-profit educational organization, the foundation was created to foster professionalism in appraising through the establishment and promotion of appraisal standards and appraiser qualifications. This is done through the two independent boards of the foundation: the Appraiser Qualifications Board (AQB) and the Appraisal Standards Board (ASB).

In August 1989, the U.S. Congress passed the Financial Institutions Reform, Recovery and Enforcement Act (FIRREA), legislation to address the financial institution crisis, and thereby gave significant authority to the AQB and the ASB. Minimum education, experience, examination and continuing education requirements for becoming a state certified appraiser are set by the AQB. In addition, standards for developing and reporting a value estimate for a federally related transaction are set by the ASB.

States would issue licenses or certificates to individuals who meet the qualification requirements established by the AQB. To ensure compliance with FIRREA requirements, a federal oversight entity, known as the Appraisal Subcommittee, was created. The subcommittee is composed of representatives from the five federal financial regulatory agencies — the Board of Governors of the Federal Reserve System, the Federal Deposit Insurance Corporation (FDIC), the Office of Thrift Supervision (OTS), the Office of the Comptroller of the Currency and the National Credit Union Administration. In addition, a representative from the Department of Housing and Urban Development serves on the subcommittee. Since the enactment of FIRREA, all states and territories have established an appraisal regulatory program and almost 90,000 individuals have been either state licensed or state certified.

This chapter explains how the work of the AQB and the ASB has had an impact on both the appraiser and the appraisal.

The Appraiser

The AQB has established minimum qualification criteria for the following categories:

- Trainee
- State-licensed residential
- State-certified residential
- State-certified general

Exhibit 15 outlines the major criteria for each classification.

EXHIBIT 15

APPRAISER QUALIFICATIONS: BOARD OF THE APPRAISAL FOUNDATION

Basic Recommended Appraiser Qualification Criteria[1]

	Classroom Hours Appraisal Education[2]	Appraisal Experience Creditable Hours	State Exam	Continuing Education
Licensed[3] Residential	75	2,000	Yes	10 hours per year
Certified Residential	120	2,000 in not less than two years	Yes	10 hours per year
Certified General	165	2,000 — at least 1,000 of nonresidential	Yes	10 hours per year

[1]Precertification or prelicensing education credit must be a minimum duration of 15 hours and include an examination. Home study educational offerings may only be approved for precertification if offered by an accredited college or university.

[2]Educational courses offered after January 1, 1991 must teach the Uniform Standards of Professional Practice (USPAP).

[3]Trainee only needs appraisal education and state exam.

State requirements for the residential and general certification must, at a minimum, adhere to AQB requirements for these classifications. The trainee and state licensed categories are only recommended to the states for their use.

The Competency Provision of the Uniform Standards of Professional Appraisal Practice (USPAP) requires that before accepting an assignment, an appraiser must have both the knowledge and experience to complete the assignment properly. This provision is enforced by state appraiser regulatory authorities.

The scope of practice for each classification varies. The federal financial institution regulatory agencies have established the following parameters:

- A *state-licensed real property appraiser* may appraise noncomplex, one- to four-unit residential properties when the transaction value is less than $1 million and may appraise any property type when the transaction value is less than $250,000.
- A *state-certified residential real property appraiser* may appraise one- to four-unit residential properties without regard to transaction value or complexity and may appraise any property type when the transaction value is less than $250,000.
- A *state-certified general real property appraiser* may appraise all types of real property, regardless of transaction amount or complexity.

The qualification criteria outlined above will remain in effect until January 1, 1998. It is the intention of the AQB to periodically review and revise the qualification criteria. As of January 1, 1998, the requirements of the criteria will be increased as shown in Exhibit 16.

The Appraisal

USPAP, the generally accepted standards promulgated by the ASB, have continued to gain increased national and international

EXHIBIT 16

APPRAISER QUALIFICATIONS: BOARD OF THE APPRAISAL FOUNDATION

Basic Recommended Appraiser Qualification Criteria[1]

Effective January 1, 1998

	Classroom Hours Appraisal Education[2]	Appraisal Experience Creditable Hours	State Exam	Continuing Education
Licensed[3] Residential	90	2,000	Yes	14 hours per year
Certified Residential	120	2,500 obtained continuously in not less than 24 months	Yes	14 hours per year
Certified General	180	3,000 — over a period of not less than 30 months	Yes	14 hours per year

[1]Precertification or prelicensing education credit must be a minimum duration of 15 hours and include an examination. Home study educational offerings may only be approved for precertification if offered by an accredited college or university.

[2]Educational courses offered after January 1, 1991 must teach the Uniform Standards of Professional Practice (USPAP).

[3]Trainee license only requires education and exam. Experience to achieve creditable hours is to be supervised.

acceptance. While regulators and other users of appraisal services have modified their requirements for appraisal or consulting services from time to time, they continue to want a credible, workable, and meaningful product. While the financial institution regulatory agencies were the first to adopt USPAP, numerous other federal and state governmental agencies have also adopted the document. In addition, associations in Canada, Mexico, Russia, Poland and Bulgaria have adopted USPAP.

FIRREA calls for the state appraiser regulatory authorities to require that certified and licensed appraisers comply with the requirements of USPAP. Questions regarding USPAP appear on state appraiser examinations. In addition, many states require periodic USPAP refresher courses.

USPAP contains 10 standards which address appraisal development and reporting for the following disciplines: real property appraisal, review appraisal, real estate/real property consulting, mass appraisal, personal property appraisal and business valuation. The standards may be altered, amended, interpreted, supplemented or repealed by the ASB after exposure to the appraisal profession, users of appraisal services and the public, in accordance with established rules of procedure.

In addition to standards, the ASB promulgates statements on appraisal standards to clarify, interpret, explain or elaborate on USPAP. Statements have the full weight of a standards rule and must be exposed for public comment before being adopted by the ASB. Statements are enforced in the same manner as standards rules by state and federal regulatory bodies. The ASB has adopted eight statements discussing issues such as review of appraisals, permitted departure from specific guidelines of USPAP and electronic transmission of reports.

The ASB also issues advisory opinions, which do not establish new standards or interpret existing standards, but are issued to illustrate the applicability of USPAP in specific situations and to offer advice from the ASB for the resolution of appraisal issues and problems. Unlike standards rules and statements, advisory opinions are not required to be exposed prior to approval by the ASB. The ASB has issued 15 advisory opinions discussing issues such as use and content of the appraisal report options of Standard 2, performing evaluations and subsidized housing.

In response to industry demands for more flexibility from the appraiser in satisfying client needs, the ASB has recently clarified allowances for the two levels of analysis in developing an estimate of value and has approved three methods of reporting its results.

Two Levels of Analysis

In developing an estimate of value, you can choose one of two levels of analysis: complete or limited. An estimate of value prepared by following all of the binding requirements and all of the applicable specific guidelines of USPAP is a complete appraisal. A limited appraisal is developed when an appraiser invokes the departure provision and departs from various specific guidelines of USPAP.

The departure provision permits limited departures from sections of the USPAP that are classified as specific guidelines rather than binding requirements. Before accepting an assignment and invoking this provision, the appraiser must make sure that the result will not confuse or mislead. The burden of proof is on the appraiser to report any departures from specific guidelines.

An appraiser may enter into an agreement to perform an assignment that calls for something less than, or different from, the work that would otherwise be required by the specific guidelines; however, prior to entering into such an agreement, three things must happen:

1. The appraiser must determine that the appraisal or consulting process to be performed is not so limited that the resulting assignment would tend to mislead or confuse the client or the intended users of the report.

2. The appraiser must advise the client that the assignment calls for something less than, or different from, the work required by the specific guidelines and that the report will clearly identify and explain the departure(s).
3. The client must agree that the performance of a limited appraisal or consulting service would be appropriate.

For the purpose of this provision, intended users of the report might include lenders, employees of government agencies, the client's partners, the client's attorney or the client's accountant. In this context, both the purpose and the intended use of the appraisal or consulting service are critical.

Three Methods of Reporting Results

The three reporting methods are the self-contained appraisal report, the summary appraisal report and the restricted appraisal report. A self-contained appraisal report contains a thorough discussion of the procedures followed and the results, the summary appraisal report discusses this information in a more summarized manner, and the restricted appraisal report presents this information in such a condensed manner that the report can only be used in specific situations.

Exhibit 17 outlines the major elements of information that are contained in each of the reporting formats.

A complete appraisal communicated in a self-contained appraisal report is expected to be a self-explanatory document that can be understood by a disinterested third party not knowledgeable about the property or the specifics of the valuation service requested. At the other end of the spectrum, a limited appraisal, communicated in a restricted appraisal report, is intended to be used and relied upon by only a single knowledgeable user. The summary appraisal report, which falls somewhere in the middle, is the most commonly used reporting option.

EXHIBIT 17

STANDARDS RULE 2-2 REPORT COMPARISON CHART

The essential difference among the three options is in the use and application of the terms describe, summarize and state. Describe is used to connote a comprehensive level of detail in the presentation of information. Summarize is used to connote a more concise presentation of information. State is used to connote the minimal presentation of information.

a) Self-Contained Appraisal Report	b) Summary Appraisal Report	c) Restricted Appraisal Report
i. identify and **describe** the real estate being appraised	i. identify and provide a summary description of the real estate being appraised	i. identify the real estate being appraised
ii. **state the real property interest being appraised**	ii. **state the real property interest being appraised**	ii. **state the real property interest being appraised**
iii. **state the purpose and intended use of the appraisal**	iii. **state the purpose and intended use of the appraisal**	iii. **state the purpose and intended use of the appraisal**
iv. define the value to be estimated	iv. define the value to be estimated	iv. **state** and reference a definition of the value to be estimated
v. **state the effective date of the appraisal and the date of the report**	v. **state the effective date of the appraisal and the date of the report**	v. **state the effective date of the appraisal and the date of the report**
vi. **state** the extent of the process of collecting, confirming and reporting data Comment:...the full extent of the process should be apparent to the reader in the contents of the report.	vi. **summarize** the extent of the process of collecting, confirming and reporting data Comment:...the full extent of the process may not be apparent to the reader in the contents of the report.	vi. **describe** the extent of the process of collecting, confirming and reporting data Comment:...the full extent of the process will not be apparent to the reader in the contents of the report.
vii. **state all assumptions and limiting conditions that affect the analyses, opinions and conclusions**	vii. **state all assumptions and limiting conditions that affect the analyses, opinions and conclusions**	vii. **state all assumptions and limiting conditions that affect the analyses, opinions and conclusions**
viii. **describe** the information considered, the appraisal procedures followed, and the reasoning that supports the analyses, opinions, and conclusions	viii. **summarize** the information considered, the appraisal procedures followed, and the reasoning that supports the analyses, opinions, and conclusions	viii. **state** the appraisal procedures followed, **state** the value conclusion and reference the existence of specific file information in support of the conclusion
ix. **describe** the appraiser's opinion of the highest and best use of the real estate, when such an opinion is necessary and appropriate	ix. **summarize** the appraiser's opinion of the highest and best use of the real estate, when such an opinion is necessary and appropriate	ix. **state** the appraiser's opinion of the highest and best use of the real estate, when such an opinion is necessary and appropriate
x. explain and support the exclusion of any of the usual valuation approaches	x. explain and support the exclusion of any of the usual valuation approaches	x. **state** the exclusion of any of the usual valuation approaches
xi. **describe** any additional information that may be appropriate to show compliance with, or clearly identify and explain permitted departures from the specific guidelines of Standard 1	xi. **summarize** any additional information that may be appropriate to show compliance with, or clearly identify and explain permitted departures from the specific guidelines of Standard 1	xi. contain a prominent use restriction that limits reliance on the report to the client and warns that the report cannot be understood properly without additional information in the workfile of the appraiser, and clearly identify and explain any permitted departures from the specific guidelines of Standard 1
xii. **include a signed certification in accordance with Standards Rule 2-3**	xii. **include a signed certification in accordance with Standards Rule 2-3**	xii. **include a signed certification in accordance with Standards Rule 2-3**
Explanatory Comments have not been included in this chart, except for excerpt of Comment on vi.		

Identical Requirements

Reprinted with permission of the Appraisal Foundation

The restricted appraisal report is not expected to be used or relied upon by disinterested third parties since it typically contains inadequate information to be of use to a reader not knowledgeable about the property or the specifics of the valuation service specified. It must contain a prominent use restriction that limits reliance on the report to the client only and warns that the report cannot be understood properly without additional information from the work file of the appraiser. It must also clearly identify and explain permitted departures from the specific guidelines of Standard 1.

Appraisal Service Options

The appraiser and the user of appraisal services have six options in identifying the appropriate level and reporting method:

1. A complete appraisal in a self-contained appraisal report
2. A complete appraisal in a summary appraisal report
3. A complete appraisal in a restricted appraisal report
4. A limited appraisal in a self-contained appraisal report
5. A limited appraisal in a summary appraisal report
6. A limited appraisal in a restricted appraisal report

To eliminate any misunderstanding, the appraiser and the user of appraisal services should be in agreement as to the level of analysis to be performed and the type of report to be prepared.

Current Status

The appraisal profession has matured a great deal in a short period of time. For the first time, the universe of appraisers providing services in federally related transactions has been identified and is maintained on a national roster. Appraising has always been a very fragmented profession, represented by numerous professional associations. Today, many of these organizations are engaged in constructive dialogue, and they are attempting to identify and achieve common goals.

While licensing and certification have established a base level of competency and accountability, differences do exist among the various states. This has slowed the goal of achieving complete reciprocity among the states. While each state appraiser regulatory program has a disciplinary mechanism in place, the disciplinary actions are by no means uniform or even roughly consistent.

Conclusions

From adversity comes change and improvement. The financial debacle of the 1970s and early 1980s has had a direct impact on improving the quality of appraisers, appraisals and appraisal reports.

The appraisal regulatory system which was put in place is a unique collaborative effort of state regulators (state real estate appraiser boards), federal regulators (the Appraisal Subcommittee) and private sector expertise (the Appraisal Foundation). In addition, costs of the federal and state regulatory programs are being funded exclusively by fees from appraisers. This self-funded, joint effort could serve as a model for other professions.

One of the foremost challenges facing the appraisal profession today is the need to educate the public about the significant improvements recently made in identifying appraiser competency and about the various appraisal products available to users of appraisal services. The public at large and the users of appraisal services in particular need to understand the importance of engaging a professional appraiser who adheres to specific performance standards. The quality product offered by such a professional is a key component of any important business decision involving real estate.

8

The Mortgage Financing Submission

Donald H. Schefmeyer, CMB, S.R.P.A., President
Action Mortgage Corporation

The mortgage financing submission, or loan package, may be defined as an analytical report with exhibits that presents information about a particular commercial real estate project, including data and reasoning to support the requested loan.

The purpose of the loan package is to underwrite a deal. Its function is to sell an investor on the deal. Functionally, at least, the submission is a sales tool. As such, it should be tailored to the specific investor or lender targeted as the most likely source of funds for the transaction. Most life insurance companies, commercial banks and thrifts, as well as conduits and REITs, have specific criteria to govern the underwriting of a particular type of income-producing property. If possible, a set of current underwriting guidelines should be obtained from the prospective lender prior to preparing the submission.

This chapter reviews the critical path followed in the preparation and presentation of loan submissions for income properties. It focuses on the general items that should be included in all packages as well as some of the specific exhibits necessary for several of the major property types.

The Loan Application

After developers or project sponsors have been contacted and preliminary evaluations have indicated that the project warrants financing, mortgage bankers must determine which of the available sources are the most likely candidates to provide the funds. Mortgage bankers know in advance the general terms and conditions under which a particular investor will make a loan. This knowledge, coupled with an analysis of the requirements for the project, enables mortgage bankers to select the appropriate application format for a particular project.

A formal application should always be taken even when the mortgage banker and sponsor (borrower) have a long-term established business relationship. Most applications take the form of a contract with general and specific terms and conditions governing both the mortgage banker's employment by the sponsor and the type of financing being sought. The application will cover the following items:

- Mortgage banker's authority from the potential borrower to arrange financing
- Exclusivity of authorization — the borrower usually makes one mortgage banking firm its exclusive agent but may limit the exclusive agency to particular sources of financing
- Consideration — covers the fee to be received for placing the loan
- Application period and cancellation provisions — the mortgage banker is the authorized agent for a specified period, and terms of cancellation are specified
- Sponsor's agreement to provide necessary exhibits and information to be included in the loan application
- Authority of sponsor to contract (for example, corporate authorization)

- Applicable governing law (regarding application)
- Assignment provisions of application

The foregoing items clarify the employment of the mortgage banker. The remainder of the application recites the general terms and conditions under which a lender will extend credit.

The mortgage banker's fees are earned at the point when a commitment for financing has been obtained in accordance with the terms and conditions enumerated in the application or upon the sponsor's acceptance of a commitment. Therefore, the application should be as specific as possible. Just how detailed an application should be depends on the following criteria:

- The mortgage banker's knowledge of a particular lender's program and commitment format
- The complexity of the financing being sought
- The sponsor's level of sophistication

An extremely detailed and specific application is a two-edged sword. It will eliminate many misunderstandings and provide a large measure of comfort about the sponsor's and mortgage banker's responsibilities to each other. However, in the likely event that the lender changes a term or condition from that which is specified in the application, the mortgage banker's fee may be at risk until the application is amended and the sponsor accepts the commitment.

At an absolute minimum, the application should address the following items:

- Loan amount
- Interest rate
- Term of loan
- Amortization schedule and payment frequency
- Escrow requirements (tax and insurance)

- Description of collateral offered as security
- Loan delivery date
- Guarantees (personal endorsement)
- Legal style of borrower: capacity, authority
- Transfer/alienation rights of mortgagor
- Copies of leases
- Prepayment privilege
- Adverse change provisions
- Utilities and services available
- Roads and access
- Plans and specifications
- Construction contracts/mechanics liens
- Inspections
- Equity kickers (if any)
- Documents required, including the survey (ALTA format), title insurance, operating and financial statements, appropriate insurance (hazard, liability, flood), appraisal report, soils report, environmental report and engineering report

Having signed up the sponsor and having obtained a good faith deposit, the mortgage banker is now in a position to place the loan with an investor.

The Loan Submission

A good loan submission is one which is effective. Depending on the complexity of the deal and credibility of the mortgage banker, a loan submission can be as brief as a cover letter with a photograph or as complicated as a full-blown analytical report with all ancillary exhibits. The extent of detail in a submission depends on the complexity of the financing and the length of time available to the mortgage banker to arrange it.

Like other financial service industries, the commercial real estate finance industry is in transition with respect to electronic communications. Some of the larger lenders (particularly life insurance companies) now request that submissions be sent on disk, backed up with hard copy. In such cases, submissions may be highly stylized, with all pertinent areas reflecting the specific underwriting format of the lender. Correspondent mortgage bankers are already using modem transfer of data to their investors and it seems likely that this trend will continue.

When developing a loan package, it is important to stress accuracy and quality. Although it is always preferable to have a complete package, quality — not quantity — is the touchstone of a good submission. A well-developed neighborhood analysis with supporting rental, sales and tax comparables is far more valuable to a lender than 10 pages of projections leading to an internal rate of return (IRR) of uncertain validity. As in a well-researched appraisal report, the best submission will concentrate on the basics.

A standard loan submission package consists of the following sections:

- Letter of transmittal (cover letter)
- Cover page (with photo)
- Project summary
- Appraisal and feasibility analysis
- Sponsor (borrower) analysis
- Rental analysis
- Underwriting
- Supporting exhibits and addenda

In a normal economy, the mortgage investment personnel in the income property departments of life insurance companies and thrifts constantly review requests from mortgage bankers, developers and affiliates. The mortgage banker's job is to get the deal reviewed as early as possible. Several things motivate a lender to pick a particular loan submission from the stack of those received. Most important is the credibility of the company and the individual mortgage banker making the submission. Also important is that the loan application package is well organized, well written and complete. Nothing is more frustrating for a lender than an incomplete package or one that has been written poorly. Be sure your submissions are written clearly and concisely, following the rules of good grammar.

Whenever possible, be brief. Most reports should not exceed 20 written pages (not counting exhibits) with emphasis on the supporting assumptions used in accurately calculating income and expenses. This support should include rent comparables, improved property sale comparables, land sale comparables, subject land acquisition history, and a project cost review. Existing properties should provide documentation, such as three to five years of operating statements, with accompanying analyses.

Letter of Transmittal

The letter of transmittal, or cover letter, is a key part of the submission package. It is the first item lenders will read, so its purpose is to excite lenders enough to make them read further. A well-crafted cover letter sets the stage for a financing request by calling attention to the project's strong points and countering any perceived weaknesses. It should address the following items:

- Basic loan terms
- Fee structure and servicing rate
- Estimated delivery date
- Mortgage banker's recommendation

The cover letter should be written immediately prior to submission to a particular lender, and it should reflect the lender's preferences and idiosyncrasies. Keep it short — rarely should it exceed two pages — and separate from the bound report.

Cover Page

The cover page of the bound report should include the project's name and location and the name of the mortgage banking firm. If available, a 5- by 7-inch color photograph should be mounted in the center. This format establishes an early visual identity with the project.

Project Summary

The project summary is the single most important page in the report. It is a one-page overview that allows a busy lender to get the facts at a glance and is easily reproduced for loan committee distribution. It should include a description of improvements, the loan request, sponsorship and tenancy information, statistics regarding costs, income characteristics and underwriting ratios. A sample of a mortgage loan summary is shown in Exhibit 18 on pages 140 and 141.

Appraisal and Feasibility Analysis

The appraisal and feasibility analysis is the research section of the report. It essentially follows the format of a narrative appraisal but does not include the certifications, limiting conditions, chamber of commerce data or other such material that is usually found in an appraisal.

Since the passage of FIRREA, it has been a requirement of federally insured financial institutions (primarily banks and thrifts), that appraisal reports be ordered directly by the lending institution, rather than by the borrower. Other than complicating the lives of potential borrowers who wish to have an appraisal report done prior to submitting it to a lender or multiple lenders, this requirement has had very little effect on the commercial financing industry. However, due to the disclosure, verification and professional practice requirements of the Appraisal Institute, appraisal reports are taking longer to complete and are becoming

EXHIBIT 18

CARMEL HIGHLANDS APARTMENTS
INDIANAPOLIS, IN

PROJECT: Contemporary styled, 260-unit garden apartment project built in 1990. Project is two-story (with hallway) frame construction with brick veneer on lower level; patios and balconies; carports for each unit. Gas forced air heat with central air. Culbhouse with pool. Project has 16 buildings and clubhouse (2,500 FS).

LOAN REQUEST: AMOUNT: $11,000,000 RATE: 7.5% TERM: 10 Yrs.
AMORTIXATION: 30 Years
GUARANTEE: Members will personally guarantee the top 25% of the loan.
FEE: PAR SERVICING FEE: 1/8% DELIVERY: Immediate (Late 2nd Quarter)

SPONSOR: Carmel Highlands L.L.C., an Indiana Limited Liability Company

Members	Percent	Net Worth	Annual Income
Bob Smith	33.33	$8 Million	$250,000+
John Jones	33.33	$7.6 Million	$225,000+
Bill White	33.33	$5 Million	$175,000+

UNDERWRITING DATA:

Site Area: 24 Acres	Cost: $780,000 (1990) Market Value: $1,200,000 (Today)
Parking: 540 Cars + 200 Carports	Parking Ratio: 3:1
No. of Units: 260	Land Cost/Unit: $3,000
GBA: 334,588 SF	NRA: 284,400 SF
% Efficiency: 85%	
Loan/Sq. Ft.: $32.88 (GBA)	

(continued)

EXHIBIT 18 (cont'd)

Unit Mix	Monthly Rent	NRA	Rent/SF
30 1BR, 1b	@ $530	680 SF	$.78
100 2BR, 1-1/2b	@ $610	975	$.63
50 2BR + Den	@ $690	1,125	$.61
50 3BR, 2-1/2b	@ $780	1,350	$.58
30 3BRTH, 2-1/2b	@ $850	1,425	$.60

Gross Potential Income:	$2,110,800
Vacancy Allowance:	($105,540)
Effective Gross Income:	$2,005,260
Annual Expenses:	($922,900)

NET OPERATING INCOME: $1,102,900

Projected Annual Debt Service ($922,900) DSCR: 1.20

Cash Flow Before Taxes: $180,000

more expensive. In cases where time is of the essence, it is wise to discuss a potential appraisal assignment with an appraiser well in advance so that timing will not be a problem.

In recent years, it has become the fashion among mortgage bankers to include a separate appraisal report prepared by a member of the Appraisal Institute (MAI) or a State Certified General Appraiser, in lieu of presenting their own field work. The excuse most often heard is that since a mortgage banking firm's fee is based on a percentage of the loan obtained, it cannot be objective when it comes to estimating value. Although the uninitiated might find this logical, it is in fact nonsense; there is no excuse for not doing your own field work.

The standard appraisal and feasibility study should follow the framework outlined below:

- Site analysis
- Improvements analysis
- Neighborhood analysis
- Area analysis
- Real estate tax analysis
- Economic analysis
- Physical analysis

Site Analysis. The site analysis should emphasize that the site is adequate to support the intended use. The following items should be addressed:

- Brief description of specific location in area
- Size (dimensions and square footage)
- Topography and drainage
- Frontage and access

- Utilities available
- Services available: police, fire and transportation
- Parking available on site
- Landscaping
- References to site plan, photo, aerial photo, survey and environmental report

Improvements Analysis. Improvements analysis should focus on the quality and cost effectiveness of the improvements. Other important aspects are the salable nature of the real estate and its potential for conversion to another use. Lenders normally prefer functional, general-purpose properties.

The improvements analysis section generally includes:

- A basic, brief description of the buildings: type of construction, gross building area and net rentable area, motif, layout and special features
- Information about major building components: foundations, floors (and coverings), walls (and coverings), ceilings, roofs (and covers), interior design (partitioning) and decoration, windows and mechanical systems (electrical, plumbing, HVAC, sprinkler and alarm)
- References to plans, specifications and photos

Neighborhood Analysis. Neighborhood analysis is far more important than overall area analysis, since it calls for specific knowledge from the mortgage banker. This analysis should proceed from general to specific observations. The lender will rely on the mortgage banker's assessment of the local market and any observable environmental obsolescence or special benefits in close proximity to the subject — medical buildings near a hospital, for example.

- Describe the neighborhood in detail: its position in the city, its general boundaries, its developed uses (commercial, retail or industrial) and its position in the life cycle (new, established or transitional).
- Describe traffic arteries: the distance to the central business district, the distance to major interchanges, and the traffic count.
- Tie in site and building sections by discussing the subject property's impact on the neighborhood (and vice versa).
- Give a mortgage banker's view of future neighborhood trends and their possible effects on the subject property.

Area Analysis. The area analysis should be brief, especially if the project is located in a primary or secondary urban area well known to the investment community at large. Presentation of all data should focus on the effect of the data on the subject:

- Location
- Population and trends
- Demographics
- Industrial classifications
- Retail sales
- Type of local government
- Major employers and characteristics of labor force
- New construction (permits and special developments)
- References to community profile, chamber of commerce data, Department of Labor data and census information
- Local newspaper articles of interest

Real Estate Tax Analysis. Real estate tax analysis is an important part of the overall income and expense analysis, since real estate taxes are typically the single highest item of annual expense. The analysis should not be overlooked, even in the case of an absolutely net lease. The discussion should reflect that the existing tax or proposed burden on the property is similar to other competitive properties.

The real estate tax analysis should include:

- The assessment and assessment methodology for land and buildings
- Ad valorem tax rates (break down)
- Special charges and flat rates: sewer, snow removal, water purification and so on
- Tax calculations
- Tax trends and whether the subject's tax burden is similar to those of competitive properties

Economic Analysis. All income-producing property is valued primarily on the basis of its capacity to generate rental income. Therefore, economic analysis, also known as the income approach, is the most important section of the submission. In this section of the report, the mortgage banker takes the estimated net operating income and converts it into a value estimate using any one of a number of conceptually defensible methods. Basically, it is an accurate and clearly developed stabilized income statement.

In certain cases, it may be useful to include discounted cash flow projections for a particular period of years from the inception of the loan. This is used as a forecasting tool by many life insurance companies that have developed sophisticated financial models. A typical 10-year cash flow projection would attempt to mimic the expected income and expenses of the project over a 10-year holding period, with the year 11's net operating income capitalized at the going-in capitalization rate. While it may seem like such a projection is of limited practical value (owing to the difficulty in predicting the future), it is axiomatic that a submission's primary goal is to satisfy a lender's requirements and obtain a commitment.

However, it is worthwhile to ponder the usefulness of 10-year discounted-cash-flow projections when viewed from the perspective of the commercial real estate cycles of the last 20 years. For example, in the early 1980s, interest rates for permanent mortgage loans were in the high teens, while the prime rate hit a high of 24 percent. In the mid-1990s, rates had dropped to the low 7% range, while the prime rate had dropped to the low 8% range. Few cash-flow models are equipped to deal with such drastic changes in any sort of meaningful way.

Yet, discounted cash flow (DCF) analysis is valuable, particularly in projecting increases in income associated with step-up leases or other regularly scheduled increases in rents or income. In most cases, lenders who utilize DCF analysis extensively will do their own projections and rely on the loan submission to give them the raw data to plug into their program.

The economic analysis section should include a discussion of stabilized income and expenses. This involves calculating gross income, vacancy allowances, expenses, net operating income and the capitalization rate. These calculations must show support for the income used, vacancy projected and all expense items, including:

- Real estate taxes
- Insurance
- Management
- Utilities
- Maintenance and repair
- Decorations
- Reserves for replacement
- Lawn, snow, trash and extermination fees
- Supplies and janitorial expenses
- Advertising
- Payroll
- Miscellaneous

Physical Analysis. Physical analysis deals with the costs associated with the development of the project. It can be a valuable check for the economic analysis, particularly in cases where the project is recently completed or yet to be constructed. Older properties typically have varying amounts of curable and incurable obsolescence, which is extremely difficult to estimate.

In physical analysis (the cost approach) the various separate depreciated costs associated with the development of the project are added together, along with the current market value of the land to produce an estimate of the total development cost. Included in this analysis are (1) indirect (soft) costs such as architects' and engineers' fees, legal and accounting, appraisal and environmental report costs, title insurance and survey costs, financing fees and interest during construction and entrepreneurial profit; (2) direct (hard) costs such as excavation and underground work, site utilities, general conditions, rough and finish carpentry, HVAC and mechanical, plumbing, electrical, building package items (cabinetry, etc.), concrete and masonry, structural steel, windows and doors, roadways and asphalt, sprinklers, landscaping and specialty items, finish decorating (wall and floor cover), etc.

In verifying project costs, it is necessary to review the contractor's sworn statement, the engineer's cost estimate and copies of the individual bids made by the subcontractors. It is helpful to check these costs by utilizing one of the popular costing services such as Marshall-Swift, Dow or Boeck.

In estimating the land value, reference should be made to the land's acquisition cost (if recent) adding for the expenses associated with rezoning, platting, various municipal approvals, etc. The land value should be able to be backed up with land sale comparables of similarly zoned land in the subject's market area. Verification must be made with either buyer, seller or selling broker.

Sponsor (Borrower) Analysis

The mortgage banker's recommendation should be based on verified facts, not hearsay. The analysis should involve four steps:

1. Describe the borrowing entity and its principals. Is it a corporation, a partnership, a limited liability company (LLC), a limited liability partnership (LLP), an individual or other legal entity?
2. Discuss the borrower's track record, management capabilities, financial strength and reputation.
3. Refer to financial statements, retail credit reports, Dun & Bradstreet reports and, if applicable, 10-K reports that some corporations file with the Securities and Exchange Commission.
4. Discuss personal endorsement, call provisions, transfer with assumption rights, prepayment privileges and special requests of borrower.

It is especially valuable when analyzing a borrower's financial condition to review a current cash flow schedule of different projects in which the borrower is involved as an owner, beneficial owner, manager or guarantor. Many times in the past, lenders have relied on a borrower's net-worth estimate and schedule of assets and liabilities, both of which were obsolete before the ink on the loan documents had a chance to dry. This is primarily a result of the way developers utilize their assets. Typically, the net worth is very high in comparison to the cash position. If a project gets into difficulties, lenders rarely find the assets and liabilities to be even vaguely similar to that represented in the original financial statement.

A cash flow schedule should be obtained on an annual basis to determine the borrower's true financial picture. This is generally unnecessary when the borrower has a high credit rating or the underlying security is backed by a lease or guarantee from a credit tenant. Exhibit 19, on the next two pages, shows a cash flow schedule format.

Rental Analysis

The rental section deals with each tenant or occupant of the property and its ability to pay the rent. The lease is analyzed with

EXHIBIT 19

PERSONAL CASH FLOW SCHEDULE

Borrower's Name: John Smith
as of January 1, ___________

Project & Location	Entity	Units Sq./Ft.	Property Type (year built)	% Owned	% Leased	N.O.I.	Debt Service
The Monroe Building Cedar Rapids, IA	Monroe Assoc.	39,000	Class A Office ('90)	50	99	532,537	346,796
Oakwood Mall Kalamazoo, MI	Oakwood Partnership	183,000	Retail ('59,'68,'75)	80	98	600,000	425,000
Jefferson Park Indianapolis, IN	The Jefferson Group	27,438	Class B ('74)	13	98	152,538	125,244
Jefferson Plaza Indianapolis, IN	The Jefferson Group	51,234	Retail ('91)	45	100	482,000	273,396
Lake Winona Apts. Madison, WI	L.W.A. Associates	310 Units	Garden Apts. ('88–'89)	50	95	1,220,000	813,672
					Totals	**2,987,075**	**1,984,108**

(continued)

EXHIBIT 19 (cont'd)

PERSONAL CASH FLOW SCHEDULE

Borrower's Name: John Smith
as of January 1, ________

Cash Flow	Income Approach Valuation	Loan Balance	Equity	Lender	Interest Rate (F/V) Term Amort.	Recourse (Y/N)	LTV	Ownership Cash Flow	Interest Equity
185,741	4,000,000	3,290,462	709,538	ABC Life	9,625 (F) 7, 30	N	83%	92,871	354,769
120,000	6,000,000	3,840,000	2,160,000	First Bank	10% (F) 0	N	64%	96,000	1,728,000
27,294	1,400,000	1,169,651	230,349	AAA Annuity	10% (F) 5, 25	N	84%	3,550	130,000
208,604	4,250,000	2,760,000	1,490,000	ZZZ Financial	7.75 (F) 25	N	65%	104,302	745,000
406,328	13,000,000	8,546,000	4,454,000	XYZ Bank	8,375 (F) 5, 25	N	66%	203,164	2,227,000
947,967	**28,650,000**	**19,606,113**	**9,043,887**				**Totals**	**499,887**	**5,184,769**
	Totals								

attention to those aspects that restrict rent payments — that is, "who pays what," cancellation rights, subordination, eminent domain and assignment. Exhibit 20 on page 152 shows a sample lease analysis form.

The most important item to be developed in the rental section is the rent roll. A typical rent roll is a lease spreadsheet that includes tenant names, leased area, lease terms, lease commencement and expiration dates, monthly rents, annual rents, rents per square foot, common area reimbursements, base year for tax and escalation payments, escalation caps and special conditions (such as kick-out clauses). A rent roll for a multifamily project includes tenant names, apartment numbers, monthly rents, security deposits, commencement and expiration dates, special charges (such as for pets or garage parking) and street rents for the units to show how close the project is performing with management's expectations.

The best rent rolls show each of these items for each year of the lease, highlighting the current year. This format enables the lender to quickly determine where the income stream is in relation to the tenancy and allows for quick DCF analysis.

Underwriting

In the underwriting part of the report, the mortgage banker analyzes the project's Net Operating Income in relation to the annual debt service projected for the proposed loan. To do this, the mortgage banker calculates the following:

- Annual debt service
- Cash throw-off (cash flow before income taxes)
- Debt service coverage ratio
- Break-even point
- Loan per square foot
- LTV ratio
- Balloon payment
- Five- to ten-year cash flow projections

EXHIBIT 20

LEASE ANALYSIS — DATA SHEET

Date:__________ Analyst: __________

Lessor:
Lessee:
Location and/or description:
Area Leased: Percentage of Total NRA__________
Lease Term & Renewals:
Lease Commencement & Expiration:
Annual Rent: Rent/Sq. Ft. __________________
Percentage Rent:
Uses of Premises & Restrictions:
Taxes Paid By: Insurance: Fire ________________
Liability ____________________
Tax Escalation Clause __Yes __ No Base Year ____________________
Operating Expense Escalation Clause __ Yes __No By __________________

Expenses Paid By: Heat __________ Water __________
(T–Tenant) Electric __________ A/C __________
(L–Landlord) Janitorial __________ Snow Removal __________ Trash Removal __________

Parking Lot: repair __________ striping __________ lighting __________ cleaning __________

Repair & Maintenance
Interior ____________________
Exterior ____________________
Roof ____________________
Glass ____________________
Structural ____________________
Decorating ____________________
Plumbing System ________________
Elec.System ____________________
Other ____________________
____
____

Tenant Contribution to Public Areas:
Condemnation Clause:
Cancellation Rights:
Restrictive Covenants:
Kickout Provisions:
Continuous Operations Clause:
Assignment and Subletting:
Subordination: Nondisturbance clause?
Purchase Option:
Date Signed:
Comments and Notes:

This analysis is for basic information only and is not to be considered a legal option.
Action Mortgage Corporation
By: ____________________

- Discounted cash flow analyses (before and after taxes)
- Sensitivity analysis

Supporting Exhibits and Addenda

The following list of necessary exhibits is reasonably complete but will not be adequate in every case:

- Legal description
- Leases and lease analysis forms
- Rent roll
- Financial statements
- Credit reports and Dun & Bradstreet reports
- Photographs (35mm, color)
- Aerial photo
- Maps (graphics, original map or photocopy)
- Site plan (survey)
- Building plans (schematics)
- Sponsor resume
- Operating statements (pro forma)
- Application
- Title policy commitment
- Appraisal report
- Environmental report
- Engineering report and inspection

Some Final Thoughts

The first order of business for a mortgage submission is to sell a deal. Never send a lender a package that could be personally delivered. Never send a submission by regular mail. The cost of using one of the overnight express services is negligible when you compare the time saved versus the fees involved. Use electronic transmission by modem or computer disk when appropriate. Try not to send a submission package to more than one lender at a time. When time constraints make this impossible, inform the lender that other people are looking at the project. No lender wants a "shopped deal."

Remember, each submission package is a direct reflection of the mortgage banker's personal professionalism, and by extension, the professionalism of the firm. A professional package enhances not only personal credibility but also the credibility of the mortgage banking firm and that of the profession as a whole.

9

Critical Legal Issues for Commercial Mortgage Bankers

Gary S. Smuckler, Partner
Pepper, Hamilton & Scheetz

This chapter describes the potential legal risks with which commercial mortgage bankers must deal. These risks are associated with four general topics:

1. General corporate issues
2. Borrower relations
3. Investor relations
4. The loan closing process

As most lawyers learn in law school, it is initially more important to spot the issue than to know the answer. The answer can always be figured out with research or the assistance of the right expert. But if the issue is missed, the legal danger may remain hidden until there is no longer time to avoid or mitigate it. Good businesspeople know that it is better to prevent legal problems than to solve them after they arise. The time and expense of preventive legal advice and compliance, unpleasant as they may be, pale in comparison to the expense, distraction and anxiety associated with litigation.

Taking all of that into account, treat this chapter as a checklist to help spot legal issues, not as a legal treatise intended to supply answers. The answers depend on too many variables for us to adequately address here. The answer to any particular issue will depend on factual matters unique to each commercial mortgage banker's situation at a given time. In addition, the law is constantly evolving. The business environment is changing too and is altering the context in which the law is applied as it changes.

Risks Associated with General Corporate Issues

Each commercial mortgage banker faces many of the same legal risks faced by other business entities. While some of these have special applications to the commercial mortgage banker, most are universal to all businesses.

Corporate Governance

The internal rules that govern the activities of each commercial banker must be updated regularly, and management must conduct the business in conformance with these rules. While most commercial mortgage banking firms are corporations governed by articles of incorporation and bylaws, several operate as partnerships; in these cases, partnership agreements take the place of the articles and bylaws. Another option is the limited liability company, an emerging form of corporate structure that is governed by an operating agreement.

Of great practical concern are the authorizations for various officers to conduct the business of the company. Those dealing with the company may request copies of resolutions or certified copies of bylaw provisions coupled with evidence of the incumbency of the individual with whom they are dealing. This is a reasonable precaution for those dealing with a business entity. In cases where an officer or employee has specific authority under the bylaws or under specific resolutions of the board of directors or other governing body, that person might have the authority to further delegate authority under certain circumstances. There should be a form of delegation that can be used quickly when needed (when key officers are out of town and specific company business must be handled while they're away, for example). The form of delegation should be readily available and familiar to the officers who execute it or function under it. When entering into important business arrangements with other business entities, commercial mortgage bankers may want to take the same precautions.

Ownership Issues

Three different types of ownership are common among commercial mortgage companies. Each presents a different set of legal issues to operational management. The three types are:

1. *Private Ownership by an Individual or Group Who Exercises Control Over the Company.* This is the simplest source of equity capital.
2. *Ownership by a Larger Company such as a Diversified Financial Company, Life Insurance Company or Financial Institution.* Although commercial mortgage banking tends to be largely unregulated, ownership by such regulated entities infects it with some degree of regulatory impact through the regulated parent, as well as a pattern of more heavily documented and formalized management of capital needs and executive decision making.
3. *Public Ownership.* The most complex legal structure, public ownership carries with it the complications of compliance with the federal and applicable state securities laws and the requirements of the exchange in which the

ownership shares might trade. Where shares are publicly traded, precautions must be taken to regulate trading in the company's shares by officers, employees and others who often have information not available to the public.

Committee Action

It is particularly important to document the proceedings of the loan committee and other operating units of the board of directors (or other governing body) and to keep accurate records on the authority of the committee, its composition and its actions. Careful documentation of the activities of the governing body and its committees is important as a matter of general corporate well-being. In the commercial mortgage field, this requirement takes on a special meaning because of the obligations that the commercial mortgage banker has to its secondary mortgage market investor, its warehouse lender (if any) and its borrowers and correspondents.

Tax Issues

Matters relating to federal and state income taxes and other taxes have fairly obvious legal consequences. Many of these issues — such as valuation of servicing, treatment of contingent liability and recognition of fee income — are intrinsically related to the operation of the company's main business and are the subject of constant industry scrutiny. Other issues, such as personal property taxation and reporting obligations on state and local levels, are generic to all businesses.

Procurement

Every business is involved in agreements for acquiring space, equipment and vital services. The terms of these agreements must be understood and complied with fully in order to heed options for renewals or terminations, miscellaneous notice requirements, limitations on the use of the equipment or facilities and so on. With regard to agreements for services (such as data processing, security and outsourced property inspections), care must be taken to ensure that the services are being delivered at the anticipated quality level and frequency and in the anticipated quantities.

Intellectual Property

Intellectual property law affects businesses — including commercial mortgage bankers — in two ways:

1. Protecting their own materials.
2. Preventing infringement on the intellectual property rights of others.

Intellectual property law involves the protection of a company's valuable intellectual property, such as trademarks, service marks, proprietary computer software, copyrighted material and trade secrets. Firms must take the necessary steps to establish this protection and must monitor their intellectual property to prevent infringement by others.

At the same time, it is important to prevent infringement on the intellectual property rights of others. The most common types of infringement are the unauthorized photocopying of protected material and the violation of software licenses, which limit the number of computers or workstations that may use a software program.

ERISA Issues

If the company maintains a 401(k) program or similar retirement benefit, careful attention must be paid to the plan document, its administration, various discrimination tests and other upkeep matters to assure that the plan, and therefore the employee's deductions from income for their contributions, are within the law.

Employment Issues

Federal, state and some local laws affect the handling and maintenance of employment records, compensation and benefits. Certain employees in this industry are customarily compensated on an incentive formula basis, often accompanied by a written contract. Monitoring these formulas and the terms of employment contracts with key individuals is essential.

Under the heading of equal employment opportunity, a variety of federal, state and local laws prohibit discrimination in personnel matters on the basis of race, religion, national origin, gender and other categories. Disputes with employees frequently permit administrative recourse to them on timetables that are very short and following rules of procedure that are to be scrupulously followed. Knowing these processes and timetables in advance of a dispute is essential.

Trade Regulation

Trade regulation law deals with unfair or anticompetitive business practices. On a federal level, these laws are enforced by the Department of Justice and by the Federal Trade Commission.

In the context of commercial mortgage banking, the most likely areas of concern involve price fixing or anticompetition actions, such as mergers and acquisitions. As the industry experiences more mergers and large-scale acquisitions, it becomes likely that monopolistic concentrations may take place. To prevent this, federal law requires various filings for transactions above a threshold size. Many states also deal with these issues.

Risk Management

Every business encounters risks. The question is which risks a commercial mortgage banker should insure against to meet requirements of secondary market investors and capital sources.

Secondary market investors and capital sources typically require errors and omissions coverage, fidelity coverage and a variety of general and civil liability plans. If the circumstances are warranted, many commercial mortgage bankers obtain life insurance coverage on their leadership and other key people.

On the servicing side of the business, hazard insurance of mortgaged property may need to be obtained on a "forced-place" basis. Because of the highly complex and specialized nature of insurance, many commercial mortgage lenders retain expert consultants to review the insurance coverage on each property prior to mortgage loan closing.

Qualification

Corporations generally qualify under the laws of each state in which they do business. The definition of doing business is a creature of state law, and commercial mortgage bankers must become familiar with the requirements of the laws in each state where they make or service loans. State laws vary dramatically as to the consequences for failure to qualify where it is appropriate to do so. For example, in one state, commercial mortgage bankers who are not qualified to do business risk the voiding of their loans; in another state, they must qualify before even taking loan applications.

This is not to say that commercial mortgage bankers need to be qualified in every state in which they make or service loans. Frequently, merely lending and servicing do not obligate the commercial mortgage banker to file state qualification papers. That is why it is so important to be familiar with the state laws. Some mortgage bankers routinely qualify in every state in which they lend or service. However, keep in mind that unnecessary qualification creates costly and time-consuming state reporting obligations.

Licensing

Well over a dozen states now require commercial mortgage bankers to obtain licenses from a state agency that regulates mortgage bankers. Licensing requirements are sometimes inapplicable due to the corporate structure of the commercial mortgage banker or its intended secondary mortgage market investor. However, the consequence of not being licensed can be fairly troublesome. A careful and systematic process for evaluating licensing requirements and maintaining those licenses in good standing (where licensing is required) is essential.

Financial Representations and Warranties

Most mortgage bankers use funds from warehouse lenders or other financial sources in their day-to-day operations and may use other debt for longer term needs. These financing agreements frequently contain detailed representations, warranties and covenants regarding corporate housekeeping and internal financial matters. It is vital that financing requirements be fully understood and processes be in place to monitor compliance.

Risks Associated with Borrower Relations

The following issues reflect special risks associated with commercial mortgage banking and, in particular, those that arise in dealing with borrowers and potential borrowers. The most common area in which commercial mortgage bankers face such potential legal risk is in the loan closing process, which is described in the last section of this chapter.

Application Agreement/Commitment Letter

The commercial mortgage banker must describe the potential loan terms accurately and completely in the application agreement.

Once the loan has been approved, the specific approved terms, including critical loan-specific details, must be addressed in the commitment accurately. Too often, lenders use long-standing form agreements that may become outdated as programs evolve and specialized loan terms are used more frequently.

Loan Documents

Loan documents must reflect the terms of the commitment accurately and completely, must comply with requirements of local law and must satisfy the requirements of the secondary mortgage market investor. As loan programs evolve, it is important that the terms of the application agreement, loan commitment and final loan documents coincide clearly and consistently.

Lender Liability

Commercial mortgage lenders need to understand the essential aspects of potential lender liability. Generally speaking, lender liability arises in two ways:

1. Through inappropriate interference in the borrower's relationships with third parties (such as tenants, management agents and third-party service providers)
2. Within the organizational structure of the borrower itself (for example, among the partners doing the borrowing)

These lender liability concerns may arise over how commercial mortgage bankers handle the terms of loan approval or over how commercial mortgage bankers exercise their rights under loan documents. For example, most loan documents give the servicer wide latitude to administer insurance proceeds, condemnation awards and other escrow amounts. In applying these fairly discretionary powers, the servicer must be attentive to the standards by which it could be judged to have unnecessarily or unreasonably interfered with the operation of the borrower and its property.

Commercial mortgage bankers need to be aware that the way in which they handle the origination and closing process may disadvantage the borrower and give rise to certain claims by the borrower. For example, a lender might give a borrower an unreasonable impression that a loan application, approval and closing can be accomplished prior to a critical time deadline which, if missed, will have a dramatic adverse effect on the borrower (such as loss of discounted payoff opportunities or default under an agreement for the purchase of property where a deposit has been tendered). Potential lender liability is always a risk when the lender knows that it is being unreasonable in expecting to complete its processes in a timely fashion, after inducing the borrower to commit to the process.

Fair Housing and Equal Credit Opportunity

Federal, state and local laws prohibit activities that discriminate in granting credit to members of protected classes. These laws generally protect against discrimination on the basis of race, gender, religion, national origin and physical disability, but may also include marital status, receipt of public benefits, sexual orientation and other grounds. A commercial mortgage banker would be in jeopardy for rejecting a loan application simply because the property's sponsor belonged to such a protected category. These laws may permit criminal enforcement and also may allow civil recovery by the person or group who has suffered prohibited discrimination. Under many of these laws, a commercial mortgage banker lending on multifamily property could also be made to suffer for denying credit on the security of a residential property because that property was occupied by individuals who belonged to such a protected category.

Risks Associated with Investor Relations

The following legal issues arise out of the special circumstances of dealing with secondary mortgage market investors.

Failure to Deliver

Specialized liabilities can arise where mortgage loans are being originated for another for cash or otherwise. Failure to deliver, on a timely basis, a loan that matches an investor's legitimate expectations will give rise to penalties, set-off fees or worse.

Mortgage-Backed Security Swaps

Swaps for familiar mortgage-backed securities (MBSs) from government-sponsored entities or private conduits carry specialized legal risk. It is necessary to be alert to the critical timing deadlines associated with this process. Most experienced players make sure there is a mechanism that enables them to postpone, at some cost, the delivery or pool certification, if necessary.

When commercial mortgage bankers have responsibility for preparing or editing supplemental prospectus materials, they must do so with the greatest of care, noting that they may ultimately have legal responsibility for inaccuracies in the disclosure materials presented to investors. The typical sale and servicing agreement places ultimate responsibility for these items on the shoulders of the commercial mortgage bankers, even if they had no role in the securitization process other than the origination of the mortgage loan and delivery for cash to the government-sponsored entity or conduit.

Recourse

Some secondary market investors agree to purchase loans on terms that require commercial mortgage bankers to share in the economic risk of default. The most common example of this is the commercial mortgage bankers' loss-sharing obligation to Fannie Mae under its Delegated Underwriting and Servicing (DUS) product line. Most investors will otherwise have a claim against the commercial mortgage banker only when a material representation or warranty in its loan sale agreement has remained uncured.

Selectivity

This concern arises when competing investors have conflicting expectations for the type and volume of mortgage loans that are to be delivered by the commercial mortgage banker. A commercial mortgage banker may have a contractual obligation to provide a certain type and proportion of its new loan production to a particular investor. This duty may rise to the level of a fiduciary obligation if the commercial mortgage banker is part of a life insurance company or pension fund management company. Therefore, secondary mortgage market investors or others may have legal recourse if they are made the victims of adverse selection in favor of another investor.

Loan Administration

A number of legal concerns arise over how a commercial mortgage lender services a loan or monitors the underlying real estate. Two common examples are the failure to pay insurance premiums or property taxes and the failure to release items such as completion/repair escrows and replacement reserves on a timely basis, especially if the funds have been collected from the borrower in an escrow account. Another common risk is the failure to learn about and take account of potential environmental hazards before commencing or carrying forward on a foreclosure proceeding.

The Loan Closing Process

Based on discussions with lawyers representing commercial mortgage bankers and key executives in the field, it is clear that the area of the greatest legal risk is the loan closing process. Practical experience bears out this proposition.

The loan closing process, often taken for granted, carries with it the highest level of risk and the highest incidence of exposure to legal risk. The loan closing process exposes commercial mortgage bankers to a full range of risks in terms of relationships with lenders, borrowers and potential borrowers each time a loan moves through the process. Correspondingly, each loan carries with it new, complex and potentially troublesome exposure to liability vis-à-vis the secondary mortgage market investor and the MBS purchaser.

Commercial mortgage bankers arrange their closing processes in a variety of ways. Each aspect of these arrangements reflects the organization's unique talents, efficiencies, economies and other needs. But each aspect of the organizational structure of the closing process also reflects the organization's tolerance for certain types of legal risk.

Selection of Counsel

It is still the custom for closings to be handled, or at least supervised, by lawyers. In many states, this is no longer the case for single family loans; however, the complicated nature of commercial mortgage lending still requires that lawyers be involved in the process. Some lenders have employed in-house counsel to oversee the process, while others routinely hire outside law firms to handle some or all of this work. While the use of an in-house attorney frequently can help keep costs down, the use of outside attorneys provides more flexibility in capacity and in making quick personnel shifts if the circumstances dictate.

Commercial mortgage bankers who operate on a multi-regional or nationwide basis often retain a local law firm to handle closings in each metropolitan area. Others hire one or more firms to supervise all closings conducted nationwide. National closing counsel must already have or must develop a network of local attorneys who can advise on local issues. While having national coordinating counsel does provide certainty and consistency, it does carry some risk of unfamiliarity with local practice. On the other hand, multiple local counsels might be highly sensitive to local variations in law and practice, but each firm will not receive the same volume of transactions as national counsel and therefore may not achieve the same consistency and efficiency.

Closing Specialists

Most large commercial mortgage bankers have an in-house closing department staffed with specialists experienced in managing the closing process and in dealing with outside attorneys, title companies, borrowers and their counsel. Other commercial mortgage bankers, generally in smaller operations, leave the in-house supervision of the closing process to the loan officer handling the loan. This is an economical approach, eliminating the cost of maintaining specialized functions, but it does create its own set of risks. A loan officer who does not perform the closing functions on a repetitive basis often will not be as familiar with the nuances of the legal requirements affecting the closing. Furthermore, not all loan officers have the self-discipline to separate their responsibilities in the closing arena from the financial incentives of a loan officer.

Division of Labor

A well-structured closing process clearly articulates the due diligence and checklist items that are to be handled by businesspeople as opposed to outside legal counsel. For example, many institutions handle zoning compliance documentation, certificates of occupancy and related issues in-house, while others put full responsibility for those items on their attorney. Either way, a clear statement of the division of labor is an important element.

Closing Style

Some lenders (particularly those on the East Coast) still prefer to conduct closings on a face-to-face basis. Many others (particularly those who operate on a multiregional or national basis) prefer to handle closings through the mail using escrow agents. Not attending the closing, some will argue, ensures that the lender will not have to deal with further attempts to negotiate loan documents at the closing table.

While the mail closing process can be efficient and reliable (when well administered), it does carry some risks. Particularly complex or unusual transactions and transactions involving particularly difficult personalities should be handled on a face-to-face basis.

Involvement by Correspondent/Broker

There is always the danger of having too many cooks in the kitchen. Whether to allow a correspondent/broker to remain involved in the substantive preparation for closing and the due diligence associated with it depends on the individuals involved. Some provide useful, knowledgeable support, while others only cause tension and confusion.

Title Agents

In most jurisdictions, closings — whether face-to-face or through the mail — are conducted by title insurance companies or their agents. If the closing is conducted through an agent, the lender must obtain some evidence — usually a letter — that the agent's activities are insured by the title insurance carrier; this letter of insured closing protection may vary from jurisdiction to jurisdiction, and is not available in all states.

The title agent's knowledge, sense of responsibility and familiarity with commercial mortgage bankers' needs also must be considered. For example, distinguishing between title agents who handle single-family loans and title agents who specialize in commercial real estate transactions is essential. The title agent is responsible for numerous activities at the closing table — completing blanks in documents, collecting proper forms of opinion, overseeing execution of loan documents and various banking functions. A mistake by the title agent can have dramatic repercussions in terms of time and expense to correct mistakes.

Preclosing Activities

The key to avoiding legal risks in the closing process is to be well organized and able to anticipate the often hectic flow of activities that leads to the closing table.

Licensing and Qualification. Licensing and qualification issues must be analyzed and resolved well before the loan commitment is issued. In some states, licensing and qualification must be completed before any applications are taken.

Preliminary Due Diligence. Common due diligence issues are more easily resolved if they are identified early in the process. The following is a list of those common issues that should be "flagged" early by the commercial mortgage banker's own underwriting and processing personnel so that closing specialists and counsel can be prepared for them:

- Title problems
- Survey problems
- Borrower organizational structure
- Environmental concerns
- Commercial tenant leases in a predominantly multifamily property

- Zoning problems
- Bankruptcy concerns

Some preliminary due diligence efforts must be directed toward the applicant. In particular, the commercial mortgage banker should alert each prospective borrower to specialized closing requirements, including:

- Standardized loan documents
- Title insurance coverage requirements
- Survey standards and required form of surveyor certification
- Required form of opinion of borrower's counsel
- Form of tenant estoppel and subordination agreement

Transmittal to Closing Attorney. A comprehensive and uniform document package, accompanied by a standardized control sheet, should be prepared and sent by the lender to the closing counsel. This package should include the following:

- *Completed Loan Commitment.* This should be a copy of the final text, as negotiated between the commercial mortgage banker and the borrower, including all supplements, addenda and exhibits. (Note: This should not be the version first sent after loan approval.)
- *Organizational Documents.* This should include the applicant's by-laws, partnership agreement, operating agreement (or the like, depending on the structure), all related documents and evidence of filing under local requirements. If the borrower's general partner or acting member or managing member is itself a corporation or other entity, all of the same documents must be obtained for that entity.

- *Title Materials and Survey.* This should include a current title insurance commitment, preliminary title report, copies of recorded exceptions and an as-built survey. If these have been ordered but not yet delivered, copies of title insurance polices and surveys from earlier, recent financing packages can provide useful preliminary information.
- *Participants List.* This list should include the full names, addresses, telephone numbers and fax numbers of all parties to the transaction and those providing key services.
- *Zoning Evidence.* Zoning evidence may take the form of a letter from the local authority or, in the case of a nonconformity, may be analytical or explanatory materials concerning the extent to which the improvement can be rebuilt if destroyed. Some circumstances require an opinion of local zoning counsel — a complex process that should be commenced as early as possible.
- *Certificate(s) of Occupancy.* These should match the size and location of the security property. If Certificates of Occupancy are not available, a satisfactory written explanation of why they are not available must be provided.
- *Underwriting Narrative (Summary).* This can provide useful background information to the closing attorneys that they might not otherwise learn from the loan commitment.
- *Commercial Leases* (if any).
- *Sample Residential Lease* (if applicable).
- *Management Agreement.*
- *Operations & Maintenance (O&M) Plan.* When the borrower is required to maintain and monitor a potential environmental hazard in place, this plan should be prepared and reviewed by an attorney.

Investor Approval of Nonstandard Items. When the transaction will deviate in a material manner from the requirements of the secondary market mortgage investor, care should be taken to see that an express waiver of that requirement is obtained from the investor.

Preparation of Loan Documents. Draft loan documents, the closing checklist and the closing instruction letter are best prepared on an automated system that assures a highly uniform product. Most firms develop standard documents that are only altered for transaction-specific matters. Marking documents with changes from one deal to the next runs the risk of creating embarrassing and potentially dangerous variations in the documents.

Introductory Conference. An early conference call or meeting with borrower's counsel and the title agent who will handle the closing is highly recommended. Such a conference will allow the mortgage lender and its attorney to establish and maintain cordial control over the process. It enables them to explain the commercial secondary market process, timetable and tolerance (if any) for changes to the key documents and to discuss any unusual issues involved in the deal.

Title Agent Approval. The title agent handling the closing should be required to review and approve, well in advance of closing, the letter of closing instructions and the recordable documents.

Closing Protection Coverage. The title insurance company whose agent will be handling the closing should provide the commercial mortgage banker (and its warehouse lender) an insured closing protection letter covering that agent.

The Closing

Once an interest rate has been selected, the timing of the process for closing and delivering to the investor becomes very rigid and failure to meet those deadlines can have dramatic and adverse consequences for everyone involved. Timely closing is sometimes jeopardized by the appearance of new, complicated issues, old issues not yet resolved or, as is often the case, mundane logistical problems. Constant and careful oversight of the process can reduce the chances of these last minute items becoming difficult problems.

Techniques for reducing risk include:

- Discuss all loan commitment special and of general conditions with the lender, borrower and both of their counsels well in advance. Make sure all parties understand and agree when and how each condition will be satisfied.
- Know the schedule, whereabouts and availability of the borrower (key principal and guarantor) so that planned vacations and other travel plans do not conflict with the latest reasonable closing date.
- Understand the reason for any deadline that is imposed on the closing.
- Understand the investor's delivery timetable and the details of its mechanical delivery requirements.
- Satisfy requirements of warehouse lender or other funding source.
- Proofread the rate-lock certification or equivalent document, and take precautions to ensure the accuracy of the monthly payment of principal and interest, yield maintenance formula and other calculations.
- Confirm that the loan amount and escrow deposit requirements did not change at the time of rate-lock due to fluctuation in rate markets or last minute repairs to the property, respectively.
- Confirm that the title agent handling the closing has complied with written closing instructions before releasing funds. When local law and custom so provide, it may be appropriate for loan proceeds to be disbursed before the title agent has completed the recording of the

mortgage instrument, as long as the warehouse lender understands and approves of that sequence and the lender has written assurance that the title "gap" is insured.

Postclosing Activities

Once the executed loan documents return from the closing they must be reviewed carefully. Some investors "table fund" (review) the executed documents before sending the closing proceeds to the escrow agent for disbursement. In many other cases, commercial mortgage bankers use their own warehouse funds to close and then deliver the executed documents to the investors who pay off the warehouse lender. In any event, the package of documents returned by the title agent must be carefully reviewed and assembled into the proper format for delivery to the investor.

The following steps may help the mortgage bankers and their counsel to reduce legal risks, delays and costs in this process:

- Conduct an immediate and detailed review of the title insurance policy, marked-up commitment, borrower's counsel opinion and all other executed documents, proofreading for completeness, particularly where blanks were to be completed or exhibits attached.
- Prepare lender's counsel opinion, legal review certification and explanatory memorandum on title exceptions.
- Prepare delivery binder(s).
- Prepare a reaction to investor's exceptions, if any.
- Track down delayed follow-up documents such as final title policy or recorded original instruments.

Overzealous Borrower's Counsel

Most commercial mortgage bankers utilize loan documents that cannot be altered without great effort; however, many borrowers' attorneys are unwilling to accept this. In fact, those attorneys have an obligation to carefully review the documents and advise the borrower of their consequences. While respecting the borrower's counsel's duty, the lender's counsel must still make it clear that very little, if any, flexibility exists concerning loan document content.

Despite standardization of loan documents in virtually all commercial secondary mortgage market transactions, it is often impossible to prevent borrower's counsel from providing voluminous comments on the loan documents. Therefore, it is important for the commercial mortgage bankers and their counsel to understand the loan documents thoroughly, even if the forms have been developed by the investor, so that the most common objections can be anticipated and dealt with swiftly.

The most common objections to loan documents stem from the following sources:

- The insertion of materiality and reasonableness standards in various places throughout the documents where the lender's sole and absolute discretion would otherwise apply.
- The insertion of provisions permitting notice of default and opportunities to cure where they do not already exist (for example, Fannie Mae and Freddie Mac multifamily programs which give virtually no opportunity for notice and cure).
- Documents that are nonrecourse to the borrower, but nonetheless contain "springing" liability for certain types of misconduct by the borrower. The scope and mechanism for that liability to "spring" attracts considerable attention from borrower's counsel.
- Provisions in the loan documents for environmental indemnification.

- The application of casualty insurance proceeds and condemnation awards.
- The requirement of most investors (Freddie Mac is a notable exception) for a form of opinion of borrower's counsel which concludes that the loan documents are enforceable. This will frequently generate a comment from the borrower's counsel that certain provisions of the documents are not necessarily enforceable under local law precisely in accordance with their terms. For example, bankruptcy courts or courts applying equitable principles may enforce the loan documents in ways that their drafters might not have expected. It is common for most investors, therefore, to allow borrower's counsel to opine that, while every provision of the document may not be enforceable precisely as written, the lender can achieve a "practical realization" of its bargain. There are numerous language refinements, and many investors anticipate it by adding it to their standard forms of opinion. Nonetheless, precise wording of the practical-realization provision is frequently the subject of extensive discussion.

Commercial Tenants

In multifamily properties, the existence of a commercial tenant (particularly one other than a laundry equipment company) can give rise to a need for unusual amounts of time and attention to analyze the lease and to assure that it is properly subordinated.

Environmental Issues

While small amounts of encapsulated asbestos-containing materials are routinely dealt with in O&M plans, other types of environmental concerns raise serious legal issues, leading to extra expenses and delays. Any transaction involving underground storage tanks, lead in the drinking water or lead-based paint may give rise to specialized negotiations and the need for specialized advice.

Borrower Travel Plans

The individuals who will be signing loan documents on behalf of the borrower are often people of means with busy schedules and, frequently, exotic vacation plans. While it is reasonably simple to arrange for documents to be executed in Palm Beach, Palm Springs or Paris, one should avoid locking into a tight closing schedule that conflicts with a fishing trip to a remote camp in northern Canada, a cruise on the Amazon or a trek in Nepal.

Discord among Sponsors

When the "borrower" is actually a group of individuals with varying personal and business objectives, it is important to monitor any last minute structural changes in the borrowing entity or authorizations among the individuals.

Completion/Repair Items

To avoid placing a large sum in a repair escrow, many borrowers work feverishly to complete required repairs before closing. As a result, the final amount to be placed in the repair escrow may vary up to the last minute and cause late changes in documents and settlement sheets.

Seniors Housing

Multifamily loan programs are becoming much more widely available for properties having special utility for seniors. As these programs evolve, it is important to monitor complex local law defining scope of service and acceptable levels of activity for various defined categories. In addition, these properties tend to have complex and extensive service contracts beyond that typically seen in the multifamily and commercial lending arena.

Multiple Parcels of Land

When the property is on multiple parcels, many investors require special analysis and title insurance coverage regarding contiguity of those parcels. In addition, multiple parcels may give rise to multiple tax lots which will be of special concern on the settlement sheet and, later, to the loan servicing department.

Access Restrictions

When the subject property does not have direct access to a public right-of-way, special problems should be anticipated. For example, creating access to a public road by means of an appurtenant easement or a condemned and abandoned adjacent parcel of unknown ownership requires special attention and expertise.

Condemnation

When portions of the subject property have recently been taken through condemnation proceedings for road widening and the like, it is important to investigate the public authority's planned follow-up activities, such as replacement of lost parking or the deposit of funds for use by the borrower in re-landscaping or reconfiguring driveways. Frequently, these funds are placed in escrow if they have not already been spent, so that the new lender can monitor their use in the restoration of the property.

Phased Properties

Properties that were developed in phases, or properties that represent only one phase of a larger multiphase development, raise special concerns. Careful attention needs to be paid to ingress and egress rights among those properties, shared access to recreational facilities, and the effect on the subject property of homeowner associations and common elements.

HAP Contract/Section 8 Benefits

When Section 8 benefits accrue to the subject property, these benefits must be evaluated carefully and, if necessary, agreements put in place so that the lender will benefit from these payments if it is forced to foreclose on the property.

Affordable Use Restrictions

When the property is the subject of a recorded or otherwise enforceable restriction mandating affordable housing, these restrictions need to be evaluated carefully. Frequently, they arise from old bond financing that may no longer be in effect. In recent years however, such restrictions arise in connection with disposition of assets by the RTC, FDIC or HUD. Particularly in the case of HUD-imposed restrictions, many investors require that modifications be made to the terms of these documents.

Transfer Tax Avoidance

In a few states (most notably New York, Maryland and Florida), specialized structures are used to avoid paying transfer tax on "old money." These structures typically involve the purchase, consolidation, extension and modification of a previous note by the new lender into a new note. Each jurisdiction documents these structures in a different fashion, requiring careful attention by local experts.

Tax-Free Exchanges

When the proposed financing is part of a larger transaction involving tax-free exchanges, careful attention and expertise in that field is needed.

Split Counsel Opinions

Borrower's counsel should only opine as to the law of the state in which the lawyers of that law firm are licensed to practice.

For example, if a borrower created under the law of New York is borrowing money on a property in Florida, the standard form of opinion might need to be split between two law firms representing the borrower: one covering New York issues pertaining to the borrower, the other covering Florida issues relating to the property.

Past Bankruptcy

When the property was the subject of a recent bankruptcy proceeding, care must be taken to evaluate the bankruptcy plan under which new financing might be taking place. Failure to follow the bankruptcy plan carefully can create serious risks to the lender.

Section Two:
Analyzing Property Sectors

10

Multifamily Property

Stephanie Polyzois, Senior Mortgage Analyst
Green Park Financial

Underwriting Multifamily Properties

In general, underwriting multifamily product is similar to underwriting all other commercial property types. The underwriting process consists of a review of the property's historic and current performance, an evaluation of the property's market and an analysis of the prospective borrowers' real estate experience and credit history. The underwriter's objectives are to identify market and borrower factors that could affect the property's performance and to formulate income projections for the property that reflect the probable influence of identified factors. The quality of the underwriting is directly related to the underwriter's ability to derive an accurate projection of a property's net operating income and to identify and mitigate market- and borrower-related risks via adjustments to the underwriting.

Distinctive Features of Multifamily Properties

Although it is appropriate to use a general underwriting framework to evaluate a multifamily property, the quality of multifamily underwriting is strengthened if the underwriter considers six distinct factors that can have a direct impact on a property's performance:

1. Economic changes
2. Changes in interest rates
3. New multifamily construction in the market
4. Decision makers
5. Changes in income levels
6. Property management's abilities and availability

Economic Changes

Economic changes affect the performance of all commercial property types; however, it is arguable that these changes have a more immediate effect on multifamily properties. The distinction between multifamily and other property types is in the timing of the effect.

Let's look at a specific example to illustrate this point. Assume that we are underwriting a property in a market where the economy is centered around a manufacturing plant that employs 6,000 people — 10% of the market's population. The plant's owners have decided to completely update the plant. As a result, jobs once filled by humans are now being done with high-tech, computer-controlled robotics, and 90% of the plant's employees are given notice that their jobs have been eliminated, effective immediately. How do these employees react? They file to collect unemployment insurance and seek other jobs in the market. Additionally, they immediately reduce their level of personal spending and eliminate nonessential expenses from their budgets.

One of the first expenses to be eliminated, either voluntarily or involuntarily, is rent. With no incoming paycheck, many renters voluntarily opt to break their leases. The penalty for breaking a lease is small, with the loss of a security deposit serving as the only deterrent. These renters will move to another market where there are more job opportunities or will move in with friends or family until they find jobs. A second group of renters will involuntarily leave their rental situations when faced with eviction notices resulting from their inability to pay rent the month following their layoff.

In this example, the impact of the reduction in market employment is felt by a multifamily rental property within the first few weeks following the layoffs. In comparison, other commercial property users in the market will feel the impact of the employment reduction much later. Retail sales may drop off as expenses are cut, but credit cards will allow the newly unemployed to borrow money and continue to make purchases. Retailers and other creditors will not feel the impact until several billing cycles have passed and credit losses begin to increase. Other property types, such as industrial and commercial properties, may not be noticeably affected.

Because economic changes have such a strong and sudden impact on a multifamily property's performance, it is imperative that the underwriter evaluate trends in the local economy and examine the economic base to gain an understanding of future levels of employment in the market.

Changes in Interest Rates

A second feature that distinguishes multifamily properties from other commercial property types is the effect that interest rate changes have on a multifamily property's performance. An increase or decrease in interest rates, specifically home mortgage interest rates, can have a significant impact on a property's occupancy level. As interest rates decrease, tenants' home-purchasing power increases. Further, as the gap between a rental payment and a monthly mortgage payment lessens, tenants are more likely to contemplate the "buy versus rent" decision. The resulting impact on a multifamily property is a sharp decrease in occupancy levels. Only when interest rates rise again or when housing prices increase will the multifamily occupancy level stabilize.

Because of the impact of interest rate changes on a multifamily property's performance, it benefits the underwriter to perform a home purchase analysis. This analysis identifies the likelihood that single family homes will provide multifamily properties with significant competition for residents. The first step in the home purchase analysis is to identify the market's median price for a home.

As an example, let's say we are underwriting a multifamily property in Oklahoma City — a market identified in 1995 as the most affordable housing market in the United States. Assume that the median sales price for a home in this market is $79,000. The average rent at our multifamily property is $450. How would a mortgage payment on the $79,000 house compare to the average rental payment? If the buyers put down 5%, they will finance a balance of $75,050. Assuming a 6.75% interest rate with no points and a 30-year amortization schedule, the monthly principal and interest payment would total $486. If interest rates were to fall to 6.50%, the monthly payment would be $475. We see from this analysis that the median-priced home is within the reach of our property's tenants, and we are safe in assuming that there are multiple properties in the market with sales prices that would result in a mortgage payment at or below the average monthly rent.

Based on the competition provided by homes available for purchase, it is imperative that underwriters evaluate affordability of homes in the subject property's market. Analyzing the property's occupancy history and comparing historical information to trends in home mortgage interest rates helps underwriters determine where a stabilized occupancy level for the subject property might be.

New Multifamily Construction in the Market

The performance of a multifamily property can be quickly and dramatically altered by the introduction of new multifamily properties in the market. In comparison to retail and office properties, whose tenants are committed to the properties under long-term leases, multifamily tenants are committed for a period ranging from only 30 days to one year. Because of this short-term commitment window, multifamily tenants are available to move to another property with little advance notice to the landlord. Multifamily tenants can be easily tempted by the appearance, floor plans and amenities offered at a new property. Furthermore, their decision to move to a new property is made easier if the new property offers concessions and move-in specials as enticements.

Because of the threat posed by new multifamily construction, it is imperative that underwriters meet with planners in the subject property's market to determine when and where new properties might be built. By identifying the location and number of additional units anticipated in the market, underwriters can address the potential impact on the subject property's occupancy in their calculation of loan amount.

Decision Makers

In the context of the following discussion, the term "decision maker" refers to the key participants in the commercial and multifamily real estate marketing and leasing process. They fall into four general categories:

1. Those people who are the target of a property's marketing effort
2. The parties who will evaluate the property and determine whether or not an interest in the property exists
3. The parties who might ultimately sign a lease
4. The parties who potentially could be occupants of the leased space

In the commercial real estate arena, the decision makers could be four different individuals or groups of individuals. Let's use the marketing and leasing of available retail space as an illustrative example. The available retail space is marketed to the real estate department of a retail chain's corporate headquarters. If the retailer's management has identified the need for a retail outlet in the subject property's market, a market demographics study will be performed by the retailer to determine the probable success of the retail chain in the market. If, after extensive analysis, it is determined that the outlet would be a profitable investment, negotiation of a lease commences. During the negotiation process, the prospective retail tenant is represented by the retailer's corporate executives and the retailer's counsel. Because of the time and dollar commitment the retailer is considering making to the new retail location, each point of the lease is carefully scrutinized and negotiated. The negotiation process can be lengthy. Once negotiations are successfully completed, the final lease will be approved and executed by the retailer's senior management. After lease execution, construction on tenant improvements can begin and, 30 to 90 days later, the retailer is able to stock and staff the new outlet and open for business.

In the retail example, we see multiple parties taking part in the decision-making process. All these decision makers have their own perspectives and objectives. The retail leasing process is lengthy and complex due to the many parties, the variety of analytical perspectives, and the time and the financial commitment of lessor and retailer involved.

In comparison, the marketing and leasing of a residential rental unit is simple and typically involves only one decision-maker: the prospective tenant. Residential rental property marketing is aimed directly at the property's prospective tenants. It is the prospective tenants who evaluate the property and determine whether or not the property fits their needs. It is also the prospective tenants who visit the property, review and sign the lease and ultimately occupy the rented space.

This consolidation of decision-making functions and analytical perspectives shortens the marketing/leasing cycle dramatically. Furthermore, the marketer of a multifamily property has an easier time in identifying and reaching decision makers. Instead of mailing leasing brochures to out-of-town corporate executives, the multifamily marketer can advertise in local apartment guides and newspapers or can leave flyers on windshields of cars parked at competitive properties.

The marketer of a multifamily property has only one decision-maker to control and "close," which makes the process less complicated. However, there is a down side to having a single decision maker. First, the multifamily property marketer typically gets only one opportunity to meet with the decision maker. During this single visit, the marketer must sell the property and close the transaction. Because only one opportunity to sell exists, first impressions generated by the property and its staff are very important. During the single encounter between the decision maker and the property marketer, the prospective tenant is sizing up the property, the quality of the staff, and the value of the rental deal being presented.

Although this distinct feature of multifamily does not have a direct impact on the underwriting, it has an indirect impact on the performance of a multifamily property. Because only one decision maker exists and because this decision maker is easily identified and accessed, the existing tenant base of a multifamily property is always subject to solicitation from other multifamily properties. This ease of solicitation, together with the short-term nature of a residential lease commitment, creates instability in a property's existing tenant base. Because first impressions are so important, tenants are easily influenced by a property's appearance and the congeniality of its staff.

To evaluate the risk of a property's tenants being lost to other properties, the underwriter should be attentive to the subject property management's capacity to manage tenant relationships and to focus on tenant retention at the property. Management's ability to perform these tasks will attract tenants to the subject property and will mitigate the loss of tenants to competitive properties. The underwriter should evaluate the attractiveness of the property to tenants, considering both the property's curb appeal and the people skills of the staff.

Dynamic Income Levels

The multifamily property owner has the opportunity to manipulate a property's income and expense levels on a daily basis. Residential unit leasing is an ongoing process, occurring daily at many properties. On short notice, a multifamily manager can initiate a "sale" to eliminate excess rental unit inventory by reducing rents or offering concessions. Conversely, if the supply of vacant units is low, the manager can increase rents and test the market's willingness to pay higher rents.

Assuming that a typical multifamily property has 50% to 80% of its units turning over to new tenants annually, these decreases and increases in rent can have a dramatic impact on a property's effective gross income for any given time period. A property's income is further affected by the rents commanded at the time of lease renewal. A healthy property that is competitive in its market will be able to increase rents at the time of lease renewal. A property at risk of losing tenants to other properties in the market may need to keep rents flat or to lower rents at the time of renewal in order to promote tenant retention.

In underwriting a multifamily property, underwriters should consider the flexible nature of a property's income. A study of rents at market comparables will provide underwriters with a clear understanding of base-line rent levels in the market. A comparison between rents at the subject property and the comparables will determine what rent levels should be used in underwriting the subject property. Often, the appropriate rent level will match actual rents obtained by the subject property. At times, however, the appropriate rent level may be higher or lower than the rents in place at the subject property.

Property Management's Abilities and Availability

Property managers at office and retail properties are responsible for tenant satisfaction during normal business hours. A multifamily property manager, in comparison, must provide residents with satisfactory levels of service 24 hours per day. In addition to the typical responsibilities of leasing, expense management, and property maintenance, multifamily management is responsible for providing residents with a safe, secure environment around the clock. Tenants consider the multifamily property to be home, and management is the host. Tenants are most satisfied at the property when they feel secure and when they believe in the responsiveness and abilities of the property staff.

Management's possession of strong people skills is the force behind tenant satisfaction and retention. Because the skills of management are tested 24 hours each day, weak management can provide tenants with numerous opportunities to decide that another property might provide a better living environment.

Because the quality of management can affect a multifamily property's performance, underwriters must carefully evaluate the abilities and performance of management at the subject property and compare the property's staff to staffs at other properties. It is beneficial to talk to tenants at the subject property. Tenants are typically forthcoming in providing opinions about the quality of the staff. The successful management team will carefully manage a property's net operating income, will have a strong leasing program and will be able to retain tenants and renew existing leases. A weaker management team will have problems obtaining an optimal income level and will have higher tenant-turnover rates.

The Underwriting Process — Getting Started

We have discussed the distinctive features of multifamily properties. It is now appropriate to return to a discussion of the general framework of underwriting. The numerical focus of the underwriting process is a projection of a property's net operating income. To arrive at this projection, the underwriter must take the following steps:

- Derive the property's gross income.
- Determine an appropriate vacancy and collection loss rate.
- Calculate an expense and reserve projection for the property.

After the underwriter has determined the property's projected net operating income, a lender can determine a preliminary loan amount.

Deriving the Gross Income Projection

Deriving a projection of a multifamily property's gross income involves analyzing historic gross rental income and identifying rental income trends at the property. If rents are consistently increasing at the subject property and are supported by rents obtained at similar properties in the marketplace, underwriters will be safe in projecting rents at a level equal to or slightly higher than rents being obtained at the time of underwriting. If, on the other hand, rents have been decreasing at the subject property or in the market, underwriters have a more difficult job. They must determine and address the cause for the decrease.

There are many potential causes for decreasing rents. Perhaps rising unemployment has driven occupancy levels down, and property management has decreased rents to attract new tenants and to retain existing ones. Perhaps home interest rates have fallen, and the property has reduced their rents to remain a competitive option for those shopping for a home. If new multifamily product has been introduced into the market, the subject property may have reduced rents to compensate for being less appealing than the newer properties in town. Other causes include weak property management and poor maintenance, which makes a property show its age.

In addition to gross rental income, additional sources of income such as parking, laundry, forfeited deposits and late fees may be included in the projection of gross income if the property's history demonstrates that these income sources are consistent.

Determining the Vacancy and Collection Loss Rate

To calculate effective gross income, a vacancy and collection loss factor is applied to the projected gross income. An underwriter's calculation of a vacancy and collection loss rate should be based on the historic rate at the property and should reflect market vacancy. Underwriters should examine vacancy trends in the market to determine whether a stabilized vacancy rate would differ from the rate currently demonstrated in the market.

The projected collection loss factor should reflect the property's historic collection loss factor and management's tenant income-qualification procedures. Those properties with more stringent tenant income-qualification standards will have smaller losses than those that include fewer hurdles in their tenant qualification processes.

Calculating Expense and Reserve Projections

In formulating a projection of expenses for the property, underwriters should review historic expense levels at the property. Also, market-expense comparables should be examined, if available, in order to determine whether or not the subject property's expenses are in line with those of other properties in the market. Expenses that are higher than market could indicate weak management practices at the subject property. Expenses that are lower than market might indicate either exceptionally strong management practices or a poorly maintained property. A property inspection will reveal whether historic maintenance practices at the property have been adequate.

In addition to expenses, underwriters calculate a per-unit reserve to be escrowed by the lender and applied toward repairs, replacements and capital improvements at the property. The dollar amount of the reserve depends upon the age and condition of the property. The purpose of the reserve is to provide the lender with assurance that the property will be well-maintained during the life of the loan, and that part of the property's cash flow will be reinvested in the property on an annual basis.

Determining a Preliminary Loan Amount

Upon completion of the steps described above, an underwriter will have a projected net operating income for the subject property. The lender is now prepared to make a preliminary determination of an appropriate loan amount on the subject property. The lender has two means of determining loan amount. The first method is the application of a debt-service coverage ratio to the property's NOI and a determination of maximum loan amount based on current interest rates and an appropriate amortization schedule.

As an example, let's assume that a property generates an NOI of $930,000. The required debt service coverage ratio is 1.25X. We are using a 30-year amortization schedule, and today's interest rate is 7.65 percent. Based on the 1.25X coverage requirement, we have $744,000 available for debt service. In dividing $744,000 by our loan constant of 0.08514, we determine that the projected net operating income will support a loan up to $8,738,000.

A second method of determining loan amount is the application of a loan-to-value (LTV) ratio to the property's value, which can be estimated by capitalizing the property's net operating income with a capitalization rate appropriate for the property's market. Let's assume that we have determined that 9.5% is an appropriate capitalization rate for multifamily properties in our subject property's market. Capping our net operating income of

$930,000 by 9.5% results in an estimated value of $9,789,000. If our LTV maximum ratio is 80%, then our maximum allowable loan would be $7,831,000.

We see from this example that the LTV ratio supports a lower loan amount than the debt-service coverage ratio does. This phenomenon reflects the fact that interest rates have fallen during the past several months to the 7.65% used in the example, and that cap rates reflect historic sales information and do not reflect the impact of the recent drop in interest rates. Had we used an interest rate of 9.25% in our example, the 1.25X debt-service coverage requirement would result in a supportable loan amount up to $7,535,000, which is lower than the loan amount supported by the LTV ratio. During times of falling interest rates, the LTV calculation will generate a more conservative supportable loan amount than the debt service coverage calculation. During periods of rising interest rates, the debt-service coverage requirement will be more of a limiting factor in the determination of loan amount than the LTV ratio.

Other Factors to Consider

The two methods described above result in solid approximations of a loan amount. The underwriters can be more conservative by increasing the coverage requirement or by decreasing the maximum acceptable LTV ratio. Regardless of the ultimate coverage and LTV ratios used to derive a loan amount via these numerical exercises, underwriters should temper this dollar amount with their knowledge of the market and the borrower. Market factors include those described earlier in this chapter, specifically the condition of the economy, the status of interest rates and projections for new construction in the market.

Borrower factors that can influence a property's performance include borrowers' character and commitment, their portfolio of other real estate holdings and their philosophy toward property ownership and management.

Borrower character and commitment are revealed through an examination of the borrowers' involvement in other transactions. Have the borrowers worked with lenders in the past to ensure that properties were operated efficiently and that adequate debt service coverage was achieved? Have other loans been paid in a timely manner? If a property is troubled, have the borrowers been willing to work with a lender on a workout plan? Answers to these questions provide tremendous insight into the prospective borrowers and serve as an accurate predictor of the borrowers' future behavior.

An examination of the borrowers' portfolio of real estate holdings will indicate whether any of their properties are cash drains that may result in diversions of cash from the subject property. A review of this information will provide insight into the borrowers' ability as investors. Are most properties covering their debt service and generating positive cash flow? Do the borrowers have previous experience as owners of multifamily properties? The best predictor of future success as a property owner is the demonstration of past success as a property owner.

Finally, underwriters should question borrowers' philosophy toward property ownership. If the borrowers have demonstrated their belief in adequate maintenance practices and have shown a willingness to return cash flow into the maintenance and improvement of a property, it is likely that they will be willing to maintain the subject property. On the other hand, if the borrowers' strategy is to pull as much cash flow as possible away from their real estate properties, this indicates a potential problem, which might induce the lender to require a reserve account.

Summary

This chapter covered the theoretical and practical aspects of underwriting of multifamily properties. In addition to reviewing the calculations involved in determining net operating income and loan amounts, we have discussed the importance of considering characteristics that are unique to the multifamily product and of analyzing market- and borrower-related factors when underwriting a multifamily loan. It is through a tempering of the numerically derived loan amount with knowledge of the market and the borrowers, that underwriters can determine an appropriate loan amount for a multifamily property and minimize potential risk.

11

Shopping Centers

Thomas Z. Minehart III, Executive Vice President
Legg Mason Real Estate Services, Inc.

Shopping Center Categories

There are many types of retail properties — the neighborhood Seven-11, the local McDonald's restaurant, the regional Wal-Mart and the downtown tri-level mall, to name a few. For the evaluation and review of retail facilities, a convenient and accepted practice is to discuss the properties in terms of the size of the center and store type. Typically, they fall into six categories:

1. The free-standing building (sometimes called the big box)
2. The neighborhood convenience shopping center (the strip center including your local grocery store, drugstore and dry cleaner)
3. The community shopping center (often a K-Mart or Wal-Mart anchored center)
4. The regional mall (two or more department stores connected by a group of in-line stores)
5. The superregional mall (four or more anchors)
6. The specialty center (the power center group such as Sports Authority, Levitz Furniture or other "category killer" stores)

The *free-standing retail building* comes in a variety of shapes and sizes, some of which are so distinctive that they are relatively worthless for a second use upon foreclosure. Often surrounded by parking intended to attract fast-service customers, these structures can be anything from a 2,000 square foot convenience chain store to a 100,000 square foot furniture warehouse outlet store. Location of the property, as always, is paramount. The nature of the structure is usually dictated by the operator, often a chain or franchise operation.

The *neighborhood or convenience center* specializes in goods and services required for daily living — mainly foodstuffs, drugs and toiletries, cleaning and laundering services and perhaps a liquor store, barber shop or shoemaker. The GLA of a neighborhood center can be a little as 50,000 square feet, but usually not much more than 100,000 square feet. Its principal stores or "anchors" are generally a supermarket and a drug store. At present, competitive supermarkets are as large as 50,000 to 60,000 square feet — much larger than 10 or 15 years ago, when 25,000 to 35,000 square feet was normal. A good center often has another anchor at the opposite end of the center from the supermarket. This anchor may be a drugstore/pharmacy or a video store of 7,500 square feet or more.

The *community center* is a retail center that is usually larger than the food-anchored shopping center. Whereas the neighborhood food-anchored center is oriented for necessary and everyday shopping, the community center is more specialized and subject to retail fashions and fads. It may include a supermarket and a drugstore, but its anchors are likely to be discount stores, such as Wal-Mart, K-Mart, or Marshall's, and perhaps a localized junior department store. In recent years, several community centers have been anchored by discount hardware chains or home improvement stores, such as Home Depot or Builders Square.

Besides the anchors, supermarket and drugstore, the community center may include restaurants, clothing stores, dry goods stores, appliance stores, electronics stores, bookstores, record or video stores and auto supply stores — together occupying as much as 75,000 to 100,000 square feet of specialty stores. A bank, fast-food restaurant and cinema may be located on the site, but may be housed in independent structures separate from the main shopping center building. Such businesses usually build their own facilities and pay land rent to the shopping center owner.

The *regional mall* is a large shopping center. It is a major operation and usually contains more than 50 tenants in addition to its anchors, which usually include two or more full-scale department stores. Regional malls may be anchored by local department stores, but are usually anchored by chain department stores such as Sears, J.C. Penney or Macy's, which provide the regional mall with its drawing power. The regional mall contains every type and description of retail and service store, including home furnishings and major appliance stores, large national chain apparel stores (for example, The Limited, Casual Corner, The Gap, Brooks Brothers and Ann Taylor), restaurants and banks and recently, medical clinics, small health spas and multiplex cinemas. Like the community center, the regional mall will contain stores that are franchises or branches of national chains, as well as satellite stores that are locally owned and operated. The anchor department stores in the regional mall are usually 100,000 square feet or more in size, and several of the large apparel and home furnishing stores may be as large as 25,000 to 40,000 square feet.

The *superregional mall* or shopping center is a special breed of retail facility which is typically found in primary or secondary cities and is centered around three or more full-line department stores of at least 100,000 square feet. The superregional center is sited on 85 acres or more and generally contains no less than 750,000 square feet. A superregional mall of today may contain as much as 2 million square feet and may serve a population of 1 million or more, within a radius of as many as 50 miles. The superregional mall will include every kind of shop; every class of restaurant; a mix of high-, medium-, and low-priced merchandise; services; and recreational facilities. The mall may contain a food court clustering as many as 15 to 25 small purveyors of food, an entertainment section and a space for special events. The market area for the superregional mall includes local residents and businesses as well as people and businesses from anywhere else within the metropolitan area, state or even nation who cannot find goods of equal variety and quality elsewhere.

The *specialty center* is exactly what its name implies: a shopping mall that specializes in one or more particular kinds of merchandise or services (food, off-price clothing, special entertainment or other specialty boutiques, for example). It is aimed at a special market and is characterized by a theme or singular design, site or environment. It rarely has anchor stores or basic merchandise and services. Some specialty centers — such as Station Square in Pittsburgh and the Union Station centers in St. Louis and Washington, D.C. — are housed in historic buildings; others — such as Harborplace in Baltimore and South Street Seaport in New York — are dramatically situated in harbors; still others — such as Yamhill Market in Portland, Oregon — profit from the ambiance of historic districts. Specialty centers can be relatively small, such as the 75,000 square foot Waterside Mall in Norfolk, Virginia; the Pavilion in Washington, D.C.; or the Dayton Arcade in Dayton, Ohio. They can also be relatively large, such as Georgetown Park in Washington, D.C., the Pike Place Market in Seattle and the Quincy Market-Faneuil Hall Marketplace in Boston.

Variations on the specialty center concept, applied on a regional basis, are the so-called outlet or off-price centers and the power centers. These centers are not traditional shopping centers in that they make no attempt to provide a broad variety of high-traffic stores. Outlet malls and power centers group tenants/discounters together in one setting because shoppers have grown fond of this style of presentation. Outlets may attract bargain shoppers and browsers while big box retailers attract the time-conscious shoppers who want to go to one special store where they know they can find specific preselected items without shopping several stores.

Location of Shopping Centers

Shopping centers should be located near their markets, within the appropriate radius of their primary market and with access to major highways. Shopping centers have become the child of the interstate highway system, and almost all centers — from the smallest neighborhood center to the vast superregional mall — are located on major state or county roads where they intersect one or several interstate highways. In many cities, malls are located directly across from each other or in close proximity, based on the theory that each stimulates the business of the other and that the cluster of shopping centers re-creates what the shopping center itself displaced: a central shopping district, surrounded by huge parking lots. Today, it is common to find a power center adjacent to a mall or in close proximity to a community center. This clustering of various centers appears to be the trend for the future.

Physical Characteristics of Shopping Centers

Some shopping centers are enclosed malls, replete with large, well-decorated common areas and with indoor, sheltered and outdoor parking. Others are merely a collection of attached stores on a common site with a communal parking lot. An important physical consideration is the placement of anchors: Anchors should be located wherever they can best attract customers not only for themselves, but also for the other stores in the center. In neighborhood and community centers, the anchors are usually at opposite ends of the center. In regional and superregional malls, the anchor stores may be at both ends and also in the center.

Perhaps the most important aspect of the physical design of a shopping center is parking. The Urban Land Institute (ULI) stipulates the following standards for shopping center parking:

- Four spaces per 1,000 square feet of GLA for malls of 25,000 to 400,000 square feet.
- Four to five spaces in linear progression — an average of 4.5 spaces — per 1,000 square feet of GLA for centers of 400,000 to 600,000 square feet.
- Five spaces per 1,000 square feet of GLA for centers with over 600,000 square feet.[1]

The ULI also advises that in centers with cinemas of more than 750 seats or in cinemas located at similar centers, three additional parking spaces should be added for every 100 seats.

Valuing Shopping Centers

The value of a shopping center, much as the value of an office building, depends on the quantity, quality and durability of its rent roll. The larger the net income from rentals generated, the greater the capitalized value of the center. Rents derived from a shopping center are directly related to the sales generated by each retailer: If sales are down, tenants cannot pay aggressive rents, and the shopping center income and value are correspondingly lower.

The Importance of Anchor Stores

Anchor stores are essential to shopping centers. Anchors are the attractions that draw the market and generate sales. For this reason, anchor store operators tend to dominate negotiations with shopping center developers. Most lenders and equity investors are reluctant to put money into a shopping center without a firm letter of commitment from an anchor or anchors, and very often, banks will even refuse to consider short-term development loans until the anchors have signed on.

Because of their importance to lenders, anchors receive favorable lease terms. For example, anchors may not have to pay percentage rents; instead, they pay only bare minimum base rent. They generally receive long-term fixed rate leases (10 to 20 years is not uncommon) and may not be subject to escalation or inflation indexing. In some cases, they are allowed to lease the property beneath their store or use it for free, or build their own store and pay no rent at all. Sometimes, they are provided all these privileges and are also included as limited or joint venture partners in the shopping center development.

Of course, anchor store operators are always looking for good locations for their stores. Projects that will locate them in the right market area to generate healthy sales and allow for the expansion of their business may negotiate better leases. Developers often have special relationships with department stores and supermarkets, and anchor retailers may cultivate partnerships and special arrangements with selected and proven developers.

Satellite, Local, Chain and Franchise Specialty Shops

Anchor stores provide the draw and take up much of the square footage of the shopping center. For example, in a superregional mall of 1 million square feet, four department stores will occupy anywhere from 40% to 50% of the total GLA. Therefore, shopping center developers and investors depend on the *satellites* — the small shops that cluster around the anchor — to generate the major part of the income stream and most of the profit from the investment. The better the sales in the small shops, the more valuable the shopping center — particularly if the square footage of the shops is down, and both sales per square foot and rents are up. Put another way, the developer's interest is to get the maximum rent and the maximum sales per square foot from each satellite or specialty store. This is why the small shops, which pay much higher base rents per square foot than the anchors, also pay a percentage of their gross sales as rent to the owner and have short-term leases so the rent may be raised to what the current market will bear once they expire.

Merchant's Associations

"Either we survive together, or we all hang separately" is an appropriate motto for both the developer-owner and the retail merchants in a shopping center. Signs, snow removal, common area maintenance (CAM), security, trash removal, advertising, special events, entertainment and common policies with respect to customers, salespeople and distributors are all handled more effectively on a collective basis, as is the relation between merchants and the owner of the center. For this reason, most shopping centers have merchant's associations. They are a necessity in super-regional and regional malls, and many community and neighborhood centers have them as well.

Shopping Center Management

Shopping center management requires more than maintenance of the center. The manager or manager/owner is responsible for negotiating the terms of new or expired leases and for keeping records concerning monthly sales data (sales per square foot) for each store in the center. Accurate record keeping enables management to assess appropriate minimum or base rents, to escalate rents when leases expire in relation to both market criteria and sales per square foot for each store and to calculate percentage rents or overages for each store.

Lease Structures

Retail leases are usually complex, including clauses relating to tenant responsibilities for store improvements, to pro rata shares of operating expenses such as utilities and to clauses about CAM, merchant association dues, hourly operating covenants, strict merchant quality requirements, sign requirements, advertising and special assessments at various holiday sale times. All of these are ways to ensure that the center generates the maximum sales per square foot.

Most tenants pay a base net rent for the space they occupy. Before accepting a tenant, the landlord will verify that the tenant is likely to generate the necessary sales to allow for the payment of the base net rent per square foot plus all tenant operating costs and a CAM contribution. In addition, the landlord will want to know that the tenant can generate enough sales per square foot to allow for the payment of a percentage rent, based on gross sales per square foot.

The percentage rent is usually established on the following basis: The tenant pays the landlord the greater of two amounts — a minimum base rent or a negotiated percentage of gross sales. The minimum base rent is usually the highest rent that the market will bear in that locale for a particular kind of retail store of a specific square footage. The percentage rent is established by negotiation, but typical percentage rent ranges are established for each type of retail trade and can easily be found in such publications as *Dollars and Cents of Shopping Centers,* published by the Urban Land Institute. If a lease calls for a rent of $1,400 per month, plus 7% of gross sales, whichever is greater, $20,000 in sales per month would be the point at which percentage rent would come into play. The minimum-base-rent/percentage-rent structure is the principal reason why shopping center leases are subject to intense negotiation, especially since both parties have so much to gain or lose either way. If the landlord accepts a low base and a high percentage rent, it is the landlord who takes on the risk of the tenant; if the landlord requires a high base rent, it is the tenant who accepts the responsibility for generating sales sufficient to pay the rent.

As with office buildings, most shopping center tenants have net leases and pay a pro rata share of the operating expenses of the center, with either a stop or base year provision. Some leases include clauses that allow for payment of pro rata share of expenses from the overage or percentage rents, when they exist.

Tenants also pay a CAM charge, which can be assessed in three different ways:

1. Pro-rata based on the percentage of the tenant's gross square footage to the GLA of the center
2. A stipulated fixed charge
3. A charge based on the percentage of gross sales per square foot

Shopping Center Income and Operating Expense

Dollar and Cents of Shopping Centers will provide anyone who is interested with a typical index of average sales per square foot by tenant, income and operating expense categories for different types of shopping centers. The information will indicate the standard ratio between income and expenses for different types of centers. Income usually includes all minimum and percentage or overage rents, common area charges, income from rent escalation clauses, income from the tenant's share of operating expenses (such as utilities) and miscellaneous items (such as vending machine income). Operating expenses generally include building maintenance,

CAM, utilities, office area services, advertising and promotion, property taxes, insurance and management fees.

The retail industry is in a state of transition. In some merchandise categories, larger stores are the trend; in other categories, smaller, more efficient space is required. Major battles are being fought for market-share locations and store positions in almost every category of retailing. Whether you are analyzing a convenience store, a specialty store or a department store, keep in mind that they all are engaged in fierce fights for survival. In order to have their tenants survive to compete in the years ahead, retail property owners must react to the changes required by their tenants in a timely manner with well-thought-out strategies.

Endnote — Chapter 11

1. *Development Review and Outlook 1983–1984,* Washington, D.C.: The Urban Land Institute (ULI), 1983, p.25.

12

Office Buildings

Thomas Z. Minehart III, Executive Vice President
Legg Mason Real Estate Services, Inc.

Downtown high-rise, suburban flex office, mid-rise and class A are just some of the terms used in describing particular office buildings. Some other terms, such as research and development, special purpose and single tenant, also help describe a particular type of office building. It would appear that there are three influences used to describe and categorize most office buildings:

1. Location — the environment surrounding the site
2. The market analysis or market *use* of the building
3. Physical characteristics, including perceived quality, amenities and internal space

Each category overlaps the other two, and complexities abound.

Describing a project by location reflects popular expectations. The downtown central business district (CBD) usually contains high-rise buildings. The suburbs used to be known for low-rise buildings, but now they may be a mix of both low- and high-rise. Office or industrial parks, usually located in the suburbs, but sometimes located downtown, include new projects, rehabilitated industrial buildings and special complexes close to universities. Research parks are usually located in the suburbs or in exurban areas, although some are located downtown.

When categorizing office buildings by market analysis, age and use of the property are major factors. New construction is self-evident. A newly constructed corporate headquarters may help identify a property type. Older buildings used to connote less desirability. However, the recent trend toward rehabilitation and energy retrofitting of older buildings has lessened this distinction. A historic building converted to a medicine building for a group of physicians is an example of a "market analysis" office building type.

Describing office buildings as class A, B or C properties is a convenient shorthand, but it can be misused like any other arbitrary stereotype. Class A buildings are prestigious and appeal to tenants who are willing to pay high rents. They have prime locations; fine and often luxurious design; the most up-to-date heating, air conditioning, plumbing, energy, security, computer and telecommunications components; numerous special amenities, such as atriums, underground parking, restaurants, retail stores and special janitorial and secretarial services, and highly professional management. Class B buildings have a little less of the above, and class C buildings provide merely adequate or even below-par office space in older and unrehabilitated buildings or in newer buildings with few amenities. Even this categorization can be considered complex because a class A building in a CBD will differ considerably from a class A building in a suburban or office park location. Further, mortgage bankers submitting loan applications for a lender's review seldom describe their client's property as other than a class A project. Moreover, in some markets, real-estate experts have resorted to describing buildings as A, AA or AAA projects.

Location

Location is critical in any analysis of an office building investment. Although a location suitable for a downtown central city office building is certainly different from one amenable to a suburban office complex, the characteristics of prime location are essentially the same.

Access to transportation is important (railroad terminals, bus terminals, suburban buses, light rail or heavy rail mass transit stations, interstate and state highways, and airports). So is availability of parking (underground or nearby for downtown locations and on site for suburban locations). Also significant is the proximity to shops, restaurants, department stores, quality hotels or motels, government office buildings, courts and other major office buildings.

Given the tendency of U.S. cities to segregate office functions from industrial or wholesale commercial activity, class A office buildings are not likely to be located near warehouses, special wholesale commercial districts, industrial shops, plants or parks. Given the tendency to segregate residential and business functions, it is highly unusual to find prime office buildings in residential areas.

Market Analysis

Market Supply

The demand for different types of office buildings varies with the market for office space. Small businesses neither need nor want the type of offices required by large corporations. Market types need and prefer to cluster together. For example, medical and dental professionals tend to group together near major medical facilities, such as universities and hospitals. The following is a standard breakdown of the market demand for offices.

- *Major corporations,* such as those in the financial, manufacturing and service sectors, seek prestigious office space for their management and consumer-oriented (public relations, sales and marketing) functions. Such buildings are typically class A, with the latest in technological and design amenities, high rents and prime locations, either downtown or in suburban locations close to regional or superregional shopping malls (such as Tyson's Corner in Fairfax County, Virginia—near Washington, D.C.), and Lenox Square Center in Atlanta).
- *Small businesses and commercial tenants,* such as independent lawyers, accountants, travel agents, employment agencies, mortgage companies, computer software firms and other small service businesses, prefer average but adequate office space, either downtown in older buildings that have been rehabilitated or in newer suburban locations, often low-rise office/industrial parks. Today, thanks to computers, fax machines and other tools, many small businesses are able to operate very well from home offices. The trend toward the home office is partly responsible for the current depressed values for office buildings in many parts of the United States.
- *Medical and dental professionals* seek convenient access to the consumer of health services, proximity to medical facilities and the sharing of technology, laboratory services, professional techniques and ideas. The high cost of malpractice insurance, the burden of patient needs, the cost of medical equipment and record keeping and the tax laws have encouraged medical practitioners to form professional associations in which many doctors or dentists share a large office suite. Professional buildings generally provide adequate office space, but not necessarily class A space with the newest technological amenities in prime locations.

- *Research and development and industrial tenants* cluster in office, industrial and research parks. Heavy industries usually house specifice types of office functions (engineering and design) in close proximity to the factory, although modern technology has rendered this unnecessary. Light industries, certain kinds of computerized warehouse distribution and high-tech research and development activities can be housed together in "smart" buildings with the latest in computerized work stations, flexible office space, telecommunications hookups and amenities such as parks, recreational facilities, nearby hotels and restaurants (the Forrestal-Scanticon and Carnegie centers in Princeton, New Jersey, for example). Although such research, industrial and office parks lack the design and architectural amenities of prestigious downtown office locations, they may equal or surpass the downtown buildings in technological advances, overall setting and convenient access to transportation, shopping, schools and prime residential housing.

Market Demand

In analyzing a potential office building investment, the current demand for the type of office structure or complex requires documentation. If there is a high absorption rate for new construction, and even for older and rehabilitated buildings, the investment risk may be low, and therefore, the project may be worthwhile. If the vacancy rate in existing and older buildings is not low and new space is not occupied, the investment risk is high and therefore, the project may not be worthwhile. Office building construction is frequently speculative and cyclical, so professional lenders know to pay attention to cycles — investing early and withdrawing from investment before the speculative peak crests, as it did in the late 1980s and early 1990s.

Physical Characteristics

Physical and Structural Design

Almost all modern office buildings — whether class A or class C, rehabilitated or new — require efficient heating and air-conditioning systems; modern, energy-efficient lighting; acoustic ceilings; carpeting; appropriate common area treatment; on-site, underground or nearby parking for downtown structures; and up-to-date, easily augmented electrical systems.

Physical design characteristics are influenced by market demand. The market for which a particular building is intended will determine its total size, floor space, elevator capacity, design, exterior aesthetics, interior material quality, architectural innovativeness, appointments, lobby and atrium size, hallway spaciousness and elevator speed.

Much more important are structural design elements and amenities that account for present and future technological progress, such as energy efficiency; security; auxiliary power sources for elevators, computers and lighting; fire protection devices; flexible office space that can be reconfigured and redesigned easily and wiring systems that can be modernized and added to so as to handle rapid advances in telecommunications (such as electronic mailing systems, teleconferencing, satellite communications and message switching systems). Office buildings are becoming, and in the future will be, information and communication service centers.

Other Considerations

Investment analysts and underwriters of existing or proposed office buildings should bear in mind other physical criteria:

- *Average Square Foot per Office Worker.* This factor generally varies with the age and size of the building. The newer and bigger the building, the more square footage per office worker; the older and smaller the building, the less square footage per office worker. The general range for buildings of all sizes and ages is 150 to 250 square feet per office worker. Equally important physical criteria include hallway widths, ceiling heights and restroom sizes.

- *Economic Efficiency.* The economic efficiency of an office building is measured by the relation between the gross building area (GBA) and the net rentable or leasable area (NRA or NLA). A building is generally considered efficient if its NRA is at least 88% of its GBA, or, put another way, if its NRA is only 12% less than its GBA. Most new high-rise buildings are 90% efficient or better. Most buildings constructed between 1920 and 1970 are at least 60% to 70% efficient. Buildings constructed before 1920 are less than 60% efficient, but most of these have either been torn down and replaced by more efficient newer buildings.
- *Parking Ratios.* Some downtown high-rise buildings do not have parking garages. Where such space is provided, one space for every 250 square feet of net rentable office area is considered reasonable. Underground garages should provide at least 300 to 400 square feet for parking spaces, depending on the size of the cars likely to be parked there and the space available for the garage. Outdoor parking spaces are usually more commodious, only because their construction cost is so much less.

Office Building Leasing Structures

The leasing of office building space is complex and can follow any one of several patterns. Office space is rented monthly and includes all usable square footage plus a floor factor. The floor factor is a proportion of the common area on a floor divided by the number of square feet per tenant, given the number of tenants who occupy the floor. In addition to monthly lease payments, tenants are also generally responsible for special tenant improvements over a basic "tenant work letter amount" or initial budget for tenant space improvements.

Leases for office buildings, as with shopping centers, can be divided into two broad categories:

1. *Gross leases* in which the tenant pays a fixed rent and the owner of the building is responsible for the property's operating expenses, taxes and capital expenditures
2. *Net leases* in which the tenant pays a pro rata share (based on the square footage of office space relative to the NLA of the building) of the operating expenses, taxes and property capital expenditures in addition to the base rent

In most new office buildings, net leases are the rule; however, each contains different kinds of escalation clauses and provisions for tenant payments of operating expenses and capital expenditures. For example, a stop lease requires the tenant to pay a pro rata share of building operating expenses only above a minimum amount stated in the lease. Another example — a base-year lease — stipulates that the tenant must pay a pro rata share of the operating expenses incurred above those in a base year (usually the year the lease was signed or the year prior to signing). Both stop leases and base-year leases are negotiable and vary considerably. Still another example is a lease that is tied to the consumer price index (CPI). If the inflation index increases, regardless of whether actual costs go up by the same amount, the lease is escalated in accordance with the CPI growth rate, thereby providing both inflation protection and potential extra profit for the landlord.

A more extraordinary example is the "net, net, net" lease. In this lease, a tenant will pay all operating expenses, taxes and insurance. Under the "absolute triple net" lease, the tenant assumes all functions of the landlord except collecting rents, paying the mortgage and earning income and profit from the investment.

To induce a tenant to lease property, the landlord will usually agree to make certain tenant improvements. These costs — which often include partitions, electrical work and occasionally plumbing — are frequently specified in terms of dollars per square foot. Sometimes a number of parking spaces will be provided without charge for the tenant's use.

Rent concessions are frequent in markets where there are high vacancy ratios in office buildings. A concession might consist of rent reduction for a period of time or an agreement to continue a fixed rent over a longer period than initially required. The underwriter for the lender must be able to factor in the cost of tenant improvements and the effect of rent concessions in determining the effective rent for the space leased. Any discounted cash flow analysis used in valuing an office property must consider all rental concessions given to retain or replace a tenant. New computer software analysis tools, such as Pro-Ject and Argus, prompt appraisers for this information and help determine net effective rental to the property owner.

Office Building Rent Rolls, Operating Income and Expenses

Today's computer software programs include prompts and procedures to show the present rental income and rate for each tenant, tenant pro-rata contributions to recover operating expenses, and renewal dates and negotiated special provisions and options for each tenant. Even when an existing multitenant building is fully occupied, a rent roll pro forma should always include a realistic vacancy factor based on historical experience and current market conditions.

In addition to rental income, including base rent and operating expense reimbursements, office buildings can yield the following kinds of additional income:

- Tenant service income, which is income from special tenant services that the landlord provides a tenant
- Miscellaneous income from vending machines, sale of utilities to tenants, rental of retail space, rental of advertising space, furniture rental, deposit forfeitures and other sources
- Parking income from underground, attached or on-site parking facilities

Landlords generally provide the following services to tenants and are responsible for the following operating expenses in whole or part: utility services, cleaning and janitorial services, elevator operation and building security. In newer, high-tech or "smart" buildings, landlords may also be expected to maintain telecommunications services and to replace and upgrade telecommunications equipment. Other typical operating expenses that may be shared by tenants include staff payroll, maintenance contracts, supplies and uniforms, repairs, real estate taxes, insurance fees, management fees, reserves for mechanical replacements, lease commissions and expenses for supplies.

13

Hotels — Risk and Reward

Peggy Berg, President
The Highland Group

Operating Businesses and Real Estate Assets

Hotels offer a unique lending and investment opportunity because both the operating hotel business and the underlying real estate are assets. In this unique property type, the real estate carries only a fraction of its potential value if business operations are poor. Conversely, a strong business operation can lend the total asset a greater value than would be evident from the cost of the building and land.

Among operating businesses, hotels are unique in that they carry a highly perishable inventory. A rentable hotel room night cannot sit on a shelf and hold value. If not rented that night, the potential revenue is lost. In fact, each hotel room must be marketed, inventoried, sold, delivered, billed for, collected on and prepared for the next rental within a 24-hour period every day of every year.

While guest room rentals are the bulk of their revenues and represent their greatest profit potential, hotels contain more than one operating business. In addition to lodging, hotels often include restaurants, banquet and catering facilities and services, lounges, a for-profit telephone company, retail outlets and a host of other businesses such as parking decks, golf courses, spas and fitness centers, salons and florists. The variations are as endless as the needs and wants of customers from every culture traveling for business or pleasure.

However, while some hotels are complicated, others are straightforward, predictable businesses. Many hotels offer an excellent and reasonably secure lending opportunity. Frequently, hotels have the capacity to offer higher returns than other forms of real estate. Hotel pricing can change quickly with market forces and inflation, providing considerable upside in good years. Hotels also have a more elastic market than other real estate: A good operator may create strong revenues, even in a down market.

The bottom line for the lodging industry is that people like to travel. They like to see new places and experience new things. As the world's population becomes more sophisticated, sees more places on television and has the affluence and ability to travel, demand for hotels will continue to grow. Providing lodging in this broad-based and constantly expanding marketplace represents a good business opportunity.

The trick is to evaluate each potential hotel lending or investment opportunity carefully. This chapter should provide you with some basic tools to undertake that process.

Recent History and Five-Year Outlook for the Hotel Industry

The hotel industry is reaping extraordinary returns in the middle of the 1990s. However, there is an atmosphere of caution in the lending community. Many have lent to this industry before, and some have been burned recently. Regardless, the risks associated with hotels are controllable, and money is increasingly available to the industry because of the strong potential returns.

Hotels, like many kinds of real estate, tend to be built as long as an enticing level of debt is available. Unfortunately, in the mid-1980s, funds remained available after the market for guest rooms was saturated. The result was a temporary oversupply. Interestingly, because of the elasticity of demand for lodging, oversupply situations are generally reversed within three to five years. This reversal recently occurred between 1989 and 1993. Now the industry is poised for an expansion that is projected to last to the turn of the century or beyond, depending on the speed with which new hotels are built.

Recent History

There are a host of reasons for periods of real estate expansion. In the case of hotels, the industry came into a period of greater demand than supply around the time that the tax law of 1982 was passed. This tax law was extremely favorable for development, and new rooms appeared in a broad variety of hotel products across the country throughout the 1980s — in both economic and tax incentive deals.

In the latter half of the 1980s, a number of factors converged to cause a collapse in this newly oversupplied industry. The tax law of 1986 undermined the financial structure of many of the newly constructed hotels, as well as hotels that had been refinanced under the tax law of 1982. The economy began to deteriorate nationally and eventually fell into recession. Hotels that were becoming financially marginal could not attract capital to reinvest into their facilities, and as the product deteriorated, their clientele eroded. Then, in late 1990 and early 1991, the Gulf War had a devastating effect on the industry because both corporate and leisure travel diminished sharply.

The combination was disastrous and was compounded by the foreclosure and disposition strategies of various lenders and the RTC. From 1989 through 1993, the RTC sold hotels at a fraction of their development cost. Lenders foreclosed in unprecedented numbers and REO hotels created an industry in workouts, as well as an excess of troubled hotels to sell. There was little equity available for investment and virtually no debt to be had. Hotel sales were difficult; reinvestment in facilities diminished further; product deteriorated and values deteriorated further. The bottom of the market for average selling prices per hotel room was reached in 1992, as illustrated in Exhibit 21.

By 1992, investors began to realize that hotels were trading at such low prices that the opportunity for high returns in a period of one to two years was extraordinary. Individuals and equity funds began buying and renovating hotels; concurrently, the economy began to improve and travel rebounded. In this period, which is graphed in Exhibit 22 on page 228, very few hotel rooms were built, except in Las Vegas. Exhibit 22 shows the changes in hotel supply and demand nationwide in the early 1990s.

Over the past four years, we have seen just over 1% supply change annually. Concurrently, demand has rebounded, markedly exceeding the increase in supply.

As Exhibit 23 (on page 229) shows, in 1995, hotel occupancy was perhaps at its highest level since good statistical data became available. Due to increased demand, hotel room rates rose at a pace well above inflation in most of the country. Performance in 1996 is expected to exceed 1995. Hotel values are close to replacement cost and the industry is on the upswing.

Increasing demand has had a very positive impact on achieved average rate, as illustrated in Exhibit 24 on page 230. While the overall average rate for the country did not decline materially during the period of recession and oversupply, it did not increase with inflation, so there was a loss in real dollars. In addition, some individual hotels lost rate. As soon as occupancy reached the low 60% range, rates began to climb again. As occupancy passed 65%, rate growth accelerated. The gain from 1993 to 1994 was 5%, compared to less than 1% from 1991 to 1992.

As long as occupancies remain at historically high levels, rates in this industry are expected to increase at a pace well above inflation.

EXHIBIT 21

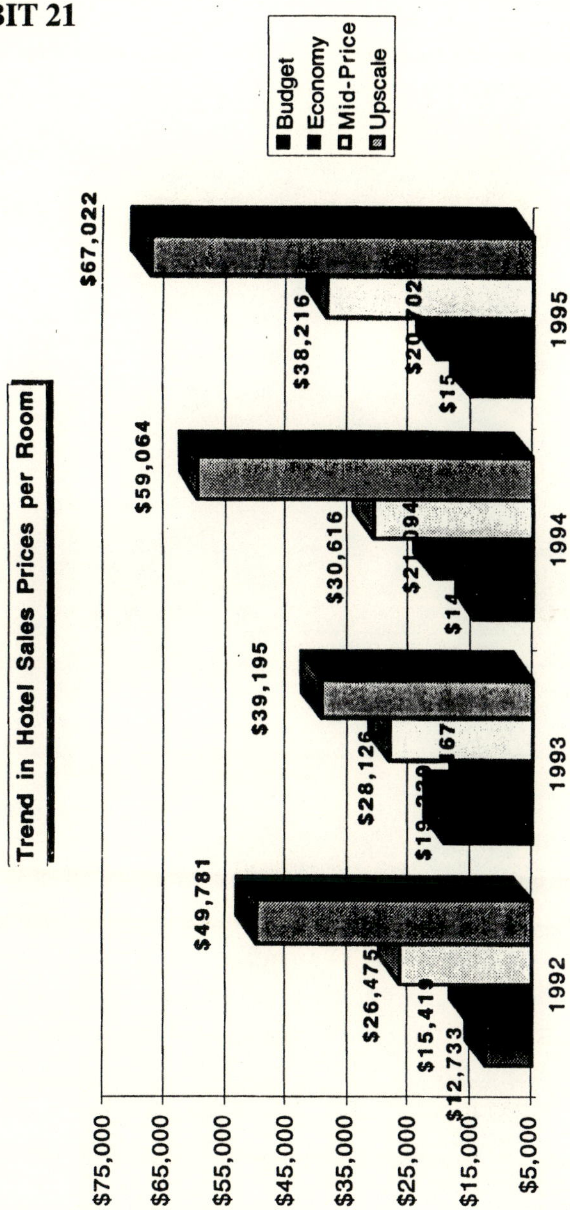
Trend in Hotel Sales Prices per Room
Budget
Economy
Mid-Price
Upscale
$75,000
$65,000
$55,000
$45,000
$35,000
$25,000
$15,000
$5,000
1992
1993
1994
1995
$49,781
$26,475
$39,195
$28,126
$59,064
$30,616
$67,022
$38,216

EXHIBIT 22

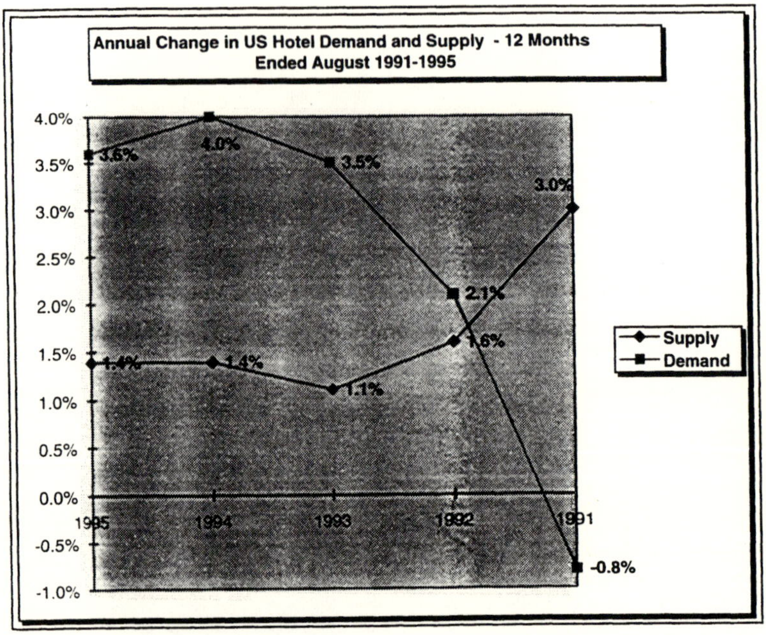

Source: Smith Travel Research

Five-Year Outlook

The five-year outlook for this industry is strong, barring economic upheaval, war or recession. Demand in most sectors of the country is expected to increase for travel-related business, holidays and vacations, gaming, conventions and corporate meetings.

While demand is expected to continue increasing, supply has begun to expand again. It is currently expanding in two ways, through redevelopment of older hotels that have needed capital infusions and through new construction of limited-service and all-suite properties.

EXHIBIT 23

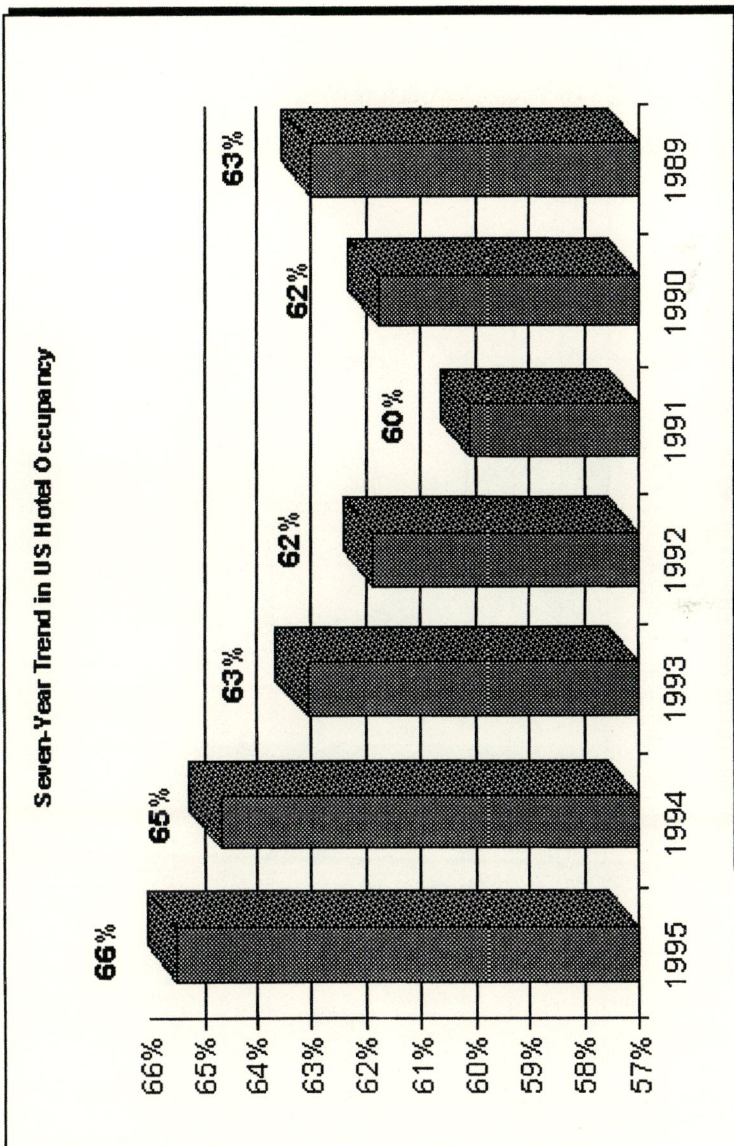
Seven-Year Trend in US Hotel Occupancy
66%
65%
63%
62%
60%
62%
63%
1995
1994
1993
1992
1991
1990
1989
66%
65%
64%
63%
62%
61%
60%
59%
58%
57%

EXHIBIT 24

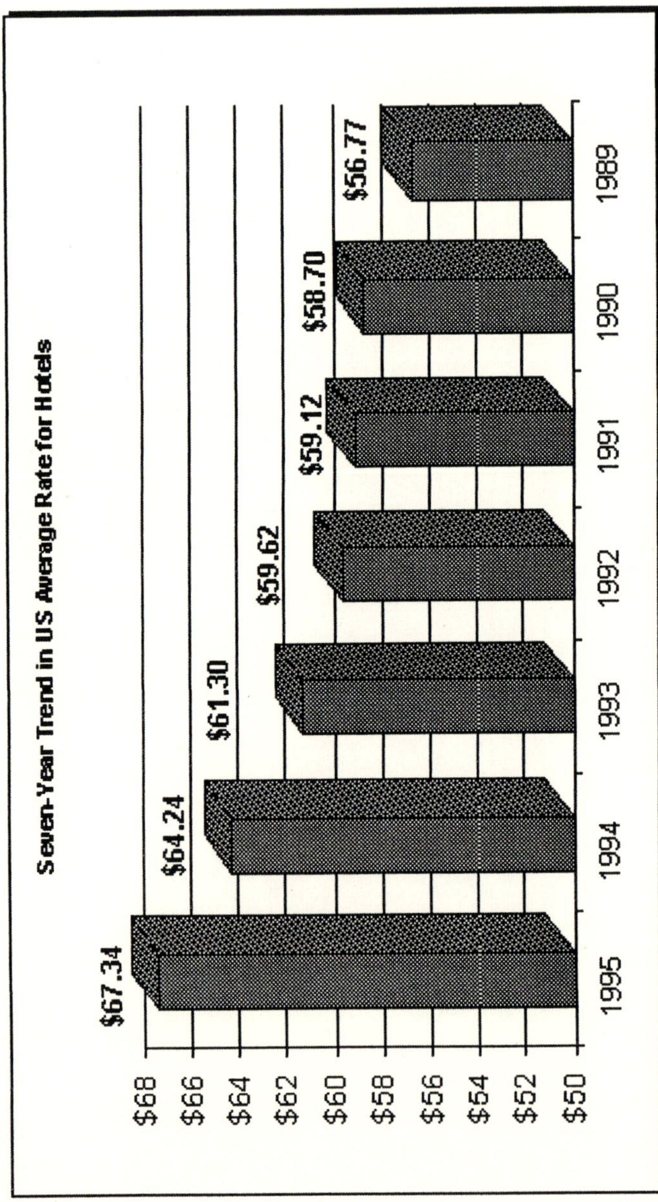

Source: Smith Travel Research

Over the next five years, demand will continue to grow, although the pace of the increase may slow. Room supply will increase faster than in recent years, particularly among strong limited service and extended stay brands. In the mid-1990s most of the increase will be among smaller hotels — generally 60 to 80 rooms.

In the latter part of the decade, the hotels developed will be larger, more sophisticated products. As funding is becoming available, full service hotels are again being built. The tax and financing structures available in the mid-1990s dictate that hotels developed will be designed for positive cash flow within about a year of operation. Large and luxury hotels tend to require a period of several years to reach market stabilization and a positive cash flow. For this reason, even most full service hotels developed in the 1990s will be smaller projects targeted for the mid market and for rapid absorption to a level of positive cash flow.

Improving Efficiency in Hotel Operations

A number of things changed in this industry during the recent upheaval. Among others, the industry became more efficient in its operations. Hotel management has been streamlined, hotel systems have become more cost effective, and technology has been put to use in a positive way. Hotels, once a predominantly family business, are operated in a businesslike fashion today, and management is more sophisticated. The trend for the next several years is to retain these new efficiencies and to take increasing advantage of technology to control operating costs. This is evidenced in reservation systems, front and back office management systems, energy management systems, new types of energy infrastructure, new building materials, new security systems, and other technological tools used by each department of the hotel.

Exhibit 25, on the next page, compares operating ratios in 1985 and 1993. Full service hotels, in particular, have made improvements in operating efficiency. Limited service hotels are

EXHIBIT 25

Trend in Operating Ratios

Statistic	1985	1993
Gross Operating Profit		
Full Service	21.5%	27.4%
Limited Service	41.7%	42.8%
Payroll & Related		
Expense as a Ratio to Sales		
Full Service	36.3%	35.7%

Sources: Pannell Kerr Forster "Trends 1985"
Smith Travel Research "The Host Report 1993"

showing a smaller improvement in ratios, but have improved enormously in product while holding to their operating ratios. Both limited and full service hotels should continue to show improvement in operating efficiency, while sustaining or improving product, over the next several years.

Trend in Operating Ratios

Overall, the five-year outlook for this industry is positive. Revenues will increase and expenses are becoming still more tightly controlled.

Key Players

In addition to lenders, owners and developers, key players in the hotel industry include management companies and franchisors.

Management Companies

While some hotels are operated by their owners, many are operated by third party management companies. These companies typically employ the hotel general manager and provide services such as accounting, marketing, technical and engineering support to a hotel for a fee.

Management fees are usually a percentage of gross revenues and may also include a percentage of net operating income. Combined, fees are likely to be in the range of 2% to 5% of revenues. The management company may be on a month-to-month contract or may have a long-term arrangement with the hotel. In the current market, long contracts tend to go with an equity investment.

Management contracts have changed considerably over the past several years and have become more flexible. Concurrently, fees have been reduced. The management company business is extremely competitive, but management makes or breaks a hotel, so selection should depend on more than price. Management companies range in size from well over 100 hotels to only one or two properties. Their access to management talent, the quality of the systems they implement, their integrity and their ability to maintain asset value while increasing bottom-line cash vary from good to bad.

Management contracts are lengthy legal documents and can be onerous. A poorly negotiated contract can result in a situation in which management has an incentive to allow the hotel to deteriorate physically and in which the owner cannot sell the property because the management contract survives the sale. It is prudent to have an attorney or experienced consultant review the terms of an agreement and negotiate on behalf of the owner.

Franchisors

Brand is an important aspect of marketing a hotel today. Hotels are retail businesses and we are a very brand conscious society when it comes to retail purchases. Most of the major hotel brands — including old-line, upscale names such as Hilton and Hyatt, roadside brands such as Days Inn and mid-market brands such as Hampton Inn — offer franchises. In the past decade, franchising has become an industry unto itself within the hotel business.

Two franchise organizations represent a large proportion of the hotels in the United States. The largest is Hospitality Franchise Systems, which currently represents Ramada, Howard Johnson, Days Inn, Super 8, Travelodge, Knights Inn, Wingate and Villager brands. The other is Choice Hotels International, which represents Clarion, Quality, Comfort, Sleep, Econo Lodge, Rodeway and MainStay brands.

Companies that own and operate, as well as franchise, include Marriott, Promus, Radisson, Hilton, Sheraton and Holiday Inn. In addition there are a number of regional or smaller franchise brands, such as Shoneys, Key West Inns, Country Hearth and Microtel. Companies like AmeriSuites, Red Roof and La Quinta are not currently franchising, although they are expanding chains.

One reason for the proliferation of brands is that franchising companies perceive a need to offer a product line, under their brand umbrella, for various levels of travelers. For this reason, Marriott supplements its full-service Marriott Hotels with mid-market Courtyard by Marriott Hotels, economy-oriented Fairfield Inns, and Residence Inns for extended-stay travelers. Each of the companies that offers a broad range of brands has a diversified product line. Exhibit 26 summarizes various hotel companies and their brands.

Most hotels will carry a brand, whether it is a proprietary sign owned by their operator, or a franchise.

Franchisors charge various fees for use of their brand and services. In general, this includes a franchise royalty fee of 3% to 6% of room sales. In addition, marketing and reservation system charges range from 2% to 5% of room sales. There may also be optional marketing programs that carry a charge and other required expenses. Total charges by a franchisor are likely to be in the range

EXHIBIT 26

SAMPLING OF FRANCHISORS AND THEIR BRANDS

Hotel Company	Brand	Product
Holiday Inn Worldwide	Holiday Inn	Mid-market full service
	Holiday Inn Select	Corporate full service
	Holiday Inn Express	Limited service
	Crowne Plaza	Upscale full service
Marriott	JW Marriott	Luxury full service
	Marriott Hotels	Upscale full service
	Courtyard by Marriott	Mid-market
	Fairfield Inn	Lower mid-market ltd. svc.
	Residence Inn	Upscale extended stay
Sheraton	Sheraton Hotel	Upscale full svc./convention
	Four Points	Mid-market full service
Promus	Harrah's	Gaming casinos
	Embassy Suites	Upscale full-service all suite
	Hampton Inn	Mid-market limited service
	Homewood Suites	Upscale extended stay
Choice Hotels International	Clarion	Mid-market full service
	Quality	Lower mid-market full svc.
	Comfort	Mid-market limited service
	Sleep	New construction ltd. svc.
	Econo Lodge	Economy limited service
	Rodeway	Economy limited service
	MainStay	Mid-market extended stay
Hospitality Franchise Systems	Days Inn	Economy limited service
	Ramada Hotels, Inns, Resorts	Economy or mid-market products
	Howard Johnson	Economy limited service
	Super 8	Economy limited service
	Travelodge	Economy limited service
	Knights Inn	Hard-budget limited service
	Villager	Economy extended stay
	Wingate	Mid-market new construction limited service
Radisson	Radisson Hotels	Upscale full service
	Country Inns	Mid-market limited service

of 5% to 9% of room sales. The franchisor will periodically inspect each hotel as part of a quality control program. The better brands require substantial reinvestment to keep up to brand quality.

Franchise agreements run from one year to 20 years. Most are for an initial period — 10 or 20 years — with an extension. It can be very expensive to terminate a franchise agreement, although it is sometimes desirable. Therefore, many franchisees negotiate periodic "outs," or opportunities to leave the system without penalty. It is prudent to have a knowledgeable attorney or consultant review a franchise agreement and assist with negotiations.

Lodging Products — Who's Doing What

The broad categories of hotel products that are being considered for development are:

- Economy
- Mid-market
- Full service
- Extended stay

Economy Limited-Service Hotels

These properties have taken the place of traditional motels. They typically offer spartan rooms with a private bath in a one- or two-story building with exterior corridor room access. Sometimes they include an outdoor swimming pool and/or offer coffee or limited continental breakfast as guest amenities. Because they cater to an extremely price-sensitive market, room rates are low. Econo Lodge, Ramada Limited, Days Inn, Motel 6 and a number of other brands fall into this category. Microtel is a new chain that is promoting newly constructed, modern, interior corridor economy limited-service hotels.

Mid-Market Limited-Service Hotels

Over the past decade some limited-service hotel brands have moved effectively into the mid-market, supplanting the position that used to be held by full-service Holiday Inns, Ramada Inns and Sheraton Hotels. While these limited-service properties do not have restaurants, they do offer a comfortable high-quality room, sometimes equipped with a refrigerator, VCR and other amenities. Bathrooms are generally tiled and upgraded from those in economy hotels. These hotels have swimming pools; more and more often, these pools are indoors. They may have a limited amount of meeting space and generally offer an extensive complimentary continental breakfast. Hotels in this category include Comfort Inns, Hampton Inns, Country Inns, Fairfield Inns and Wingate Inns. Courtyard by Marriott is generally considered the top end of this kind of product.

Mid-market limited-service hotels are the fastest growing segment of the hotel industry today in terms of new development. And because this segment is also the most rapidly expanding in terms of both business- and leisure-travel demand for guest rooms, it offers good upside in terms of rate in many cases.

Full-Service Hotels

There were virtually no full-service hotels developed in the United States, except in Las Vegas, between 1990 and 1995. During that period, these properties were difficult assets to hold, and many were sold at prices below half their replacement cost. While the financial performance of full-service product was poor in the early 1990s, performance has improved radically. Full-service hotels include Hiltons, Holiday Inn's Select and Crowne Plaza brands, Hyatts, Marriotts, Radissons and Sheratons.

Mid-level and upscale guests have a strong preference for good-quality full-service hotels. Properly operated, these hotels offer a sense of service and provide a degree of comfort that is not available in a limited-service product. The market today is demanding good-quality full-service product and is finding it scarce. Unfortunately, many full-service hotels have not been maintained to an acceptable standard and are not satisfying these potential guests.

One advantage to full-service hotels is their ability to house group meetings and conventions — one of the fastest growing segments in the industry. Full-service hotels create their own demand in this segment, attracting guests who would not otherwise be visiting.

The demand for full-service hotels is slowly being met by the complete renovation and repositioning of older properties. Purchased at discounted prices in the early 1990s, these renovated hotels are now providing exceptional returns to their owners and good value to their guests.

Over the next several years, it is likely that new full-service hotels will be developed. Although these properties can be operated more efficiently than they could have been 10 years ago, in most markets, rates have to increase above 1996 levels before new development can be economically justified. Rates are increasing rapidly, and this opportunity should be available soon.

Extended-Stay Lodging

Some travelers find themselves away from home for longer than a week, but less than the six months or year required to make it convenient to rent and equip an apartment. Extended-stay lodging is designed for these travelers and is available at price points ranging from $150 to $800 a week. The best known extended stay brand is Residence Inn by Marriott, which appeals to an upscale market.

A number of new companies and brands are entering the extended stay market, most at a moderate to economy price point. These include MainStay, Candlewood, Homestead Village, Extended Stay America, Suburban Lodge and Studio Plus.

These properties are crossovers between hotels and apartments. Less-expensive projects operate more like apartments, while higher priced properties have a shorter average stay, operate more like hotels and offer more amenities. Over the next several years, extended stay will evolve into its own industry. Product will be available at several price points in cities throughout the United States. This industry is expected to show explosive growth and high returns in the latter part of the 1990s.

To date, debt funding has been difficult to secure. One of the largest players is a real estate investment trust (REIT); two other players have successfully gone public to raise capital. As these new products roll out profitably, debt for new construction is expected to become available.

Evaluating Hotel Pro Formas

Operating expenses for today's standard franchised hotel product are reasonably predictable, and good data on comparable products is available. Smith Travel Research maintains a large database of annual hotel operating statements and provides composite averages for defined samples of hotels for a small fee. Exhibit 27, on the next two pages, compares an aggregate average hotel income statement for limited-service hotels to the same for full-service hotels within the United States.

Smith Travel Research and most of the larger hotel operators use the "Uniform System of Accounts for Hotels" promulgated by the American Hotel & Motel Association. Although there are classification differences from operator to operator, the Uniform System has provided comparability across hotel statements for over 70 years. Key issues to consider in evaluating a hotel statement include the following:

- Room revenues are the product of occupancy and average daily rate. A statistic that has more recently become popular is "RevPar," which is the gross revenue for a

EXHIBIT 27

INDUSTRY AVERAGES — STATEMENTS OF OPERATING INCOME AND EXPENSES — 1994

Revenue	Full-Service Hotels Ratio to Sales	Full-Service Hotels Per Available Room	Limited-Service Hotels Ratio to Sales	Limited-Service Hotels Per Available Room
Rooms	67.6%	$20,094	94.7%	$14,321
Food & Related	21.4%	$ 7,229	0.0%	
Beverage	5.1%	$ 1,763	0.0%	
Telephone	2.6%	$ 809	2.2%	$ 364
Minor Departments	2.1%	$ 892	1.2%	$ 226
Rentals & Other Income	1.2%	$ 427	1.8%	$ 258
Total Revenue	100.0%	$31,214	100.0%	$15,169
Departmental Expenses				
Rooms	26.4%	$ 5,247	26.6%	$ 3,656
Food & Beverage	82.2%	$ 7,163	0.0%	
Telephone	60.5%	$ 442	71.4%	$ 198
Other Departments	1.6%	$ 693	0.6%	$ 115
Total Departmental Expenses	42.0%	$13,545	27.2%	$ 3,969
Total Departmental Profit	58.0%	$17,669	72.8%	$11,200

Source: Smith Travel Research "Hotel Operating Statistics — 1994"

(continued)

EXHIBIT 27 (cont'd)

INDUSTRY AVERAGES — STATEMENTS OF OPERATING INCOME AND EXPENSES — 1994

Revenue	Full-Service Hotels Ratio to Sales	Full-Service Hotels Per Available Room	Limited-Service Hotels Ratio to Sales	Limited-Service Hotels Per Available Room
Undistributed Operating Expenses				
Administrative & General	9.8%	$2,919	9.9%	$1,453
Marketing	5.9%	$1,886	5.0%	$ 795
Franchise Fees	1.4%	$ 333	2.1%	$ 304
Energy	4.9%	$1,384	5.5%	$ 768
Property Operations & Maintenance	5.3%	$1,610	5.1%	$ 761
Total Undistributed Expenses	27.2%	$8,132	27.6%	$4,081
Gross Operating Profit	30.8%	$9,537	45.2%	$7,119
Management Fees	2.1%	$ 646	3.6%	$ 499
Income Before Fixed Charges	28.7%	$8,891	41.7%	$6,620
Property Taxes	3.2%	$ 989	3.7%	$ 550
Insurance	0.9%	$ 255	1.2%	$ 165
Reserve for Replacement	1.3%	$ 378	0.8%	$ 91
Available for Debt Service & Fixed Charges	23.3%	$7,269	36.0%	$5,814
	70.8%		73.2%	
	$78.67		$54.44	
	293		129	

given room for a year divided by the number of rooms in the property.

- Food and beverage revenues come from restaurants, lounges, banquet facilities and room service. A hotel with an established clientele usually maintains its level of food and beverage sales. However, major property overhauls tend to reconfigure food and beverage space and may sharply affect revenues. Also, high-energy lounges can be strong contributors to a hotel's food and beverage performance, but may not sustain a consistent volume.
- Hotels, as providers of telecommunications services, are likely to see major changes over the next several years. In general, we expect telephone revenue potential to increase as telephone companies provide more sophisticated services for a fee.
- Other income and operating departments in a hotel include a host of other businesses, salvage sales, leases, interest and dividends. Sometimes these line items include short-term or one-time income that cannot contribute to the property's long-term ability to pay debt.
- Rooms department expense is shown as a ratio to departmental sales, rather than to total revenues. Both the dollar expense and the ratio are higher for luxury hotels than for economy properties, reflecting the high cost of providing amenities and services. The rooms department expense ratio has come down in recent years as hotel operations have become more efficient, and as revenues have increased. However, increasing requirements by chains with regard to items such as continental breakfast and room amenities are likely to keep costs increasing at least at the level of inflation. Reservation charges from a franchise company will often be categorized in the rooms department.

- Food and beverage department expense, also shown as a ratio to departmental sales, is one of the hardest areas to control in a hotel. Even a well-run department is likely to see some variation in expense ratios. In general, successful lounges and banquet operations are more profitable than in-house restaurants. Hotel companies are aggressively working to find technology, new brands and new systems to improve food and beverage department profits.
- Telephone departments in hotels routinely had a loss of more than 40% in the early 1980s. Today, it is not uncommon for a hotel to report a profit of 40 to 50 percent. The change has been remarkable, and profits are likely to increase in dollar amount, if not as a ratio to sales.
- Administrative and general expense should be evaluated as a dollar amount and not as a ratio to sales. In addition to standard expenses, this figure may include part or all of a franchise fee, part or all of a management fee, outside accounting charges, unusual legal expenses, cars and other benefits for owners, and insurance. From an analytical perspective, most of these items do not belong in this department. Insurance, in particular, should be evaluated to make sure coverage is reasonable and costs are competitive.
- Marketing expense is vital to a successful hotel, and a property that shows a reduced marketing budget is not unlikely to see a decline in revenues within a year. Marketing for a limited-service hotel may include little more than billboards. Conversely, marketing for a full-service hotel or resort is a major undertaking and may include staff of more than a dozen, sophisticated advertising, public relations and telemarketing. The marketing assessment charged by a franchise company may appear in the marketing department, as may some management company charges, which may distort this figure.

- Management fees are the contract charges from a management company. If not shown in a hotel's income statement, often a lender will impute these fees.
- Franchise fees are the contract charges from the hotel's franchisor. If not shown clearly (broken out of the rooms, administrative and marketing departments), often a lender will impute these fees.
- Property operations and maintenance costs tend to be slightly higher in the first two years of operation. After this, operations and maintenance costs decline for a short time and then increase as the hotel ages. There is a debate within almost every hotel operation about which expenses should be classified within the property operations and maintenance department and which should be classified as capital expenditures, or CapEx. Both should be covered in the statement. A management agreement that is very specific in this area helps prevent asset deterioration and long-term problems between ownership and management.
- Energy includes gas, electric, water, sewer, disposal and other energy-related items. Energy expense has become more controllable in recent years as HVAC and other technologies have improved. However, these benefits are only available for hotels that invest in good equipment.
- Property taxes are different in every municipality and cannot be compared to industry averages, but should appear in all hotel income statements as a line item. Property tax consultants are used to track taxes and negotiate with local municipalities.
- Insurance may just include property and extended coverage insurance or may also include a complete package with liability and worker's compensation. Traditionally, liability and worker's compensation insurance have been classified in the administrative and general department while property insurance appears as a line item; however,

this distinction has blurred as bundled plans have become more prevalent.

- Lenders used to require a 3% CapEx (capital expenditures/reserve for replacement) reserve, but did not require that reserve to be funded; the result was disastrous. Actual CapEx expenses are predictable, and the availability of funds for CapEx is vital to a hotel's ability to compete beyond its seventh year in operation. Reserves need to be adequate, planned to coincide with the life of the components of the hotel, and funded.

A limited-service hotel should reach stabilized occupancy during its first year in operation and should have the positive cash flow to cover debt service within a few months of opening. A full-service hotel, conference center or resort may take several years to reach stabilized occupancy and to develop its room rate. Its operating ratios will tend to improve each year as it approaches stabilization. This type of property usually will not provide debt service coverage during its first two years of operation.

Historic Performance vs. Future Financial Projections

In general, financing an existing hotel based on historic cash flow results in a situation where the hotel covers its debt service readily following implementation of the loan. However, in the latter part of the 1990s, many markets will come out of the period of rapidly inflating room rates and will find that their pace of room rate gains are close to the level of inflation or lower. In many markets, new hotels will open and competition will force occupancies down. Also, many hotels that were acquired will start running into product quality issues. Even a well-renovated older building is likely to need considerable ongoing CapEx to remain competitive. As these issues play out, financing on a trailing income stream will become more dangerous. Every hotel should be evaluated for its CapEx needs, market potential and financial situation going forward.

Hotel Lending

From 1989 into 1994 there was virtually no funding available for hotels. During that period very few hotels opened, except in Las Vegas, and of those developed, almost none were over 65 rooms. Refinancing for existing hotels was also extremely difficult to secure, and property values were so low that the refinancing options available were distasteful.

Funding is now available for acquisition and refinancing of hotels with an operating history. Financing is also available for new construction of small hotels. Larger new construction projects are just beginning to surface and are expected to become more prevalent toward the late 1990s.

J.M. Madderra/Corporate Realty, Real Estate Investment Bankers, publishes a periodic "Interest Rate Survey." The hotel interest rates in its February 1, 1996 newsletter are listed in Exhibit 28.

An interest rate survey developed by InterBank Mortgage Company and summarized in Exhibit 29 (on page 248) shows additional details. As would be expected, actual rates and spreads will vary by institution depending on loan size, project quality, location, LTV ratio, debt service coverage ratio, age of hotel, type of hotel, hotel market, owner experience, management company experience, credit and financial statement considerations and overall perceived risk of the loan.

Construction financing remains difficult to obtain, and for hotels there is only about a 70% loan to cost. In general, conduits will finance 70% LTV, but will go up to 75% on exception. Lending rates are among the highest for any construction type. Affordable

EXHIBIT 28

INTEREST RATE SURVEY — HOTEL/MOTEL

Funding Source	Treasury Spread	Fixed Prime Loan Rate 5 Year	Fixed Prime Loan Rate 20 Year	Maximum Loan to Value
Conduit	275–325	8.0%	8.6%	75%
Credit Company (Participating)	250–350	7.7%	8.3%	80%
Life Insurance Company	225–325	7.5%	8.1%	70%
Construction Loan	370–435	9.3% floating		70% LTC

Note: Subject to errors, omissions and change.
Source: J.M. Maderra/Corporate Realty

EXHIBIT 29

INTEREST RATE SURVEY

Lender Type	Loan Size	Treasury Spread	Fees	Maximum Loan to Value*	Minimum Debt Coverage	Typical Term	Typical Amortization
Conduit	$1 million+	350–375	1.5–2%	70%	1.50	10 years	20 years
Conduit	$5 million+	275–325	1–1.5%	70%	1.40	10 years	20 years
Life Co.	$10 million+	225–250	0–1%	70%	1.35	10 years	25 years
Credit Co.	$10 million+	250–350	1–2%	75%	1.30	5–7 years	20 years
Banks**	$1 million+	250–300	1–2%	75%	1.30	5 years	20 years

* Up to 75% on exception.
** Construction loans not included. They are relationship oriented with banks and require a minimum 25% equity on loans under $5 million and 35%–40% equity on larger loans.

Source: InterBank Mortgage Corporation, March 1996

housing, garden apartments, retail centers and free-standing credit, all had interest rates 0.7% to 0.9% lower, with approximately half the equity requirement for a hotel loan. However, average contract interest rates for hotels are at their lowest point in a decade. According to Sonnenblick-Goldman Company, the average contract interest rate for hotels has dropped to the 8% range after hovering around 10% for several years until 1993. However, many loans are still in the 9% to 9.5% range.

Although financing can be difficult to obtain, owners and developers are finding this an attractive time to secure debt.

Small Hotel Deals

In the past five years, and continuing into the latter part of the 1990s, many small hotel projects were financed with the assistance of the Small Business Administration (SBA). These projects tended to be hotels with about 60 rooms each and total project costs, including land and soft costs, of $2.5 million dollars or less. These projects required at least 30% equity, generally raised from family and other private investors. As lending to the hotel industry becomes more competitive, equity requirements are expected to come down to the 20% range. Debt is typically from a local bank, which may also be an SBA lender. Depending on the status of SBA loans, some $400,000 to $750,000 is guaranteed by the SBA with the balance of the debt provided by the bank or SBA lender. Lenders active in the hotel industry for this kind of project include VST, PMC Capital, The Money Store and local banks. Once the hotels have an operating history, they have often been refinanced either through a local bank, a credit company or a conduit.

Acquisitions and Refinancing

As a result of the recent period when financing for hotels was virtually nonexistent, interest rates became high. Wall Street sensed an opportunity and developed conduits for hotels. The conduits typically do not finance new construction; however, they can finance up to 80% of the value of hotels with an operating history. Typically, they will fund the loans with a bank credit line and then sell accumulated portfolios off to the public. Conduits are a source of refinancing for owners who have developed several smaller hotels during the last few years. In the period from 1990 to 1996, hotels throughout the United States were acquired — largely with equity — renovated and turned around. Many of these properties are being resold or refinanced as they establish an operating history. Conduits are funding acquisitions and refinancings as well. According to "E&Y/KL Real Estate Forum," commercial mortgage-backed securities for hotels were estimated to total about a billion dollars in 1995.

Conduits and life insurance companies tend to look at projects in the $2 million to $10 million range, but conduits will fund larger projects as well. Pension, life insurance and credit companies are more likely to be interested in projects over $10 million. Credit companies have had limited interest in hotels in recent years and tend to be participating lenders. They are beginning to look hard at hotels on a straight debt basis today. Life insurance companies had been active as hotel lenders, and then most left the market when they became more active as sellers of the REO portfolios. More recently, their interest has increased. Life insurance companies and pension funds are generally expected to increase their activity in the hotel market during the late 1990s. There are institutional investors who are also becoming more active in the hotel market because of the loan spreads available. Most active hotel investors — including GE Credit, Heller Financial and Nomura — have strong backgrounds in the industry.

As of this writing, lenders:

- Base lending decisions on trailing 12-month performance
- Prefer three years of operating history

- Will add management and franchise fees into the expenses section of an income statement if they have not been included
- Will add 4% to 6% CapEx annually into the expenses section of an income statement if it has not been reserved for replacement
- Require a debt service coverage ratio of 1.4 to 1.5
- Apply cap rates of 10% to 12% depending on the quality and age of property
- May lend 60% to 75% of appraised value or 70% to 80% of value based on a capitalization of trailing 12-month performance (deals less than $5 million tend to require 25% to 30% equity and deals over $5 million require 40% to 50%)
- Prefer branded, standard products

Equity Funding

Equity has become perhaps the largest source of funding for hotels. There are three major components to the equity currently in the market:

1. Equity raised for an individual project — the 20% to 40% required to secure funding for new development. As the property value increases, this equity is taken out.
2. Equity funds assembled to take advantage of deeply discounted hotel prices during the early part of the 1990s. Funds have acquired hotels of all types and have been actively renovating and repositioning these hotels. It has not been uncommon for returns on these projects to exceed 30% annually when they are renovated and reopened under aggressive management. However, hotel prices have already more than doubled and some have tripled. There are now more dollars available than there are strong turnaround opportunities. Eventually, the funds

are likely to sell their hotels or convert them to another financial structure.

3. REITs. Hotel REITS were popular in the 1970s and became inactive around 1975; these were set up as mortgage REITs. Hotel REITS — now set up as equity REITs — resurfaced a few years ago when a small hotel company called Jamison Inns went public. Hotel REITS require a complicated structure under which the REIT leases the hotel. These REITs do not lend on hotels, but they do make acquisitions. Management is through a separate company. As of this writing, there are 11 hotel REITS, representing $2.5 billion in hotel equity ownership. These REITs continue to be active buyers of existing, performing hotel product. REITS include short-term and medium-term notes, convertible and nonconvertible bonds, preferred and perpetual preferred stock, and credit lines with equity take-outs.

A Hotel Financing Package

Most hotel projects seeking funding for this year, and for the next several years, will be clearly defined products. Each of the major brands has introduced distinct prototypes and has specified the facilities and amenities that the hotels within their brands will require. For these standard products, development and operating expenses are predictable, given competent management.

Dangers of the marketplace revolve around the stability and future potential sources of demand for the hotel, changes in the competitive market, community development, the operator's skill and the need to keep a hotel's physical plant competitive. Each can be controlled to a reasonable degree. The package of information submitted to a lender should address each of these risks, as well as the project potential. A discussion of the components of a good lender's package on a hotel follows.

The Summary

The first page of the financial package should summarize the situation. Included should be the:

- Name and address of the hotel
- Number of rooms for each kind of product
- Age and condition
- Additional facilities
- Size of the land included
- Name and address of the management company
- Summary of the occupancy, average rate, gross revenue and net income for trailing 12 months and three calendar years (if available)
- Projections (if the property has not yet been built)
- Value at a 10% to 12% cap or an appropriate figure for the hotel, based on actual operating performance
- Loan request and debt service coverage ratio
- Name and address of the borrower

A map and pictures of the hotel should follow after the summary.

Related Materials

In addition to the materials presented in the summary, each lender will have additional items required for due diligence. Other materials that may be requested are outlined as follows:

- Three years (or as close to three years as possible) actual monthly operating history

- Copy of the franchise agreement and three most recent inspection reports from the franchisor
- Copy of the management agreement, if any
- Information on the management or management company. Management risk is controlled by having an owner or management company that will monitor on-site management; implement internal controls and monitor the operation daily; do capital planning; provide marketing and maintenance support and respond quickly if a problem arises. A well-operated hotel might have 35% of its revenue available for debt service. Conversely, a poorly operated hotel can have a negative cash flow. A lender may request information on management expertise and operating history.
- Historic and projected capital budgets (CapEx). Hotels wear out. Everything in a hotel has an anticipated life, and those lives can be very short—three to five years for soft goods such as bedding, drapes and carpet. Capital expenditures will exceed 10% of development cost or 30% of its revenue in some years in a well-maintained hotel. The cost of bringing a poorly maintained hotel up to industry standard can be considerably higher. Accordingly, a knowledgeable lender will want to know what has been spent in the past three to five years on CapEx and what the CapEx needs will be for the next three to five years. Exhibit 30 and Exhibit 31 (shown on page 256) show typical projected CapEx for prototype limited-service, mid-level and full-service hotels. Because of the potential magnitude of CapEx, a reserve for replacement of 4% to 6% of gross revenues should be required annually. This reserve should be shown in the historic statements and in any projections presented to a lender.
- Environmental Phase I report
- Engineer's report

EXHIBIT 30

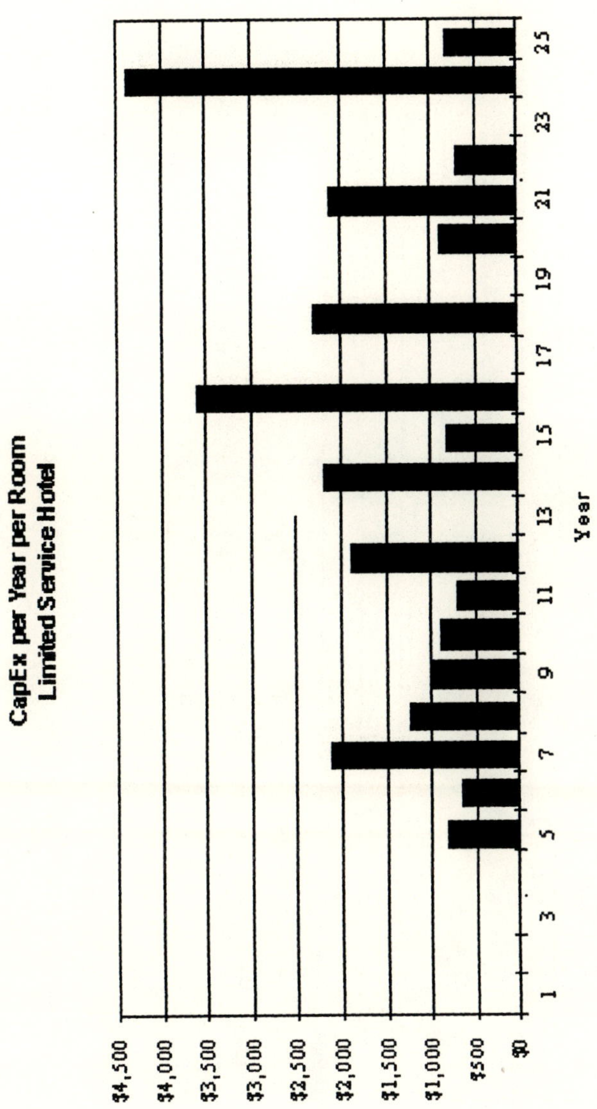

Source: International Society of Hospitality Consultants

EXHIBIT 31

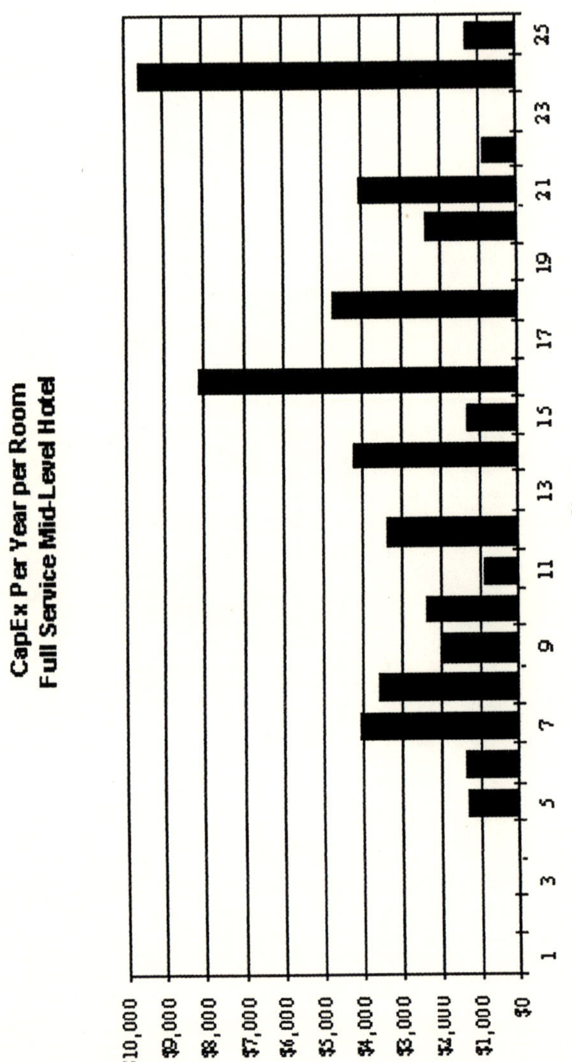

Source: International Society of Hospitality Consultants

- Certified Public Accountant's "review" of the prior year operating results
- Site plan or survey of the property
- Plans and specifications for a renovation or new construction project
- Borrowers' resumes, including recent balance sheets and experience with hotels
- Detailed property description
- Statement of the planned sources and uses of funds, including a breakdown of equity and debt sources, a property acquisition plan and a cost breakdown for new construction or renovation
- Terms of existing financing
- Existing lender reference
- STAR Report for the hotel and its competition. These are two to three page statistical reports showing the performance of the hotel in comparison to a sample of competitive properties. STAR Reports are available from Smith Travel Research.
- Market study. For a new construction hotel, large acquisition or major renovation, a market study is used to show the lender the pros and cons of the location, current and anticipated characteristics of the community, details of the competitive hotel market, likely sources of demand for the hotel and market potential for the hotel in terms of projected mix of business, occupancy and average rate.
- Appraisal. A lender is likely to require an appraisal and should commission this analysis directly from an appraiser with hotel expertise.

Lenders in this industry are responsive to the requirements of rating agencies because many loans will eventually be sold. Accordingly, the lender will need a loan package that meets rating agency requirements. There are guidelines for rating commercial mortgage-backed securities. Standard and Poor's, Fitch Investor Services, Duff and Phelps Credit Rating Company and others publish their rating guidelines for larger loans and pools of loans.

The U.S. lodging industry more than doubled aggregate profits from 1993 to 1994, as shown in Exhibit 32. In 1995 and 1996, profits are expected to exceed 1994's levels.

Lenders are still cautious. However, as a result of increasing profitability, debt is becoming more available to the industry. The outlook for financing for the hotel industry for the next several years is improving.

For Further Information

Assistance and information on hotels is available from a variety of sources. Some important references for this industry are:

- *American Hotel & Motel Association* is the national association representing the industry. It publishes a variety of materials including the "Uniform System of Accounts for Hotels" and the "Directory of Hotel-Motel Companies." Its address is 1201 New York Avenue, Suite 600, Washington, DC 20005-3931; its telephone number is (202) 289-3100.
- *Hotel & Motel Brokers of America (HMBA)* is a professional society of brokers specializing in hotel properties. You can write to HMBA at 10220 North Executive Hills Boulevard, Suite 610, Kansas City, MO 64153-2312 or call (816) 891-7071.
- *International Council of Hotel and Motel Management Companies (ICHMMC)* is a branch of the American Hotel & Motel Association for management companies. It can assist with information on management companies, the services they provide, management contracts and fees.

EXHIBIT 32

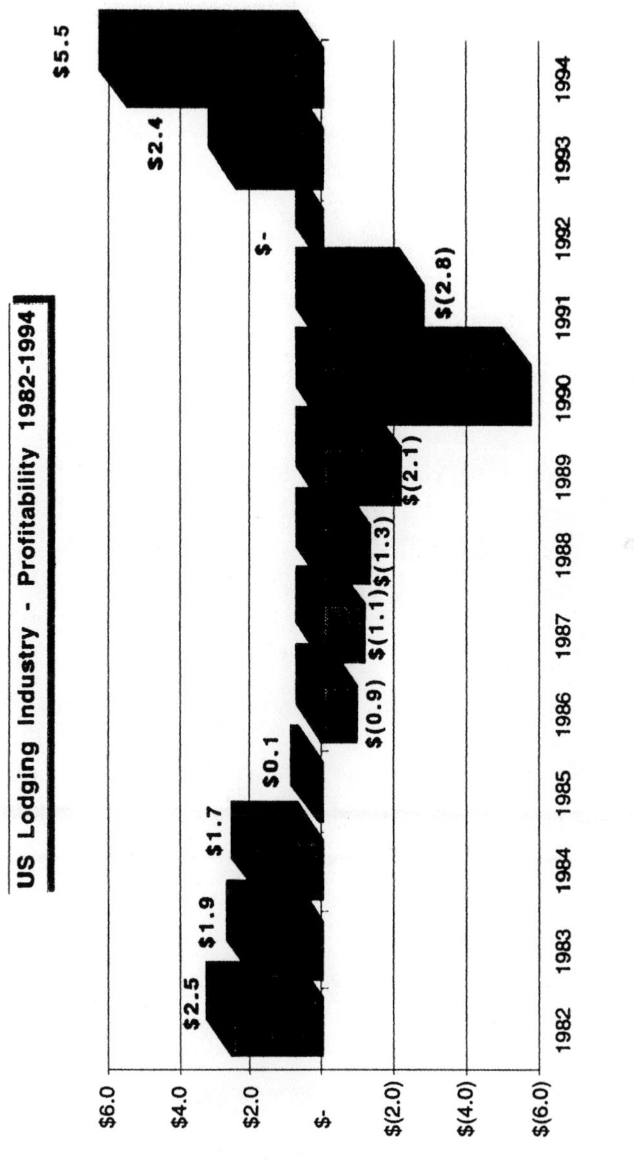

Source: Smith Travel Research

You can write to ICHMMC at 1500 South Highway 100, Suite 375, Minneapolis, MN 55416 or call (612) 591-7640.

- *International Society of Hospitality Consultants (ISHC)* is a professional society of the leading consultants to the industry. Their membership directory lists leading appraisers, market analysts, financial and feasibility analysts, attorneys, designers and other professionals serving the hospitality industry. "CapEx," a report on capital expenditures in the hotel industry, is available from ISHC, as is a member directory. You can contact ISHC at 1080 Brookfield, Suite 200, Memphis, TN 38119 or call (901) 683-1806.
- *J.M. Madderra/Corporate Realty* publishes a periodic interest rates survey newsletter that includes hotel/motel rates and rates for other real estate types. You can write to J.M. Madderra/Corporate Realty at 1515 Poydras Street, Suite 1875, New Orleans, LA 70112 or call (504) 585-2611.
- Interbank Mortgage also publishes financing statistics. Their address is 6190 Powers Ferry Road, Suite 100, Atlanta, GA 30339 or call (770) 955-2470.
- *Smith Travel Research (STR)* is a company that compiles statistical data on the hotel industry and maintains databases of monthly occupancy and rate performance (published in its STAR Report) as well as annual financial performance (published in its HOST Report). You can contact STR at 105 Music Village Boulevard, Hendersonville, TN 37075; the telephone number is (615) 824-8664.

14

Industrial Property Analysis

W. Thomas Gardner, Investment Officer
State Farm

Analyzing industrial properties has taken on a whole new meaning in the last five years. Gone are the heady days of the 1980s when everything was going up, up, up, and no one thought it would ever change. The real estate depression that followed changed all that. Today, we have an industry emerging from that depressed state. The players are beginning to show a cautious optimism that the dreary days of recession are behind us, and it is time to assemble the pieces of a shattered industry.

However, there is evidence of a more pragmatic approach in the industry. Real estate professionals are more into the nuts and bolts of property analysis than they had been over the last 15 years. Lenders, developers, investors and appraisers are rethinking the analytical process that drove the real-estate-loan boom of the 1980s. More precise guidelines have been developed and are being followed carefully to ensure accurate assessments of investments and to protect against the problems of the recent past.

Changing Environment: 1970 to Present

The Past

Twenty-five years ago, the industrial property industry was fairly simplistic, compared to what it is today. Industrial buildings, although recognized as a highly specialized type of real estate, were basically boxes of various sizes and shapes, categorized as general warehouses, research and development (R&D) facilities or industrial production buildings. Each type of property had its own unique characteristics. The analytical approach was heavily skewed to the property type rather than to the tenants who would occupy the facility.

The financial structure of the property's owners and lenders was also fairly simplistic. Typically, developers would construct facilities on a speculative basis (no tenants at the time of construction) and finance the construction with a bank loan. During the construction process, the developers would lease the property and seek a permanent loan to "take out" the construction loan once construction was complete. The typical source for this permanent loan was either an insurance company or an S&L.

Then, there were some changes going on that were forerunners of things to come. Developers began to look for new sources of equity money as projects got bigger, encompassing hundreds of acres and millions of square feet of development. The timetable for completing such developments was measured in years instead of months and required a new sophistication in financing. The joint venture emerged as a viable business option. Joint ventures took many shapes and forms, but typically involved a developer, who provided the development expertise, and a money partner, such as an insurance company, that would provide the up-front equity money needed to get the project off the ground.

At about this time, a new source of financing also was emerging. REITs provided another source of the capital needed to finance the construction boom. Structured for equity or debt,

REITs, along with joint ventures, demonstrated the creativity of the real estate industry. One of the beneficiaries of that creativity was the industrial property.

The Present

The past 25 years have brought change in the industrial market. This change can be seen in the following areas:

- *Types of Properties.* Most industrial buildings are located in industrial parks today. As our economy has transformed from manufacturing and heavy industry to high-tech, industrial buildings have adapted to industrial parks. Tenants are more compatible with one another and can be located side by side. Driving through an industrial park today, you usually cannot tell whether a building is used for manufacturing activity or product storage. The growth of flex buildings and R&D facilities has also had a great impact on the industrial market, making us more acutely aware of specific tenant requirements and their impact on a project. The computer also has had an impact on the industrial building industry, revolutionizing the way our economy operates.
- *The Players.* Industrial players include owners, financiers and operating personnel. Ownership is changing as Wall Street has created new vehicles for property purchases. Pension funds and foreign investors see opportunities in the real estate industry brought on by depressed prices in the early 1990s. S&Ls, as we once knew them, no longer exist. Many insurance companies have dropped both debt and equity investments in real estate. Other insurance companies still are involved, but have been joined by new players, most of them created by Wall Street, including a revived REIT industry. The result is an increase in absentee ownership and a need for professional operating

personnel to handle the management and leasing for owners. Many of these professionals are former developers who have decided to remain in the management and leasing business.

- *Government Regulations and Legal Concerns.* The government is concerned about our quality of living. Consequently, the industrial market must deal with such regulations as the Americans with Disabilities Act and Environmental Protection Agency requirements. These and other legal issues have increased overall awareness of these issues and also have increased the necessity of seeking expert legal counsel.
- *Industrial Property Variables.* The activities housed in industrial buildings today are still manufacturing and storage for various products, materials and inventory. However, there has been a great shift in the American economy away — from heavy industry, such as steel manufacturing, into the computer age and high-tech industry. Therefore, the type of space tenants require for industrial buildings has changed dramatically. Tenants are more specific in their space needs and often require special improvements — such as additional lighting, refrigeration, added insulation and clear air systems — over normal building standards. Consequently, the "spec" building of the past is more difficult to produce today.
- *Industrial Property Assessment.* To outline the complexity of industrial building analysis today, Exhibit 33 shows one life insurance company's industrial property assessment list. This is a basic checklist of items to consider when studying any standard industrial building, including environmental issues, site factors and building characteristics. However, today's buildings would not completely fit into a simplified assessment such as this;

EXHIBIT 33

INDUSTRIAL PROPERTY ASSESSMENT CHECKLIST

Review of Geotechnical Investigation (Soil Report)

- Identify engineer recommendations regarding foundation design (soil-bearing capacity), floor slab design and paving specifications.
- Confirm plans and specifications have incorporated engineers' recommendations.

Review of Site Plan

- Identify items that will restrict the use of the property in terms of access or building use, such as topography, configuration, detention ponds, wetlands, easements and floodplain.
- Identify site items that will affect the ability to attract tenants to the building, such as truck access to the four sides of the building (including the long side), parking layout and site access from major highways.
- Indicate land coverage.

Analysis of the Quality of Building Structure and Building Materials

- Specify future maintenance characteristics of exterior materials, including roofing, exterior walls, paving, concrete strengths (for example, floor thickness).
- Describe energy efficiency of building envelope, particularly the roof insulation.
- Identify building items that will affect the ability to attract tenants to the building, such as building depth, bay size, clear height, overhead doors (number and size — dock high and at grade), building sprinklers, skylights, building size and aesthetic qualities (general appearance, landscaping, irrigation, street exposure and showroom space for retail tenants).
- Address environmental issues on- and off-site that will affect the environmental integrity of the site, such as soil or groundwater contamination, UST, Asbestos, PCBs, lead and radon.
- Indicate ADA compliance.

they are far more complex and require the analyst to evaluate the type and needs of tenants occupying the building.

Industrial Building Categories by Tenant

It is fairly easy to describe the function of an industrial building; it is quite another thing to try to categorize industrial buildings. Their physical characteristics have changed dramatically over the years, and there is no stable platform for categorization based on physical characteristics. It is easier to categorize them by tenant. Even though the specific requirements have changed, building categorization by tenancy has remained fairly constant.

Please note that a building does not necessarily remain in one category for its entire life. The reason for this is the industrial market: A building that attracts a single tenant in today's market may be more attractive and profitable if leased to multiple tenants in the future. However, not all buildings will have the flexibility or the design characteristics to be recategorized. Characteristics, such as bay depth, number of overhead doors and building configuration, will affect the use of the building.

The most important factor in analyzing an industrial building is the building's revenue-generating potential. Owners want to maximize profits, and therefore, they will seek the tenants who enable them to achieve that. To figure out who the appropriate tenants are requires a financial analysis of the property that — much like the appraisal process — will determine the highest-and-best-use of a property.

Single Tenant

A single tenant property is designed specifically for one tenant, yet has characteristics that make it economically feasible to allow multi-tenant use. Design characteristics used to determine if a building belongs in this category include building size, bay depth, overhead doors and their locations, lot size, location of building on the lot and ceiling height.

Multitenant

Multitenant is the most generic and flexible of all industrial properties. It is a building that is readily adaptable to a variety of tenant needs. The tenants determine what features are important. Consequently, it is important to study the specific market where the property is located to ensure optimal use of the facility.

Special Purpose

A special purpose facility is designed to meet the specific needs of a single tenant or industry. Its best use is very limited in scope, and the likelihood of that use changing is small. One example of such a facility is a building used by a particular couscous manufacturer. This particular building — a 60-foot wide, 250-foot long building, with a 36-foot ceiling, two overhead doors (one at each end of the building), no windows and a small, 20-foot by 30-foot office area with a 10-foot ceiling — was constructed to house the couscous manufacturing machinery. At the time, this building was the only couscous production facility in the United States.

Special purpose is the most inflexible category of industrial properties. Recognizing this, it is important to determine the longevity of demand for this type of product. If only one tenant wants it, you want to make sure that tenant will be around for a long time.

Build to Suit

A build-to-suit property is designed to meet the specific requirements of a tenant. Its design features could include any or all of the three previous categories. Recognizing this is important because it determines the property's future market appeal. If it were the special purpose couscous facility, its appeal to other tenants would be very limited; therefore it would be important to analyze the financial strength of the borrower and the tenant and to require the tenant to sign a long-term lease in order for you to feel comfortable that they would be around for a long time. On the other hand, a tenant may want a general purpose property that would be easily adaptable for a wide variety of tenants. This situation puts you in the best of both worlds because you have a fully occupied building, probably on a long-term lease, and yet you still have a building that could meet a wide variety of tenants' needs if the original tenant vacates.

Flex Buildings

Flex buildings are hybrid buildings — a mix of industrial, office and retail. They are designed to accommodate a variety of tenants' needs. The one common trait among flex buildings is that they have warehouse space. They are designed to accommodate a variety of tenants' needs. With the right building dimensions, they can even provide mezzanine space.

There are two concerns when dealing with flex space. The first is determining what type of tenant will be attracted to the space. If a tenant is going to sell a product from the location, the tenant should locate in a retail area. If the majority of the space is office fit-up, a manufacturing area may not appeal to many of the other tenants. The important thing is to adapt the building and the tenancy to the environment. For this type of building to be placed in the industrial category, it must meet the description of an industrial building: its primary purpose being either manufacturing or storage for products, materials or inventory.

The second and probably more important issue is what I call good flex/bad flex. Good flex occurs when, as the building matures, tenants' demands for improvements increase and the rent paid for the improvements becomes more profitable. For example, let's say that the initial tenants in the building required 10% of the space finished as office area; over time, these tenants (or new tenants) might require more office area and therefore might pay a rent that would increase the return on the investment to the owner. Bad flex is the opposite; over time, there is less demand for tenant fit-up. Not only do rents decline, but the owner has to remove improvements, such as office space, in order to attract tenants. This was one of the problems created during the real estate crash of the 1980s. To get a better understanding of this situation, read the case study on fluctuating tenancy in Exhibit 34, shown on pages 270 through 272.

Major Factors in Industrial Property Analysis

Once the property has been designed and categorized, all that remains is to analyze the factors that influence the viability of the project. The purpose is to determine if the category or type of building under consideration — single or multitenant, special use or build to suit — maximizes the use of the property. You cannot assume that any industrial building placed in an area of industrial buildings maximizes the use of the property; although the uses may be similar, similarity is not necessarily the same as maximization of use.

Before analyzing these factors, you must establish criteria or standards against which you can measure the particular project. For example, if you are interested in projects in communities with populations of more than 1,000,000, a project in Peoria, Illinois, would not be right for you. Likewise, if you decide the project must be located in an industrial park, you can eliminate any projects located elsewhere. The importance of these criteria is that they act as guidelines and they aid you in establishing benchmarks for your analysis.

EXHIBIT 34

A SIMPLIFIED ANALYSIS OF AN INDUSTRIAL PROPERTY

This example assumes that the developers/owners conducted a thorough analysis of the major industrial factors and then decided to construct the building described below, anticipating certain leasing activity.

Building Description: The building is a 100,000-square-foot bulk warehouse constructed in accordance with the appropriate bulk warehouse design criteria. The building is located on a 6-acre tract of land (.38 FAR). Five tenants are interested in leasing space but tenant finish requirements vary. Market rents for this type of space range from $2.75 to $5.00 per square foot because most tenants in the market area have tenant fit-up that varies from 10% to 25% of their space.

Question: Can this building be constructed and offer rents competitive within the market?

Assumptions:

Land Cost	$50,000/acre
Basic Building Cost	$20/square foot
Site Improvements	$100,000
Tenant Improvement Cost	$5/square foot

Tenant Requirements: The five tenants interested in space have the following requirements:

Tenant	Lease Terms	Total Square Footage (SF) Needed	Finished Area
A	5 years	20,000 SF	-0-
B	5 years	20,000 SF	2,000 SF
C	5 years	20,000 SF	2,000 SF
D	5 years	20,000 SF	6,000 SF
E	5 years	20,000 SF	3,000 SF

(continued)

EXHIBIT 34 (cont'd)

Step One: Determine the basic project cost.

Land Cost — 6 acres @ $50,000/acre	$ 300,000
Basic Building Cost — 100,000 SF @ $20/SF	$2,000,000
Site Improvements	$ 100,000
Basic Cost	$2,400,000

Step Two: Determine an expected rate of return on the investment.

If you desired a 12% return, you would have to design a lease structure that would allow a net income sufficient to realize that return.

Investment x Expected Return = Net Income
$2,400,000 x 12% = $288,000 or $2.88/SF

Charging a rent of $2.88/SF would provide a proper return for Tenant A. However, the other four tenants have additional costs in the form of tenant improvements. To realize a 12% return on these tenants' areas requires higher rents.

Keep in mind that these tenant improvements are for one particular tenant. Not only should a 12% return be realized, but the investment in those tenant improvements should be recaptured over the lease term. Also, the tenant improvements will have to be amortized over that tenant's lease term to allow the owners to recapture their investments in these additional costs and theoretically, to provide them with funds to refit the space for future tenants.

Utilizing this approach, the remaining four tenants would be charged the following rents to realize a 12% return:

Tenant B: 2,000 SF finished area x $5/SF = $10,000 additional cost
Additional rent of $2,670 ($1.33/SF) is necessary to recapture $10,000 investment @ 12 percent.
Total Rent = $2.88 + $1.33 = $4.21/SF

(continued)

EXHIBIT 34 (cont'd)

Tenant C: Same rent as Tenant B: $4.21/SF

Tenant D: 6,000 SF finished area x $5/SF = $30,000
Additional rent of $8,000 ($4/SF) is necessary to recapture $30,000 investment @ 12 percent
Total Rent = $2.88 + $4.00 = $6.88/SF

Tenant E: 3,000 SF finished area x $5/SF = $15,000
Additional Rent of $4,000 ($2/SF) is necessary to recapture $15,000 investment @ 12 percent
Total Rent = $2.88 + $2.00 = $4.88/SF

This analysis of the five tenants indicates the amount of rent that must be charged to each tenant in order for the owners to realize the expected return of 12 percent. The range varies from $2.88/SF for Tenant A with no tenant improvements to $6.88/SF for Tenant D with $30,000 of tenant improvements.

Assuming that 12% is an adequate return, charging Tenant D $6.88/SF is a realistic rent. However, a market analysis indicated that rents for this type of space were $5/SF maximum, even with 25% tenant finish. If the environment is static, at the end of five years, Tenant D's space will lease for no more than $5/SF. For this reason, the cost of each tenant's improvements must be recaptured over that tenants' lease term, and the owners' investment must be maintained at a level to realize an adequate return.

Location

In analyzing location, you must consider the market in general and the subject property's specific location and how it relates to its surrounding environment. Demographics on the metropolitan area, county and immediate neighborhood of the subject property are helpful. Also helpful is a market study about the type of property under consideration. There are several national firms that provide such studies for major metropolitan areas. These studies should include current occupancy and vacancy rates, historical absorption of space and current market rents.

Building Design

Analyzing the building design involves evaluating it against any significant preestablished guidelines for the building type. Exhibit 35, on the next page, lists the specific design criteria and building standards that one life insurance company uses to evaluate bulk warehouse space.

Tenancy

For the most part, the tenancy will be determined by the type of building. A single-tenant building will have one tenant; a multi-tenant building will have several tenants. Beyond that, it is important to analyze the leasing risk of the property. Just as the study of building specifics clarifies the cost of the project, analyzing the tenants and their leases will clarify the profitability potential of the project.

In analyzing the tenants, it is important to assess each tenant's financial strength, particularly as the dependency on that tenant for project viability increases. For example, a generic building does not require dependency on initial tenancy because it is compatible with a variety of tenants' needs; in this case, a good market analysis to determine market acceptance is as important as the building.

EXHIBIT 35

BULK WAREHOUSE DESIGN CRITERIA

Bulk warehouse projects should be a minimum of 100,000 square feet and should be capable of serving tenants in the 10,000- to 50,000-square-foot range. Single-user buildings will be considered if they meet multiple tenant requirements. A park setting is preferred. Manufacturing and storage of hazardous materials is not acceptable.

Shell:	Decorative tilt-wall concrete, precast-concrete or brick-over-block walls; steel structure; minimum 5.5-inch concrete slab floors; built-up roof. Structure must meet current energy code.
Building Depth:	150 to 200 feet; 200 to 250 feet preferred.
Column Spacing:	40 feet by 40 feet minimum.
Clear Height:	18 to 24 feet for smaller buildings; 24 to 32 feet for larger buildings over 100,000 square feet.
FAR:	Minimum: 40 percent.
Parking:	At least 3.5 spaces per 1,000 square feet of rentable office area and 1.0 space per 1,000 square feet of warehouse area.
HVAC:	Standard roof-mounted units with electric air conditioning and gas heat in office areas; gas-fired unit heaters in warehouse areas. Electric heat is not acceptable.
Electrical:	High-efficiency interior and exterior lighting; adequate power capacity to accommodate typical tenants (preferable five watts per square foot); three phase available; meters for each tenant area.
Plumbing:	Sprinklers (high density if required by market); adequate restrooms to meet code and ADA requirements for each tenant area; overhead or under-floor water and under-floor waste properly located; irrigated landscaping (if applicable).
Loading:	Dock high with minimum 120-foot concrete truck court. Front or dual loading is acceptable, depending on market.
ADA:	Building must be accessible and must meet current applicable ADA requirements.

It is also important to analyze each lease to determine economic factors — such as longevity, rent, and who accepts responsibility for each expense — and noneconomic factors, such as condemnation and casualty. As the property becomes more specialized, the leasing risk becomes more significant. For example, the lease on a special purpose facility will be scrutinized in much greater detail than a lease on a generic, multi-tenant building.

Ownership

It is important to analyze the owner of an industrial property not only from a financial standpoint but from an expertise standpoint as well. Owners are responsible for the management and operation of their real estate. Their abilities in these areas will determine the profitability of the project. Traditional developers/owners typically have their own management and leasing teams on site and have daily contact with the property. In contrast, foreign buyers and REITs typically hire professional management and leasing personnel to carry out these functions for them. It is essential to recognize that real estate needs leasing and management regardless of who owns the property.

Legal Issues

Over the last 25 years, there has been a dramatic increase in government regulation of real estate. Industrial real estate analyses now require professional legal advice on property-specific issues. Following is a list of legal issues that affect industrial real estate:

- Environmental matters, including Phase I, contamination from off-site migration and tenant and user activities.
- Stand-alone parcel or part of industrial park? What are the applicable covenants, conditions and restrictions (CC&Rs)?

- Utility easements: Are utilities from public or private sources? Are easements from publicly dedicated rights-of-way or across adjoining private property?
- Shared driveway agreements: Maintenance? Insurance?
- Zoning: Evidence of compliance?
- Building setbacks: Zoning or CC&Rs?
- Truck turnaround: Any encroachments on adjoining property?
- Platted lot lines or metes and bounds legal description: As-built survey should confirm absence of strips or gores.
- Nonconforming uses: In the event of a casualty loss, restoration must be done according to zoning and building codes.
- Common ownership of security property and adjoining property: Must view properties as under separate ownership and document all necessary easements and other agreements.
- Flood-zone areas: Elevations of ground floor, parking lots and other building and site features.
- Necessary approvals by property owners association.
- Access from dedicated roadways or private streets?
- Legal description of property: Must include all easements necessary to provide access from publicly dedicated rights-of-way; have title insurance to ensure access, zoning (if possible) and compliance with CC&Rs.

Conclusion — Value and Risk

A thorough analysis of a property should not only provide an understanding of the value of the property, but also an understanding of the level of risk inherent in the property. Not all properties have the same level of risk; the level of risk is determined by the industrial factors — such as location, building design, tenancy and ownership abilities — that will influence the dependability of the income stream. In order to analyze and assess the risk inherent in a property, it is imperative to focus on pricing, financing and determining an appropriate lease rate for a tenant.

15

The Senior Care Market

Stephen F. Wood, CMB, Chairman
Vista Commercial Mortgage Group, LLC

Life expectancies are increasing with healthier lifestyles and advances in medical science. However, medical problems still exist and accompany longevity in many cases. More people are living longer, and they are demanding greater choices and flexibility in dealing with infirmities. Not only are seniors themselves seeking new delivery systems for housing and health care, but payors — government and private alike — also are looking for greater efficiency. In response to these market demands, and aided by a general climate of deregulation, many different types of housing and health care providers for seniors are emerging.

This chapter will examine the factors influencing the senior care market and the different types of care being provided today. The chapter also will examine mortgage underwriting considerations for these types of properties within the changing dynamics of the health care and long-term care industries.

Demographics

Several demographic dynamics are influencing senior health care. First, the median age of the U.S. population is increasing from 34 in 1994 to a projected 35.5 for the year 2000; it will peak at 39.1 in 2035 before decreasing slightly to 39 by 2050.[1] This projection alone suggests that the population is getting older. There are other dynamics to consider, as well. The birth rate in the United States declined to the zero population growth rate in 1930 and remained there until the end of World War II; thus, beginning in 2005, the over-75 cohort will be level for 15 years, before expanding greatly beginning in 2020, as shown in Exhibit 36. With demand flattening in 2005 (only on a national level — some regions may experience growth in the over-75 cohort after 2005), facilities that provide services in this market must establish market share and position before demand decreases in order to remain viable over the long term.

These population dynamics suggest that the industry's growth will slow during the period from 2005 to 2020. Slow growth generally leads to consolidation in industries, as participants in the market seek economies of scale to continue individual firm profit growth. During industry consolidation, firms that have established market leadership will acquire or otherwise force out weaker industry participants.

Industry Changes: 1985 to 1995

Regulatory Changes

Momentum has been building under Democratic and Republican administrations alike for a reduced federal government role in private enterprise. Regardless of what impact reductions in the federal deficit have on specific programs, such as Medicaid and Medicare, clearly, there will be less federal oversight. The corollary to reduced government involvement is reduced reimbursements to providers of health care of all types. Individual states will

EXHIBIT 36

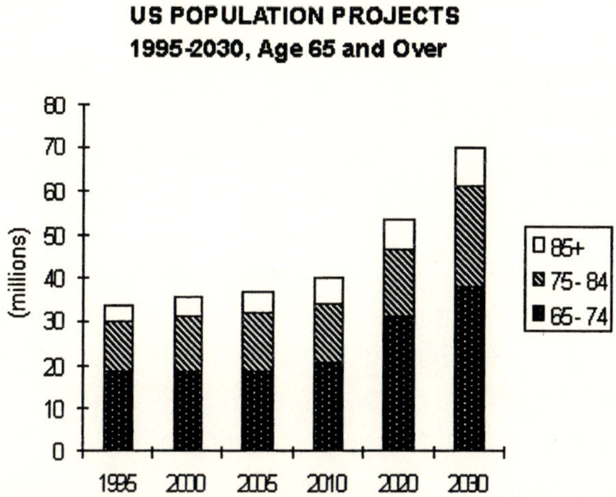

Source: U.S. Bureau of the Census, Current Population Reports

regulate and subsidize to some degree, but the overall trend points to less government involvement.

Where regulations have been relaxed (or, in some cases, circumvented), new services have been developed. In the 1970s, essentially one type of service flourished — nursing homes. Later, other classes of services, such as assisted-living, came into being. By looking at other deregulated industries, such as airlines and telephone companies, one can see the variety of services offered on the open market. Deregulation allows the market to function and allows entrepreneurs opportunities to profit from innovation. History has shown, however, that the boom in new services offered immediately after deregulation is often followed by industry consolidation. Market forces will dictate that some players acquire smaller players and that some participants will not adapt to the new environment.

Emergence of Managed Care

The retreat of government has allowed the emergence of managed care as a way of paying for health care of all types. It is likely that future health care reform initiatives will include some sort of managed-care or preferred-provider plan, which several states are currently trying.

This change in the health care industry has brought about significant changes in acute (hospital) care, but also affects long-term care. To shorten hospital stays, many plans are signing up long-term care providers to care for patients at a lower cost. The negative side to this trend is that preferred provider plans rely on capitated programs which can reduce facility revenue. The net effect of managed care is impossible to predict, as it will be unique for each particular facility.[2]

Industry Consolidation

Some of the predicted consolidation has already occurred over the past 10 years. The American Seniors Housing Association (ASHA) reports that 40% of respondents to a survey of senior executives in the industry are actively seeking to expand their businesses through acquisitions.[3] Furthermore, roughly one-third of all properties in the market have been acquired from the original owner. The ASHA also reports that over 40% of firms have been in business for 5 to 10 years and that 38% have been in business for more than 10 years. This indicates that the industry has matured somewhat over the past 10 years, as part of an ongoing cycle of growth and consolidation.

Factors that have an impact on the seniors housing market represent both threats and opportunities for current market participants. Clearly, established providers will have the greatest opportunity to use these trends to build competitive advantages. Being aware of how a specific factor may affect a particular project will enable lenders to make appropriate investment decisions.

The Spectrum of Long-Term Care Options

Changes in the market have led to a spectrum of long-term health care offerings. These market offerings now cover seniors throughout their retirement and are defined according to the level of assistance given. The most intense level is just short of hospitalization, while the lowest level merely gives retirees a place to live during their senior stage of life. There are now specialty centers for certain infirmities, such as Alzheimer's disease, as well as others that offer many different types of senior care.

Because the variety of offerings is a relatively recent phenomenon, a body of terminology has not been established yet. Different types of care go by different names that roughly describe what they offer; however, this lack of nomenclature often confuses those not familiar with the industry. Thus, the following five sections define broad classifications of services and provide some background on how these classifications have evolved.[4]

Independent Living

Independent-living facilities provide the lowest level of care for seniors. Also known as adult congregate living facilities (ACLFs), they are typically apartments in retirement communities with some amenities not found in conventional apartments. In this type of seniors housing, residents are usually ambulatory and do not require assistance with daily activities. The monthly rental fees include services, such as meals, housekeeping, linen service, organized activities and transportation.

Because of the low level of health care services provided, independent-living projects will look most like traditional residential properties to analysts. However, several special factors must be considered when underwriting a loan for this type of facility. The development cost for an independent-living facility is higher because of special features, such as wide doors with easy-turn handles, shower grips and call buttons in each apartment. Further, these facilities usually have more common areas relative to the units; these common areas include kitchen, dining and lounge areas.

Two lessons learned from the late 1980s' overdevelopment of this type of facility are that marketing costs are very high and that lease-up takes considerably longer than in a traditional residential development. This is because of the specialized nature of the product and the need for personal selling. Seniors tend to be cautious about deciding to move to a new residence. In many cases, they may be leaving homes where they have lived for decades. It is a difficult, emotional decision — one that makes seniors look at several offerings on the market and return several times before committing to a move.

Operating expenses on a per-unit basis also are higher than those for traditional apartments. These expenses will vary depending on the types of services offered (such as transportation and housekeeping) and whether the services are included in the rental fee.

Independent-living facilities are typically not required to have a certificate of need (CON), which means that only the market regulates supply. This lack of regulation also means that independent-living facilities do not rely on reimbursement programs for revenue.

Assisted Living

Assisted-living facilities provide assistance to residents in the activities of daily living: bathing, dressing, preparing meals and taking medications. As with other types of care, assisted living goes by several different names, such as personal care, board and care, residential care and sheltered care. Assisted-living services are frequently provided within one section of an ACLF or even within a nursing home facility. Free-standing assisted living has been called the hottest area of seniors housing, and several providers have gone public recently. Some well-known names, such as Marriott, have entered the market in a significant way.

The assisted-living industry is largely unregulated at present. However, because of the amount of care given, it is possible it could be subject to regulation in the future. Such regulations could require facilities to provide for financially challenged patients or could establish reporting requirements to ensure the quality of care.

Assisted-living projects tend to include a greater business element than independent living and also have some unique considerations. Because the product type is new, lenders must continue to monitor its acceptance in the market. Assisted-living facilities offer many services that seniors formerly received from other institutions, primarily intermediate-care nursing homes. Lenders must monitor the evolution of product offerings and how this evolution affects other segments of the industry. The development cost, lease-up, marketing and common area considerations of independent-living projects apply here too; however, staffing expenses per resident are greater in an assisted-living facility, where personal care is a primary component.

Nursing Homes

Nursing homes are facilities with licensed nursing beds. Nursing homes are the traditional long-term care facilities, yet nursing homes are very different from those of 10 years ago. Today, patients may have private or semiprivate rooms, and ward-style nursing homes are becoming increasingly rare.

Nursing homes not only provide intermediate assistance; they also provide skilled nursing care, such as administering medication and monitoring patients' conditions. Skilled nursing care increasingly offers a wide variety of ancillary services, which enhance overall revenues. Intermediate care is becoming obsolete as assisted-living facilities are taking care of a greater number of ambulatory patients who have less need for skilled nursing care.

Nursing homes are very different from lower-intensity seniors housing for a variety of reasons. In most states, nursing home development requires state-issued certificates of need

(CONs). The net effect of CON regulation is to limit the supply of nursing homes in the market. Nursing home stays are becoming shorter, and nursing homes are becoming halfway houses between hospitalization and other forms of long-term care. Nursing homes rely largely on reimbursement programs such as Medicare and Medicaid. These programs have complex record-keeping requirements and other regulations, which affect nursing home profitability. In recent years, there has been a strong trend toward consolidation in order to cope with such regulatory matters more efficiently.

Subacute Care

Subacute care is an emerging class of care for patients who need extensive rehabilitation or who have complex medical needs. This class of care is perceived to cost less than hospitalization, partly because of the lower overhead associated with a dedicated facility. Since hospitals have been forced to cut the lengths of stays, subacute care facilities have soared in popularity.

More than any other class, subacute care facilities have ties directly to acute care hospitals; in fact, many are being created as wings of hospitals, circumventing licensing restrictions on nursing beds. Due to the nature of patients and the kinds of services rendered, subacute care facilities often contain more medical equipment per bed than any other class. Like nursing homes, they generate revenues more from health care services than from rental fees.

Continuing Care Retirement Community

The continuing care retirement community (CCRC) is a concept that was developed in the early 1980s to provide the full spectrum of care to seniors. The concept suffered early setbacks, especially due to overbuilding. However, the concept is gaining in popularity as facilities improve their quality and unbundle the services they provide. Such facilities may include independent- and assisted-living apartments, a nursing home and a subacute care wing. They are subject to different degrees of regulation and have income from a variety of sources. Because of their hybrid nature, CCRCs are generally best analyzed by breaking them into their constituent parts and analyzing each individually.

Sources of Income

To analyze a long-term care property, it is essential to understand the source of revenues. Different types of projects will have different payment mixes from various sources, including Medicaid, Medicare, the Veterans Administration (VA), private insurance and the residents themselves. The situation is more complicated for facilities that offer several levels of service — each level has its own distinct mix of patients.

This section describes the various payors and what each covers. It is an overview intended to help analysts understand the different revenue streams in senior care facilities, even though the dynamics of those streams are unique in each case.

Medicaid

Medicaid is a program jointly funded by the states and the federal government. Its purpose is to provide health care services to the needy. Within broad national guidelines set by the federal government, each state:

- Establishes its own eligibility standards
- Determines the type, amount, duration and scope of services
- Sets the rate of payment for services
- Administers its own program[5]

Increasingly, states are turning to HMOs or other managed care models to curtail the costs of providing health care. Thus, loan analysts must be aware of state regulations affecting long-term care facilities. At a minimum, analysts should understand the percentage of patients who rely on Medicaid programs, what services are covered and at what rates. Additionally, the analysts should request copies of the facility's Medicaid reimbursement forms and preferred provider agreements with state Medicaid agencies.

Medicare

Medicare is a federal health insurance program primarily for people over 65, but also covering those under 65 with certain disabilities. Medicare has two parts: hospital insurance (Part A) and medical insurance (Part B). Part A helps pay for inpatient care in hospitals, skilled nursing facilities and psychiatric hospitals and for some hospice and home health care arrangements. Part B helps pay for physician services and many other medical services not covered under Part A. Unlike Medicaid, Medicare is administered by the federal government's Social Security Administration and is not need based.

Nursing home patients must meet several requirements in order to receive benefits under Medicare. To qualify for Part A, skilled nursing patients must:

- Require daily skilled care, as certified by a medical professional
- Be in the hospital for at least three consecutive days prior to discharge
- Be admitted to the nursing facility for the same condition within 30 days of discharge from the hospital

Part A pays a set amount for long-term care services. It pays 100% of the approved amount for the patients' first 20 days of care, but requires a copayment for the next 80 days. Unless the patients are hospitalized again, they must pay the full amount after 100 days. Part B pays 80% of the approved amount for several ancillary services after a $100 deductible is paid.

Medicare pays a facility an interim rate for services based on that facility's prior year costs. At year-end, the facility submits a cost report detailing actual costs (including some capital reimbursements) and is reimbursed the difference. However, these costs are often disputed and can be delayed. Analyzing a loan, particularly on a skilled or subacute nursing facility, requires a detailed examination of the Medicare cost statements and reimbursement history.

Veterans Administration

The VA contracts with some nursing homes to admit VA nursing home patients for a set daily rate that includes all services necessary for the particular patient, even medicine and laundry services. Therefore, facilities that admit VA patients usually screen such patients carefully to make sure the nature of the service required by the patient will not cost more than the flat daily rate provided by the Veterans Administration.

Private Insurance

Private insurance is a relatively new source of revenue for seniors housing. The first private insurance policies were basic "Medigap" policies that helped Medicare patients pay deductibles and copayments. The policies have evolved since then, and many major insurance carriers now offer policies — such as long-term care insurance, hospital indemnity insurance and specified disease insurance — that can take effect before Medicare. Of these policies, long-term care insurance is the most significant to the providers industry because many extended care services are not covered by Medicare. Thus, this industry trend logically coincides with the emergence of assisted-living facilities because services provided there may be covered by a private insurance policy, but not by Medicare.

Since the private insurance industry has been trying to establish itself with seniors, it has avoided using preferred provider plans. Such plans restrict the doctors and facilities patients can choose and, therefore, are unpopular with seniors and their families. This trend is positive for long-term care facilities because it keeps the potential market for services greater.

Private Pay

Patients and their families shoulder some of the burden for their stays in long-term care facilities. The amount coming directly from the patient depends on the type of facility and the services rendered. Fortunately for the loan analyst, private payments are the most straightforward revenue streams in seniors housing because they do not involve complicated chargebacks and adjustments.

By their nature, independent-living facilities generate the bulk of their revenue through rental fees from the patients; very little of their revenue comes from reimbursement programs because they provide little in the way of health care. In a typical arrangement, residents pay an entrance fee and monthly rent, plus addition fees for additional services.

In contrast, skilled nursing patients pay copayments and deductibles for their stays. They also pay for any ancillary services not normally included in the daily rate, such as physical therapy or counseling, personal laundry services, vending machine snacks, guest meals and pharmacy items.

Underwriting Considerations

Underwriting a mortgage loan for any long-term care facility is unique in that the loan must be considered on two levels. On one level, the facility is an operating business with business risks that affect its operators' ability to make payments. The facility may be owned by one party and leased to another. Because of the special purpose of the property, it is important to look at the underlying strength of the business. On another level, the facility is a commercial property with a set of cash flows (lease payments) over time. Approached from this level, loan underwriting considerations are more conventional.

Management Considerations

In any industry facing consolidation, strong management is the key to success. In an industry such as senior care, where external forces (regulatory and demographic changes) and internal forces (acquisitions and new delivery methods) are at play, the management strength becomes doubly important. The question for the loan analysts is how to evaluate management.

Independent versus Chain Operation

A facility may be run independently or as part of a chain. Both independent management and chain operation have advantages and disadvantages.

Single-facility management usually indicates an owner-managed property. There is often deep commitment both on personal and financial levels by the owners/managers to provide the best possible service. However, the independent facility frequently does not achieve economies of scale with respect to purchasing and may require greater staffing. These inefficiencies may be offset by the facility not having to pay management fees to support the overhead of a multifacility operation. Also, analysts will find it much more difficult to analyze a proposed owner-managed facility that has not yet been built than to analyze a chain property because there are no other facilities by the same owner/manager to use as models.

Multifacility management applies to a chain of properties under common ownership and to individually owned properties under long-term management contracts. A chain operation generally has a track record to provide a level of comfort in its ability to acquire, develop and manage facilities. The chain should be able to exploit economies of scale in purchasing, training, bookkeeping and regulatory reporting that are not achievable in independent operations.

Years Experience

Regardless of whether a loan will be for a chain or independent facility, analysts should carefully examine management's experience. Some lenders now require both owner and manager to have at least five years experience with the type of facility under consideration. In examining the experience, ask about the team in place at the facility and not just about the top individuals. A group that has worked together longer generally indicates past success and greater stability.

Management by Owner or Third Party

Whether a facility is managed by the owner (regardless of its status as an independent or multifacility property) or a third party has important implications for the loan. An owner/manager certainly has a greater financial interest in improving performance than a third-party manager. However, should performance drop, an owner/manager may be less willing to change management. Loan analysts should pay close attention to the remedies provided in the loan documents with respect to management changes. The covenants may give the lender the right to approve all management changes.

Marketing Considerations

In addition to how a facility is managed, how the facility is marketed plays a significant role in project success. Unlike traditional apartments, seniors housing is more than just floor plans. The facility's reputation, customer base and amenity offerings relative to the competition are important.

The Market

A seniors facility is likely to draw a high percentage of residents from its immediate community. The definition of this community may be only the surrounding neighborhood in high density areas, or it may be several towns in a rural area. Regardless of the definition, demographic data should be used to quantify the potential market and the potential future market for the area. The market study for skilled nursing facilities should also examine the percentage of private-pay patients, because these patients deliver a higher margin than those treated under government reimbursement programs.

Marketing Program

To understand what kind of marketing program is appropriate, it is important to recognize who the market for the services is. Marketing to the resident is more important for those types of senior housing that provide less skilled nursing — that is, assisted- and independent-living facilities. In these cases, the residents themselves and their families will choose a facility, often based on repeated visits.

Those facilities that provide more skilled care need to have strong ties to hospitals and an excellent presence in the community. With these facilities, patients may have no choice about where they will go and may be strongly influenced by the recommendation of the hospital, doctor or social worker referring them.

Level of Integration

One key element of the marketing program is the level of integration of services. Many facilities now offer a broad spectrum of care types from independent living through subacute care. These facilities are pursuing a strategy to provide services from retirement to death and must be able to show advantages at each level of care. The drawback to this strategy is that if there are better alternatives available at one level, say assisted living, seniors may move to one of the better facilities rather than to the combination facility. Thus, a pyramid effect can take place: without permanent residents cycling through from lower levels of care, higher level units and beds may remain empty.

Facilities that provide only one (or two) levels of care face a different set of marketing challenges. These facilities need only have an advantage over other competitors in that class of care to attract patients. For many licensed nursing homes, proximity to an acute care hospital is enough of an advantage. However, in a less regulated class such as assisted living, the facility may need to differentiate itself from competition by offering as much or more than competitors.

Competition — Existing and Potential

The loan analysis should include a thorough assessment of competing facilities. The evaluation should include comparisons of unit size and mix, rent per unit, range of services, actual and perceived quality of services, health care arrangements, location, amenities, common area design, management and ownership and operating expenses.[6] Marketing issues will continue to increase in importance throughout the period of industry consolidation. Therefore, it is essential that lenders closely examine each of these interrelated issues.

Furthermore, the underwriting analysis should consider the potential threats to the facility's market. It is essential to examine whether there are other facilities in the area that might offer the same services, even if they currently do not. This sort of analysis will reveal if a hospital's excess capacity threatens a stand-alone subacute facility, for example.

Location

Long-term care facilities do not require high visibility, ease of access and proximity to population centers as many types of real estate do. However, the location must be pleasant and quiet, preferably in a residential neighborhood. A skilled nursing facility should be located close to at least one hospital and should have a transfer agreement with that hospital, allowing free transfers of patients to and from the hospital. All kinds of facilities may benefit from being close to a hospital because medical doctors are more likely to refer patients for the sake of convenience. Independent- and assisted-living facilities should be located near essential services and recreational activities.

Design

The design and construction of a facility dictate the nature of the services that may be provided and the type of patient who may be attracted to the facility. A high-quality nursing facility with a high percentage of private rooms is likely to attract a higher percentage of private-pay patients. For independent- and assisted-living facilities, where the resident has more choice, higher quality designs will be more successful in competing for new tenants.

Nursing and Acute-Care Facilities

Suburban nursing homes are typically one-story structures with one or more wings. The wings should have central corridors branching from a highly visible nursing station, which can serve 50 to 60 beds. Multistory facilities may be appropriate in urban areas, but in such facilities, reliable elevators and more intensive safety provisions are essential. In nursing facilities, total floor area, including common areas, usually averages 250 to 300 square feet per bed.

Parking requirements are not as critical as for other types of real estate. On-site parking for employees, visitors and physicians is usually sufficient. The amount of parking required will vary depending on zoning regulations, the availability of public transportation and other factors.

Independent- and Assisted-Living Facilities

The layout of an independent- or assisted-living facility will reflect the range of services provided. Often, two- or three-story apartment wings are attached to a common area. The corridors should be short, since the residents will typically make at least one trip per day to the common area. Apartments may be studios or one- or two-bedroom units and may or may not contain kitchens. The smaller units tend to be closer to the common areas since these typically house the more frail residents. The apartments should be equipped with call buttons that are monitored 24 hours a day, and all areas should be handicapped-accessible. As with nursing homes, these facilities do not require extensive parking, since residents typically do not drive. Parking is necessary only for visitors, employees and facility-owned transportation.

Valuation

Selecting an Appraiser

Underwriting a loan on a long-term care facility requires a detailed appraisal of the facility. The appraiser — whether on the lender's staff, through the correspondent or independent — must be familiar with the industry. There are some firms that specialize in senior care appraisal and are familiar with the nuances required in the subjective judgment of the valuation.

Analyzing the Appraisal

In analyzing the appraisal, it is important to note that the cost approach does not set the upper limit of value on a long-term care facility. There is considerable expense in the initial staffing, lease-up and marketing of a facility, which may not be included in the cost approach. This expense is typically more significant for seniors housing than for traditional apartments. Additional value may result from limitations on new facilities by the CON process, which creates virtual franchises for some types of facilities in certain areas.

Therefore, the income approach and the related market approach are more appropriate measures of value than the cost approach. Typically, long-term care facilities are valued on a per-bed or per-unit basis; however, this valuation may vary significantly among facilities depending upon the nature of operations. For facilities that offer multiple types of care, it may be appropriate to apply different valuation multiples for different wings.

Analyzing Land Value

Land value is a relatively insignificant portion of the overall value of a seniors housing project. Many properties are located in lesser traveled areas or in rural areas where land values are low, but the locations are satisfactory for use as nursing homes. Skilled and acute care facilities, however, benefit from being located in a "medical" neighborhood, where land prices may be high, but are justified by the ancillary revenues produced by such facilities.

Analyzing Net Operating Income

From a loan-underwriting standpoint, the net operating income (NOI) for a senior care facility — as for any other type of facility — is the key figure. There are a number of considerations in analyzing NOI:

- *Reimbursements.* Net operating income should represent the cash flow available to service the proposed debt after all other cash expenses and reserves. Getting to the bottom line for cash flow in some senior care facilities can be difficult. In facilities where significant revenues come from reimbursement programs, for example, adjustments may be recorded in the year in which they are received, rather than the year in which they were incurred. Thus, loan analyses should pay careful attention to real cash flow, as opposed to conventional "revenues less expenses" calculations of net operating income.
- *Vacancy Allowance.* A reasonable vacancy allowance should be included, taking into account the history of the facility and competing facilities in the area. In many areas, strong demand for services cause facilities to operate at virtually 100% of capacity with a waiting list. Nevertheless, because of potential competition and the relatively high turnover in senior care facilities, a vacancy factor of at least 5% is imputed by most lenders.
- *Staffing.* The NOI analysis should look at staffing as a major portion of operating expenses. In addition, the analysis should look at historical staff turnover and any union contracts that could affect operating expenses.

- *Other Expenses.*The expenses utilized in projecting NOI should include a liberal reserve for replacements and supplies. In addition, a professional management fee of 5% to 7% should be imputed even if the facility is owner managed, since professional management could become necessary in the event of default.

Minimizing Risk

In addition to a mortgage on the real estate involved, it is very important for the lender also to have a security interest in nonrealty items, including all furniture, fixtures and equipment. Such items comprise a significant portion of the initial cost of the facility and are essential to its operation.

In addition, when management fees are paid to a related party, it is desirable to require the management entity to subordinate all or a portion of its management fee to the debt service. This is particularly true when the management company is affiliated with the ownership entity.

State Regulations Overview

It is important to remember that many kinds of long-term care services are regulated at the state level. This regulation generally applies more to nursing homes than to independent- or assisted-living facilities; however, the loan analysis should include an overview of the applicable state regulations for the facility. This analysis should address:

- Current reimbursement climate and system used in the facility's area
- Proposed changes in current regulations

- CON moratoriums that block competition with the facility
- A review of the most recent surveys by the regulators

Funding Sources

A variety of traditional and nontraditional sources of financing exist for long-term care facilities. These sources change over time as the industry moves into and out of favor with particular lenders, especially in response to tax law changes. However, the clear trend is toward more sophisticated financing vehicles that reflect the higher degree of business risk involved in these types of loans.

Currently, there is a HUD program for financing new construction of nursing homes and refinancing of existing facilities. HUD insurance protects the lender and may render the loan available for inclusion in mortgage-backed securities. The program requires additional processing time, but may provide the necessary credit enhancement for marketing tax-exempt or taxable bond issues for financing.

Life Insurance Companies

Some life insurance companies have traditionally been lenders to the independent facilities or small chains. However, most have abandoned the industry because the business risk has become too complex and the level of acuity too high.

Real Estate Investment Trusts (REITs)

Since the mid-1980s, specialized REITs have provided financing to the industry through traditional mortgages or purchase/leaseback arrangements.

Conduits

Conduits for securitizing mortgage loans have increasingly brought funds from the capital markets into the commercial mortgage market. Some of these conduits also specialize in loans to this industry.

Tax-Exempt Bonds

Nonprofit entities [501(c) (3)s] may qualify for nursing home financing by issuing tax-exempt bonds through a municipal entity (typically the health facilities commission in the community). These bonds may be issued with or without credit enhancements and usually provide nearly 100% financing for acquisition or development costs at attractive interest rates. It is not unusual for owners of nursing homes to sell some or all of their facilities to nonprofit entities for an attractive price, while they continue to manage the facility under a lucrative management contract.

Banks

With a proliferation of larger, corporate care givers, banks have become a source of funds both for acquisition and new development. With consolidation in the banking industry progressing rapidly, many banks have specialized health care lending groups for this purpose. Typically, they deal with corporate owners of multiple facilities.

Summary and Conclusion

The senior care industry will continue to undergo many changes beyond the turn of the century. Changing demographics, government regulations and types of care available will keep the industry in a state of flux and should provide a backdrop for significant consolidation. Successful lenders to the industry must remain abreast of the types of care available and the sources of income to pay for them. They must pay careful attention to management and marketing issues for facilities and must analyze the valuation and NOI thoroughly before committing to lend. Given that these factors are taken into account, several types of investors may participate in the growth of this dynamic industry.

Endnotes — Chapter 15

1. United States Census, *Population Profile of the United States: 1995.*
2. Industry analysts have widely differing views on these effects. Capital Valuation Group argues in "Value Influences Past, Present and Future" (1995) that managed care is a long-term negative because it brings more regulation and lowers revenues. Joseph T. Howell, on the other hand ("Seniors Housing and Health Care in 1995: Key Trends and How They Are Transforming the Industry," 1995), believes managed care will be beneficial to firms who become integral links in managed care networks.
3. American Seniors Housing Association, "The State of Seniors Housing 1994," 1995.
4. These definitions draw heavily on those provided by Roth, Herman and Urban in "Value Influences Past, Present and Future," Capital Valuation Group, 1995.
5. For additional information, take a look at the Social Security Administration Internet home page at the following address: http://www.ssa.gov/hcfa/medicaid/mover.html
6. Philip A. Brooks, "Keys to Underwriting Seniors Housing Transactions: Marketing and Management," August 1995.